That Eminent Tribunal

NEW FORUM BOOKS   *Robert P. George, Series Editor*
A list of titles in the series
appears at the back of the book

That Eminent Tribunal

JUDICIAL SUPREMACY AND THE CONSTITUTION

Christopher Wolfe, editor

PRINCETON UNIVERSITY PRESS

PRINCETON AND OXFORD

Copyright © 2004 by Princeton University Press

Published by Princeton University Press, 41 William Street, Princeton, New Jersey 08540

In the United Kingdom: Princeton University Press, 3 Market Place, Woodstock, Oxfordshire OX20 1SY

All Rights Reserved

Library of Congress Cataloging-in-Publication Data

That eminent tribunal : judicial supremacy and the constitution / Christopher Wolfe, editor.
   p. cm.
  Includes bibliographical references and index.
  ISBN 0-691-11667-9 (cloth : alk. Paper) — ISBN 0-691-11668-7 (pbk. : alk. paper)
  1. Judicial power—United States. 2. Judge-made law—United States. 3. United States. Supreme Court. 4. Constitutional law—United States—Interpretation and construction. I. Wolfe, Christopher.

KF5130.T48 2004
347.73'12—dc22

                                    2003063293

British Library Cataloging-in-Publication Data is available

This book has been composed in Sabon

Printed on acid-free paper. ∞

www.pupress.princeton.edu

Printed in the United States of America

10 9 8 7 6 5 4 3 2 1

Contents

Contributors

HADLEY ARKES is Ney Professor of Jurisprudence at Amherst College and author of *First Things* (Princeton University Press, 1986) and *Natural Rights and the Right to Choose* (Cambridge University Press, 2002).

GERARD V. BRADLEY, Professor of Law, University of Notre Dame, is author of *Church-State Relationships in America* (Greenwood Press, 1987).

GEORGE W. LIEBMANN is an attorney and author of *The Gallows in the Grove: Civil Society in American Law* (Praeger, 1997) and of *The Little Platoons: Sub-local Governments in Modern History* (Praeger, 1995).

MICHAEL W. MCCONNELL, Professor of Law, University of Utah, and currently Judge of the Tenth Circuit U.S. Court of Appeals, is the author of articles in the *Harvard Law Review*, *Yale Law Journal*, and *University of Chicago Law Review*.

ROBERT F. NAGEL, Ira C. Rothgerber Professor of Constitutional Law, University of Colorado, is the author of *Constitutional Cultures* (University of California Press, 1989) and *The Implosion of American Federalism* (Oxford University Press, 2001).

JACK WADE NOWLIN, Jessie D. Puckett, Jr. Lecturer in Law and Assistant Professor of Law at the University of Mississippi Law School, is the author of articles in the *Kentucky Law Journal*, the *Oklahoma Law Review*, and the *Notre Dame Law Review*.

STEVEN D. SMITH is Professor of Law, University of San Diego School of Law, and author of *Foreordained Failure: The Quest for a Constitutional Principle of Religious Freedom* (Oxford University Press, 1995) and *The Constitution and the Pride of Reason* (Oxford University Press, 1998).

JEREMY WALDRON, Maurice and Hilda Friedman Professor of Law and Director of the Center for Law and Philosophy at Columbia University, is the author of *Liberal Rights* (Cambridge University Press, 1993) and *Law and Disagreement* (Oxford University Press, 1999).

KEITH E. WHITTINGTON, Associate Professor of Law, Princeton University, is the author of *Constitutional Interpretation: Textual Meaning, Original Intent, and Judicial Review* (1999) and *Constitutional Construction: Divided Powers and Constitutional Meaning* (1999).

CHRISTOPHER WOLFE, Department of Political Science, Marquette University, is the author of *The Rise of Modern Judicial Review* (rev. ed., Rowman and LittleField, 1994) and *How to Read the Constitution* (Rowman and Littlefield, 1997).

MICHAEL ZUCKERT, Professor of Government, University of Notre Dame, is the author of *Natural Rights and the New Republicanism* (Princeton University Press, 1994) and *Launching Liberalism* (University Press of Kansas, 2002).

That Eminent Tribunal

Introduction

Christopher Wolfe

> At the same time the candid citizen must confess that if the
> policy of the government, upon vital questions, affecting the
> whole people, is to be irrevocably fixed by decisions of the
> Supreme Court, the instant they are made, in ordinary
> litigation between parties, in personal actions, the people will
> have ceased, to be their own rulers, having, to that extent,
> practically resigned their government, into the hands of that
> eminent tribunal.
> —Abraham Lincoln, First Inaugural Address

IN THE PAST generation, an abundance of scholarship has clearly described the profound transformation in the role of the Supreme Court
(and the judiciary in general) in American public life. While the Court has
always played a significant role in our political system, it has not always
wielded the broad policymaking power it regularly exercises today.[1]

The scope and character of judicial power today is fundamentally inconsistent with the separation of powers embodied by the American
founders in our Constitution. Current judicial excesses are not merely an
aberration from our ordinary political arrangements, but raise the
specter of establishing a new form of government. Even many of those
who are opposed to judicial usurpation today are under the impression
that it is merely a particular group of unusually "extreme" judges that account for this phenomenon. They fail to understand that extreme notions
of judicial power have become entrenched in our legal and political system. And, as Lincoln argued, in regard to the *Dred Scott* case—with
all the respect properly owed to the judiciary as a coordinate branch of
government—to treat the Supreme Court as the *final* or *ultimate* authority on constitutional issues is to resign our self-government into the hands
of "that eminent tribunal."

At times in the past thirty years Court watchers have predicted a fundamental shift in the Court, a retrenchment of judicial power, due largely
to the appointments by Republican presidents who have stated their desire to appoint judges who will interpret the law rather than make it. But,

typically, those terms in which the Burger Court or Rehnquist Court handed down decisions that seemed to portend a withdrawal from judicial pretensions have been followed by other terms in which such pretensions have been reasserted. The current composition of the Court (and, even more so, the lower courts) gives little hope for fundamental change.

In particular, there is something quite distinctive about the Court's continuing injection of its power into so-called culture war issues (symbolized by cases such as *Roe v. Wade* and *Planned Parenthood v. Casey*) that have become so prominent a part of American political and social life since the 1960s—matters regarding life and death, family and sexuality, church and state. According to many of its critics, the Court's "privacy" decisions (regarding, for example, abortion and homosexuality) have, in the name of individual autonomy, undermined the moral framework of society by depriving state and local governments of their legitimate power to provide social supports for traditional morality. Similarly, in their view, the Court has barred state and federal efforts to provide for a reasonable accommodation of religion, pursuing instead a conception of church-state relations that radically privatizes religion and creates a "naked public square." Even liberals who approve of many of the policy outcomes that have been generated by the courts in these and other areas sometimes question the constitutional and moral legitimacy of achieving these outcomes by judicial fiat.[2]

The debate is not merely about how the Supreme Court should use its authority to resolve authoritatively our great constitutional questions, and whether it has used this power well or ill. The question is *whether* the Supreme Court has such authority, especially in light of the fact that the Constitution for at least the first century was generally understood to give *no one branch* such final authority. Phrased more positively, the legislative and executive branches and state governments have legitimate constitutional authority to participate in the resolution of our great constitutional questions, rather than simply waiting to receive answers from the Supreme Court. In this respect, it could be said that the central question about judicial power today is how to limit it effectively in order to reestablish a full measure of republican government in the United States.

It should not be surprising that this will be no easy task. First, elite intellectual opinion is strongly behind the courts—as one should expect it to be, given that courts are often an effective vehicle for giving elite intellectual opinions the political power that they cannot win through elections. Second, the legal profession as a whole has been educated by a corps of legal intellectuals and scholars, the vast majority of whom are committed to modern notions of judicial power that are quite incompatible with the traditional American separation of powers. And, third, the "new class" professionals—such as journalists, those working in the entertainment media, and writers and artists—whose power and influence turn on the ability to manipulate information, and who typically tend to support liberal intellectuals, also tend to weigh in against any efforts to restore a proper balance between judges and the political branches.

Even recent "conservative" judicial activism in some areas of the law has led to only limited reconsideration of the scope of judicial power. Certainly we do not hear many scholars calling for a wholesale reconsideration of the Court's liberal precedents from the last generation or two. More often, there is criticism of particular decisions, and, in some cases, a call to recognize a broader power in other branches to qualify or limit what the recent, more conservative Court has done, in order to undermine those decisions (but usually in ways that protect the earlier and more academically popular fruits of judicial activism). If this qualified reconsideration of judicial supremacy is welcome, it does not go nearly far enough.

This book, drawing on scholars with divergent political views, lays out the problem of judicial imperialism today—what it is, what its sources are, some of the key arguments made on its behalf, and the appropriate responses to those contentions.

Gerard V. Bradley opens the volume with an analysis of the claims made by defenders of the Court, and by the Court itself, in the landmark joint opinion in *Planned Parenthood v. Casey*. He describes the way in which the Court has identified its own authority with that of the Constitution, after having detached the Constitution from any concrete content and arrogated to itself the power of defining its alleged majestic generalities. The Court effectively tells Americans, "We will be your Court and you will be our people." To those who object to this arrogation of power, there is a twofold response. The power of the Court to strike down laws on the basis of something other than the Constitution is said to have been popularly ratified (in some unspecified manner), but popular opposition to controversial Court decisions is downplayed on the basis of the Court's superiority to the people in elaborating our national principles: "the Court has constructed around its rulings a seemingly impregnable rhetorical fortress, pouring the hot oil of principle on the heads of rabble ascending the walls, cutting off the legs of highbrow critics with the whipsaw of popular ratification." But, then, how is it possible to know what the law is, until the "winners" have written their histories?

Robert F. Nagel locates the source of *Casey*'s claims for the Court in the fear that the nation lacks a sufficient ground for unity without judicial supremacy. What explains *Casey*'s concern about a "jurisprudence of doubt" is something deeper than precedent: "the authoritativeness and supremacy of the judiciary's interpretive function, not respect for precedent, is the operative concern." The Court is the vehicle by which the nation can "see itself through its constitutional ideals," and the capacity for this kind of collective self-perception is nothing less than the capacity for a national identity. What is at issue is not just the operational integrity of our constitutional system but the existence of the political culture upon which that system rests. This fear of disintegration appears regularly among scholars and Court watchers, and has been particularly salient in cases involving race, such as *Cooper v. Aaron*, and the culture war, such as *Casey*. The shadow argument of *Casey* "is that the Court's interpretation must be accepted, not because it is right, but because dissensus on an issue deemed crucial and unresolvable will tear the country apart." But there is a terrible irony in all this: our devotion to judicial supremacy, exemplified in the centralized imposition of questionable policy by *Roe v. Wade*, may stimulate further opposition that makes nationhood seem more precarious than it is, thus inducing ever more nervous reliance on national judicial power.

Michael Zuckert takes another swing at *Casey*, arguing for a more limited understanding of it. Despite the apparent magnitude of its surface claims (for example, in its famous "mystery passage"), *Casey* should be understood more narrowly—as an example not of "Nietzschean autonomy" but of "hermeneutic Socratism"—not radical autonomy on fundamental issues, but a sort of openness to competing answers. But in the end hermeneutic Socratism is inadequate: first, as a judicial and political action, it failed in its goal of eliminating a "jurisprudence of doubt," since it only stimulated further controversy; second, it is inadequate as a general constitutional theory, because it is has too open-ended a theory of rights, and too little appreciation for the role of government in protecting rights; and third, it is ill equipped to resolve the abortion controversy, providing inadequate resources to address the two fundamental questions that are decisive of the issue: whether the rights of the fetus counterbalance the woman's generalized liberty right, and whether there are other considerations of the public good that counterbalance the woman's generalized liberty right.

Hadley Arkes contends that judges seem willing to snatch questions such as marriage, sexuality, nature, life, death, and the very definition of a human being out of the political arena and reserve it to their own hands, "removing from the arena of public deliberation questions that were once thought to be at the center of our public lives." Their holdings on abortion—especially recent lower-court decisions on prohibitions of partial-birth abortion, at a point where the act is indistinguishable from infanticide—have cast doubt on human beings' natural rights, making such questions a matter for political authority. We are no longer as certain as we used to be about what constitutes "nature" and human beings, or perhaps (even if we think we understand what a human being is) "we think that our judgment here may be a matter of opinion or convention—or even a certain tribal preference for our own species—and so we are content to leave to the decision of the community, or the political process, the authority to determine just who is a human being." That is to say, we assume that there is no intrinsic meaning or dignity that attaches to the notion of a human being: this judgment is a matter dependent wholly on the positive law. Judges are thereby at war with jurisprudence itself, for the law is no longer committed, as part of its central mission, to the protection of human life, it being no longer clear that there is a body of natural rights that forms the grounds of our rights, and our jurisprudence. This new jurisprudence can therefore be characterized as "antijural jurisprudence," since it detaches itself from the premises necessary to the notion of lawfulness, leaving us with the forms but without the substance of law.

George W. Liebmann discusses the effect of judicial interference on subordinate and mediating institutions, and what should be done about it. He describes the deleterious effect of judicial interference in state and local governments, various professions (law, medicine, social work, schools, the mass media), economic units (especially by perverse statutory construction), and the family (with the extolling of the individual rights of family members above interests of family solidarity). These unfortunate judicial interventions have been tolerated because of the fixation on the economic by both the Right and the Left, and have been hastened by their association with the pursuit of racial equality (aspects of which have only helped to make slum inhabitants wards of the state, due to a fostering of extreme individualism). Government should start by obeying the admonition to "do no harm." Its contribution to equality should come in the form of a fair tax policy applied to income above subsistence. Other efforts of egalitarianism generally end in tyranny and partiality. "The road away from our present discontents," he argues, "is found not in invention of new 'rights' but in respect for what was once thought to be a distinctive American value, what Justice Black called 'the right of each man to participate in the self government of his society.'" Repudiation of various judicial doctrines is necessary to help prevent the United States from falling into the error of France described by Tocqueville: a prejudice against local discretion (characteristic of both the Left and the Right, the Jacobins and Economists) leading to a capricious and arbitrary central administration that undermined respect for law.

Steven D. Smith inquires into the capacity of the legal academy to shape the law. The first category of the more obvious ways of influencing the Supreme Court—for example, scholarly publications and supplying "the courts with law clerks freshly trained to see the law the way the professor sees it"—are very limited, Smith believes. Even the capacity to bestow praise and blame on judges, which is likely to have a greater impact, at least on some judges, is still limited and somewhat haphazard. A second, and much more important, form of influence on the courts is more indirect: the legal academy's inculcation of a "culture of rationalism." This rationalism has three principal components: a discourse of instrumental rationality; a perpetual roving commission to ferret out decisions based on tradition, faith, and emotion; and deference to the opinions prevalent among an educated class. This culture has various unfortunate consequences, and finally results in a kind of arrogance that disparages tradition, faith, and intuition as sources of decision, or as modes of living. This culture and its consequences help to explain an otherwise puzzling phenomenon: how it is that personally modest judges become aggressive intermeddlers in the social order.

Jack Wade Nowlin rejects an argument, put forward by advocates of a "moral" reading of the Constitution, that judges have special powers of moral insight, concluding that it has insuperable theoretical and practical difficulties. The obvious and familiar arguments in favor of a special judicial power of moral insight in fact paint a skewed and idealized portrait of judges and courts. On the one hand, the inference of moral "expertise" from a tendency to reach the "right" answers as defined from a particular "thick" or substantive moral standpoint—liberal judges are moral "experts" from a liberal standpoint—is indistinguishable from special pleading and therefore cannot serve as a general argument for expansive judicial power. But, on the other hand, one cannot draw a clear connection between the ability to engage in "thin" sophisticated moral reasoning and the discovery of right answers to difficult moral questions. Moreover, other aspects of the judicial process—such as the primacy of legal interpretation and the practical political constraints on judicial power—suggest that judges typically do not, and indeed cannot, openly engage in sophisticated moral reasoning or develop sophisticated, critical, reflective, reasoned, and coherent moral theories. Judicial moral analysis is inexorably understated, incompletely theorized, and distorted by legal materials (*Roe* and *Casey* providing notable examples).

Michael W. McConnell is not surprised by the fact that justices (and lawyers and law professors) take a "generous" view of judicial power, but he puzzles over why "the People," whose democratic authority has been wrested away by nine lawyers wearing robes, put up with it. His answer is that the Court is the beneficiary—in high schools, colleges, and even law schools—of a "celebratory history" of the Court as a defender of the Constitution and the agent of beneficent social reform. After summarizing this history, McConnell sketches a (more accurate) counterhistory, in which most political actors, including the Supreme Court itself, have *not* viewed the Court as the body with exclusive authority to tell us what the Constitution dictates. Moreover, this counterhistory would recognize that the Court has made mistakes, not just on peripheral questions, but on some of the most important moral, political, and constitutional questions that our society has had to face. *Dred Scott*, decisions dramatically narrowing the proper scope of the Fourteenth Amendment and helping to usher in Jim Crow, and the oft-cited laissez-faire cases of the early twentieth century are only some examples of such decisions. The Warren Court engaged in activism that was legitimate, activism that was politically desirable but illegitimate, and much that was neither wise nor legitimate. The Burger Court "exacerbated the worst tendencies of the Warren Court," and the Rehnquist Court, while pulling back, has not reconsidered precedents and carries on "the vision of the Justices as the high priests of our constitutional religion." Especially given that bad judicial decisions are much more difficult to change than legislative ones, a "more balanced" understanding of constitutional history calls for "greater humility in the exercise of judicial review."

Jeremy Waldron asks how republican government can be squared with a political system in which important issues of public principle are decided finally by majority voting in panels of professional judges, appointed for life, whose decisions are made after, and whose decisions prevail over, decisions made in legislative assemblies by the accountable representatives of the people. He considers arguments that judicial review is compatible with republicanism inasmuch as it represents the view of the people as to how their self-government should be conducted, that it promotes republican values by improving the quality of public debate on matters of principle, and that it is necessary as a means of safeguarding a republican framework. Each of these arguments, he argues, betrays the idea of republican government in the light of something that seems to the proponent more important—popular sovereignty, scholarly culture, or procedural respectability. Republican government is a demanding ideal, requiring risks based on faith in a people's ability to govern themselves. The worst form of republican apostasy is to worry that important social issues may not be settled according to one's own views, and therefore to refuse to submit to social decisions with which one disagrees. Such a stance fails to respect the elementary condition of *being with others*, which is both the essence of republican politics and the principle of mutual recognition that lies at the heart of the idea of citizenship.

Keith E. Whittington writes in response to the increasing academic criticism of an "activist" Rehnquist Court—not because of decisions like *Planned Parenthood v. Casey* (which largely garners the approval of the legal professoriate)—but because of its federalism cases. The recent Supreme Court has increased judicial review of national, as opposed to state, action, and has shifted from a focus on individual rights to matters of constitutional structure. What Whittington particularly puts his finger on is a key difference in the nature of recent judicial activism: unlike *Casey*, which had the effect of "stopping political debate and legislative action," recent decisions such as *Lopez* "are about redirecting political activism into different channels," that is, from national to state channels. The result of this difference is that the policy consequences of federalism-oriented judicial activism are rather modest, and do not involve the much more substantial threats of judicial supremacy inherent in earlier forms of activism(à la *Casey*). Whittington is careful to note that we might still want to criticize recent activism qua activism, but he says that we should at least understand the magnitude of its implications for "judicial imperialism."

In the final chapter, I discuss the academic charges of "conservative judicial activism" leveled against the Rehnquist Court. I begin by detailing a specific understanding of what constitutes judicial activism, focusing especially on the transformation of judicial review from an interpretive to a legislative power, and by offering a few observations on just who constitutes "the Rehnquist Court," since various combinations of justices on that Court can produce quite different sorts of opinions. After reviewing some significant cases from the Burger Court (which help to identify the jurisprudential approach of key Rehnquist Court members), I then examine the Rehnquist Court's takings clause jurisprudence (contrasting *Lucas v. South Carolina Coastal Commission*'s search for an "intelligible standard" favorably with *Dolan v. City of Tigard*'s balancing), its free exercise jurisprudence (defending *Smith*, but arguing that *Boerne* is only accidentally right in this particular case and that its broader argument is unsound), and *U.S. v. Lopez* (suggesting that, despite the importance of constitutional standards for federalism, the judiciary lacks manageable standards for the exercise of judicial review). On the whole, I conclude, the critics have substantial grounds for their accusations of judicial activism, and it appears that the Rehnquist Court has not, unfortunately, marked a significant retreat from the activism inherent in modern forms of judicial review.

What practical measures can be taken to rein in judicial imperialism, and whether and when political conditions will exist to make them a reality is unclear. It is vital, however, for those who value republican government to recognize the necessity of achieving that aim. A lack of awareness about the scope of contemporary judicial power will make it impossible to mobilize the necessary political support even to consider significant limits on court power. And a fatalistic acceptance of extraordinarily broad policymaking power in the hands of unelected and virtually unaccountable judges is not consistent with the profound attachment to self-government that is embedded in the very foundation of our nation's political principles. A dedication to those principles should impel us to persevere in efforts to restore "that eminent tribunal" to its proper and limited role in our system of government.

The chapters in this volume (with the exception of chapters 10 and 11) are based on papers delivered at the American Public Philosophy Institute conference "Reining in Judicial Imperialism," and the editor wishes to acknowledge the support of the Lynde and Harry Bradley Foundation, the John M. Olin Foundation, and the Lehrman Institute that made the conference possible. I am particularly grateful for the assistance of Diane Sehler, Bill Voegeli, and Lew Lehrman and Dick Behn.

I also wish to thank Robert George, Bill Kristol, and Leonard Leo for their assistance in the conceptualization and organization of that conference.

A previous version of chapter 2, "Nationhood and Judicial Supremacy," appeared in *The Implosion of American Federalism* by Robert F. Nagel, copyright 2002, published by Oxford University Press.

And finally, I want to thank Chuck Myers of Princeton University Press for being a most supportive editor throughout a long and sometimes trying process of bringing the book to publication.

NOTES

1. See Robert Bork, *The Tempting of America* (New York: Free Press, 1990); Raoul Berger, *Government by Judiciary* (Cambridge: Harvard University Press, 1977); Christopher Wolfe, *The Rise of Modern Judicial Review* (New York: Basic Books, 1986).

2. See, for example, Mark Tushnet, *Taking the Constitution Away from the Courts* (Princeton: Princeton University Press, 1999); and Gerald Rosenberg, *The Hollow Hope* (Chicago: University of Chicago Press, 1991); as well as Jeremy Waldron's contribution to this volume.

CHAPTER 1

Is the Constitution Whatever the Winners Say It Is?

Gerard V. Bradley

IT WAS THE day before *Roe v. Wade's*[1] twenty-fifth birthday, the day most of us first heard of Monica Lewinsky. But on January 21, 1998, *two* tales of sex and constitutional crisis were told in Washington, D.C. Here is the one you have heard less about.

On that cold, clear morning Missouri senator John Ashcroft convened a hearing of his Subcommittee on the Constitution. The subject was *Roe*. The occasion was noteworthy, in part, for the appearance of "Jane Roe"—Norma McCorvey—as a witness *against* the holding that the Supreme Court entered in her favor a quarter century before. More telling than Ms. McCorvey's testimony was an exchange between the chair and Georgetown law professor Michael Seidman. Seidman had come not to bury *Roe v. Wade*, but to praise it. Ashcroft put this question to him: now that slavery is outlawed, is there a circumstance other than abortion where the law gives one person life or death authority over another?

Seidman did not directly answer his distinguished interlocutor. But he defended *Roe*, in a three-part argument, the last part possessed of two sections. The whole ensemble is a nearly perfect expression of what has been on offer from the Supreme Court, not just on abortion but about much of constitutional law since *Roe*. In fact, Seidman's apology succinctly explained the deepest justifications for the Court's whole privacy jurisprudence over the last half-century, and for the Court's authority to make it.

Here is Seidman's tour de force.

PART 1

Suppose the state of Missouri were to decide that it was underpopulated. And in order to deal with the underpopulation, the state decided that they were going to, against the will of women, artificially inseminate them and force them to bear children that they don't want to bear.[2]

Get it? Senator Ashcroft did not. "Professor," he said, "that's sort of an interesting hypothetical." But what has it to do, he wondered, with the uniqueness of a private franchise to terminate the lives of the unborn?

Strange as Seidman's response thus far considered may seem, he merely adapted a statement of the Supreme Court. In *Planned Parenthood v.*

Casey (the 1992 case that reaffirmed *Roe*), three Republican appointees—so-called centrists—said that, but for the abortion license established in *Roe*, "the state might as readily restrict a woman's right to choose to carry a pregnancy to term as to terminate it, to further asserted state interests in population control, or eugenics, for example."[3]

And so, it seems, we are somehow to equate forced impregnation with abortion with the freedom to bring a child to term and delivery. Or, more exactly, we are to fear that the "state" does.

Casey may mark the high (or low) point of an improbable judicial agnosticism about moral values. But not its birthday. Justices have spoken this odd language of moral equivalence since the end of World War II, though with settled frequency as part of the *ratio* of cases only since the sixties. The classic statements include "[O]ne man's lyric is another man's vulgarity" (to sustain a ruling in favor of public display of this sentiment: "F——k the draft").[4] Also memorable is William O. Douglas's passionate defense of constitutional protection for publications "of value to the masochistic community or to others of the deviant community."[5] One of my favorites in this line of colorful phrases never made it into a Court opinion. A brief in the important but neglected *Burstyn v. Wilson* case said that "one man's sacred cow is another man's casual repast."[6]

Now as a purely descriptive matter, there is some truth in these assertions. People do in fact believe all sorts of things. But the justices have not been doing sociology; they have not been merely describing. They mean by these statements and others like them to articulate a theory of value. That theory is a subjective one. The Supreme Court over the last generation or so has declared that no one exercising public authority may act on the basis of the conviction that, regardless of what somebody believes about, say, abortion or adultery, such acts (as abortion or adultery) are objectively wrong, and worthy of discouragement by the state for that reason (though not for that reason alone). Note well: the Court does not speak solely for itself, and announces no rule of peculiarly judicial restraint. The Court announces a rule of constitutional law. Legislators and governors and school board members and the President and everyone else acting as part of the state shall act as if forced impregnation is the same as abortion as bringing a baby to term.

We shall revisit this theory of value, stated a little differently, when we come to part 3b of Seidman's argument.

Why? That is, why has the Court adopted and imposed upon others this particular theory of moral value? Sex, mostly. More exactly: at least since the mid-1960s the justices have determined to liberate the libido from legal constraints rooted in the moral common sense of the American people. (Why they have decided to do so is a question whose answer is beyond the scope of this paper.) All the odd talk about the relativity of moral judgment—from Seidman, from the *Casey* opinion writers, from William O. Douglas—is the answer to this question: *how* could the Court manage to pull off such an audacious undertaking?

Here is the predicament that the Court presented itself. In *Roe* and *Casey* the justices wanted (for reasons we leave aside) to justify liberty for acts that most Americans morally condemn, and would legally prohibit, on grounds that include precisely these acts' objective immorality. The Court's odd theory of moral equivalence nullifies this popular judgment by *declaring* that the asserted objectivity is illusory. The Court says: assertions of moral objectivity amount to, or underwrite, the imposition of one's value judgments upon another. "One man's lyric . . ." In such case, the imposition is an unconstitutional abridgement of liberty.

But upon what did—does—the Court base its declaration? The place to begin the search for the requisite authority is the Constitution.

PART 2

Now, the fact of the matter is, the Constitution says no more about the [forced impregnation] than it says about abortion. There's nothing in the Fourteenth Amendment that says a word about it, nothing in the intent of the framers that we can find that they thought about that problem.

Is this not a concession that the Court's rulings in favor of moral subjectivism are adrift from the constitutional text, as understood by the "framers" (that is, those who put the text into the Constitution)? Is not the concession necessary, because the proposition conceded is obviously true?

Casey is one important piece of evidence for the advisability of the concession. In that case the "centrists" (though on this point they could easily have spoken for almost all those who have served on the Court since World War II) derived a principle of decision—a broad liberty of self-definition—not from the text or history, but from their own decisions going back twenty-five years.[7]

Almost any Establishment Clause case is a good illustration, too. A prominent academic lawyer's struggle with its text exemplifies the struggles of the Court. Yale law professor Stephen Carter describes himself as generally an originalist in matters of constitutional interpretation.[8] He concedes an important point about the meaning of the Establishment Clause: that provision was designated by its framers *not* to disestablish any church, much less for the sweeping purpose—to separate religion from public life—that the Court has recently found there. The historical evidence rather shows that the clause was not meant to lay down *any* concrete norm having to do with church and state. The text, which prohibits "laws respecting an establishment of religion," protected state autonomy from the national government in matters of religion. The Establishment Clause was a jurisdictional directive: states were permitted to retain their establishments of religion, if that was their preference, and Congress was denied the authority to interfere.

Carter concedes that this interpretation of the Establishment Clause is sound. But he does not approve of it. So, he says, the "original understanding may no longer bind because contemporary reality is so sharply discontinuous with the world of the Founders."[9]

Maybe the "worlds" are "discontinuous." Maybe not. The question is, however, how does a judge's reckoning (for Carter means to endorse the recent judicial turn away from the historical understanding of the clause) of such large matters make for judicial amendment of the Constitution?

Someone might object that strict adherence to the Constitution's text does not exhaust the possibilities of meaningful, and adequate, constitutional fidelity. Indeed, the main direction of the Court's argument for the content of the new master norm—the agnosticism of the *Casey* court—is fidelity to something deeper and broader and more important than the text, but still meaningfully in, or close enough to, the Constitution to justify judicial imposition of it upon a recalcitrant polity. And so, the canonical justification for the Court's nonestablishment doctrines and tests has not been the text but the "principle" or value the text expresses (or is otherwise related to): separation of church and state, or a cognate principle.

Is the objection valid? There is indeed an important distinction between norms, rules, or standards—all of which are specific enough to actually guide decisions in concrete cases—and principles. A "norm" (or rule, or standard) capable of guiding decision annexes, to some specific description of an act, an evaluative directive: this act—described thus and so—must not (or must be or may be) done (under the following conditions, by these specified persons). "Jaywalking is prohibited" is a rule, not a principle, and it says do not walk across the street except at corners.

A "principle" justifies or explains or supports a norm. The Fifth Amendment contains a norm having to do with an act (compelling one to be a witness against oneself), and a directive: it is not to be done. This norm can be subsumed under one or more principles—that it is unfair to make one the instrument of one's own indictment, or to make one choose from among contempt, perjury, or conviction. The Fourth Amendment says, in its legally operative part, that no warrant may issue, save upon certain conditions. This norm is no doubt a concretization of the broader, justificatory principle we find preceding it in the text: no unreasonable searches or seizures. And perhaps that is a specification of a (very broad) principle or value, call it privacy. Another example: the "rule against hearsay" is a specification of the norm that precludes unreliable testimony, all to ensure that there is, in principle, a fair trial, an entitlement of defendants by dint of the Sixth Amendment.

The move from principle to norm is not deductive. It is not a matter of compelling inference. The move is much freer, much more creative, than that. The move from principle to norm is guided by reason, but the reality is that a broad range of possible specifications—corresponding to the universe of act descriptions and to the menu of evaluative directives—are all more or less consistent with a given principle, or cluster of principles. A relatively small number of imaginable specifications will be ruled out as entirely unreasonable, as simply incompatible with the governing principle.

So, persons equally devoted to providing a fair trial might disagree about whether there should be a rule against hearsay and, if there is to be such a rule, what exactly that rule should prohibit. Or persons equally devoted to providing a fair trial to criminal defendants might disagree, as our Supreme Court did before *Gideon v. Wainwright*,[10] about whether an attorney is essential to a fair trial. But note well: one who moves from principle to norm is exercising a legislative-like authority. One who moves back from norm to principle, and stands there with norm production in mind, has (re)claimed legislative-like prerogative. "Legislative" denotes the implementation of a value ("privacy," "equality") by picking an act out of the universe of acts and affixing a directive norm to it.

When the context is constitutional, the stakes are higher. One who goes back to the text to embrace what one asserts to be its animating values or goals or to deal with the evils that called forth the textual response stands in the Framers' shoes. One who does so is set to write the Constitution anew. Think of it this way: one stands in the shoes of those who, having set down the broad goals of the national government in the Preamble, proceeded to answer the question: what will best serve those goals here and now, by writing the rest of the Constitution?

This was precisely the move that freed the Warren Court from the Constitution. Beyond the text, the Warren Court members rightly observed, lay some values and principles. Maybe those values included, as those justices said, privacy, liberty, tolerance, diversity. But the Warren Court acted as constitution maker, and not as interpreter, in reducing the text to jurisdictional charter to bring forth a law of religious liberty for our time, or a contemporary law of search and seizure, or of confessions. So, if it is the case that all one can recover (or confidently say one recovers or prudently recovers) from the Constitution and in its originating context *is* a broad principle, then the Constitution calls for implementation that is legislative in character.

That the judiciary should exercise this legislative-type authority is a proposition to be argued for. Citation to the *Marbury* declaration about judges saying what the law is[11] do not constitute argument. And, taken simply as authority, the meaning of the declaration is scarcely univocal; *if* it is to be taken as authority for the proposition that courts have legislative authority (along the lines I have sketched), then *that* interpretation would have to be argued for.

"The independence of the judiciary" is no more transparently a proper, adequate authority. That our judiciary is independent I do not deny: Article III judges enjoy tenure and salary protection, and they do so for a reason. But that reason, or rather those protections, presuppose the contrary of the authority they would justify. Put differently, for our Constitution makers the judiciary's independence presupposed the definiteness of the law to be faithfully (apolitically, if you will) applied. The Framers did not endorse—they could scarcely imagine—an insulated judicial prerogative to determine what the law should be.

To return to the main story. We have been considering the possibility that the Court's denial of legitimacy to certain products of the democratic process—those that presuppose the truth of an objective moral norm regarding (assertedly) harmless sexual acts—is required by the Constitution. The best defense of this position, we have seen, claims no more warrant than that provided by principles outside but near the text. I have argued that this will not do: the authority to specify those principles—granting but not conceding that the Court has identified the relevant nearby principles—is the thing to be justified. The so-called defenses assume this authority. Besides, it can hardly be imagined that the Framers of our Constitution entertained, as a pertinent background principle, the moral relativism of our modern Supreme Court.

PART 3A

And yet, I really seriously don't believe that anybody in this room would say that it was unjustified judicial activism for a court to strike a law like that down.

Is the Court's authority the product of a popular referendum? If so, when was it held? What, exactly, was the proposition approved? Are the justices collaborating with the (some? a few?) "people" in a continuing constitutional convention? If so, why cannot the people have it both ways? Why cannot they have a Court that does *both* of the following: strikes down China-type family policies—Seidman's nightmare—*and* strikes down abortion-on-demand, which *Roe* gave us but which the people never supported?

More exactly: Seidman took Ashcroft's question to be an invitation to defend *Roe*. Seidman introduced the forced impregnation hypothetical to begin this defense. He asserted that some authoritative group of people would condone judicial invalidation of that heinous law, even if, he implied, there is nothing in the Constitution that warrants that judicial act.

Let us grant these points. How does granting them commit one to the proposition that Seidman means to defend, which is the correctness of a decision—*Roe*—to strike down the popularly enacted antiabortion laws of all fifty states? Indeed, where in the premises granted is (*a*) a jurisdiction to decide, in any fashion, questions other than the one about techno-rape, and (*b*) to decide any question at all except morally correctly? Put differently, why can't one grant Seidman's premises, and applaud one decision because it is morally correct, and condemn another because it is morally incorrect?

Again, the central question is begged. And there is a deeper problem. By putting part 1 together with part 3a, we have the curious proposition that "the people" invest great authority in the courts to protect them from the depredations of "the state." Who is the "state," but the people? Have the people hired judges to protect them from themselves?

PART 3B

   And the reason [the people in this room] would say that [i.e., that it was justified judicial activism to enjoin forced impregnation] is because the issue of
   whether individual parents decide to have children is a matter that ought not
   to be decided by the legislature in Missouri or by the legislature in Congress. It
   ought to be decided by individuals.

Now Seidman seems to rely upon a simple but profound norm of political morality, quite entirely distinct from 3a, the plebiscite. Where does this principle of individual autonomy come from? The Constitution? No. See part 2. Have the people approved it? If they had, they would scarcely need judicial protection from the "state." See discussion of 3a.

Indeed, part 3b appears to restate part 1. If so, the colorful statements of moral equivalence reviewed in 1 are now seen as a theory of value, not sociology. That theory assigns value not to the propositions people affirm (or deny), but the *fact* of *their* affirming (or denying). For the final time, where does this subjectivist theory of value, or very strong doctrine of moral autonomy, come from?

What is the pedigree of this strong autonomy principle? During its long trek through the privacy cases the Court veered, incrementally but consistently, towards grounding them, in no recondite or technical sense, in the raw significance of the decision to the decider. By the time of the *Webster* case,[12] the 1989 decision that was widely expected to sound the death knell of *Roe*, this development was aptly described in a law professors' brief as the right to "self-definition in matters of value and conscience, and self-determination regarding ways and walks of life."[13] The *Casey* justices spoke of the deeply personal and highly spiritual nature of a woman's decision to abort, concluding that the abortion license was within the liberty "to define one's own concept of existence, of meaning, of the universe, and of the mystery of human life. Beliefs about these matters could not define the attributes of personhood were they formed under the compulsion of the state."[14]

How then do all parts of the argument fit together? We see finally that 3a and 3b are *not* alternatives. Seidman, here faithfully echoing the Court, has set up a rhetorical field bounded by 3a and 3b. Defenses of the modern judicial project oscillate between them as the needs of the argument determine.

Listen carefully to the absolutely pivotal oscillation in the following sampler of prominent defenses of the Court since the heyday of Earl Warren.

John Rawls: "The Constitution is not what the Court says it is. Rather, it is what the people, acting constitutionally through the other branches, eventually allow the Court to say it is."[15] But who decides whether the people have acted "constitutionally," and how long is "eventually?" And more. Rawls defends, in *Political Liberalism*, the possibility of unconstitutional constitutional amendments, procedurally impeccable alterations invalid because of conflict with what he calls "entrenched" constitutional provisions, like free speech.[16]

Ronald Dworkin: "[T]he Constitution insists that our judges do their best collectively to construct, reinspect, and revise, generation by generation, the skeleton of freedom and equality of concern that its great clauses, in their majestic abstraction, command."[17] Amendment and impeachment—which is to say, popular checks upon our Constitution— Dworkin reduces to the level of "theory": the "main engines for disciplining judges are intellectual rather than political or legal." The "whole American community" must hold the judges to certain intellectual standards. So the guys down at the barber shop and the soccer moms do not discipline judges by, somehow, voting against them, but by writing critical law review articles.

William Brennan, in an important speech at Georgetown University while a sitting justice: "When Justices interpret the Constitution they speak for their community, not for themselves alone. The Justices must render constitutional interpretations that are received as legitimate." How is legitimacy established? In what does it consist? "Successive generations of Americans have continued to respect these fundamental choices and adopt them as their own guide." Brennan called for "contemporary ratification" of the court's handiwork.[18] But he never got around to calling a ratifying convention.

Casey: the American people's aspiration to live according to the rule of law "is not readily separable from their understanding of the Court invested with the authority to decide their constitutional cases and speak before all others for their constitutional ideals. If the Court's legitimacy should be undermined then, so would the country be in its very ability to see itself through its constitutional ideals."[19]

Perhaps most notably, again from *Casey*: "Our Constitution is a covenant running from the first generation of Americans to us and to future generations. Each generation must learn anew that the Constitution's written terms embody ideas and inspirations that must survive more ages than one."[20] The Court is telling us: "We will be your Court and you will be our people."

We are free, it seems from this rhetoric, to ordain the order that suits our age—but we are, paradoxically, trustees of our descendants. But we must, it also seems, hold back (something) that is appealing to us (curbing the Court) because of what it might work for our descendants. But they will, it also seems, have a complete liberty to discard the work of their ancestors—*us*—just as we may of ours.

This much is clear: the Court has constructed around its rulings a seemingly impregnable rhetorical fortress, pouring the hot oil of principle on the heads of rabble ascending the walls, cutting off the legs of highbrow critics with the whipsaw of popular ratification.

These matters are not the concern solely of constitutional lawyers; they are not just "academic" questions. Everyone needs to know what the law is. Was George Wallace, standing at the doors of the University of Alabama, engaged in the legitimate process of coming to constitutional conclusions or interpreting constitutional ideals, or was he defying the law? Are antiabortion demonstrators participating in a constitutional conversation, or are they breaking the law? Is constitutional law knowable only after the winners have written their histories?

NOTES

1. *Roe v. Wade*, 410 U.S. 113, 93 S.Ct. 705 (1973).
2. "Twenty-Fifth Anniversary of *Roe v. Wade*: Has It Stood the Test of Time?" Hearing before the U.S. Senate Committee on the Judiciary Subcommittee on the Constitution, Federalism and Property Rights, 105 Cong. 20 (1998) (Statement of Professor Michael Seidman).
3. *Planned Parenthood v. Casey*, 505 U.S. 833, 859.
4. *Cohen v. State of California*, 403 U.S. 15, 25, 91 S.Ct. 1780, 1788 (1971).
5. *Ginzburg v. United States*, 383 U.S. 463, 489, 86, S.Ct. 969, 973 (1966).
6. Brief of the Committee on Constitutional Liberties of the National Lawyers Guild as Amicus Curiae at 5, *Burstyn v. Wilson*, 343 U.S. 495, 72 S.Ct. 777 (1952) (522).
7. See *Planned Parenthood v. Casey*, 112 S.Ct. 2791, 2805–7 (1992).
8. Stephen L. Carter, *The Culture of Disbelief* (New York: Basic Books, 1993), 298.

9. Ibid., 119.

10. *Gideon v. Wainwright*, 372 U.S. 335, 83 S.Ct. 792 (1963).

11. *Marbury v. Madison*, 5 U.S. (1 Cranch) 137, 177 (1803).

12. *Webster v. Reproductive Health Services*, 492 U.S. 490 (1989).

13. Brief of Attorneys for a Group of American Law Professors as Amicus Curiae at 6, *Webster v. Reproductive Health Services*, No.88-605.

14. *Planned Parenthood v. Casey*, 851.

15. John Rawls, *Political Liberalism* (New York: Columbia University Press, 1993), 237.

16. Ibid., 239.

17. Ronald Dworkin, *Life's Dominion* (New York: Knopf, 1993), 145.

18. William J. Brennan Jr., "The Constitution of the United States: Contemporary Ratification," in *Interpreting the Constitution*, ed. Jack N. Rakove (Boston: Northeastern University Press, 1990) 23, 25.

19. *Planned Parenthood v. Casey*, 868.

20. Ibid., 901.

CHAPTER 2

Nationhood and Judicial Supremacy

Robert F. Nagel

EVEN CRITICS of *Planned Parenthood v. Casey* must admit that the opinion of the Court has an earnest, almost yearning quality.[1] The justices manifestly *want* the American people to understand weighty and difficult matters. They discuss at length not only the immediate legal basis of their reaffirmation that the Constitution protects the right to abortion but also the deeper institutional and political bases of the rule of law and, indeed, of "the country's understanding of itself." Accordingly, beginning with the first sentence—"Liberty finds no refuge in a jurisprudence of doubt"—the language of the opinion is both portentous and elusive. The justices take us into their confidence; they risk much. They reveal what to some is stupefying arrogance and to others selfless heroism.

They do not, however, reveal the full range of considerations that drive their thinking. I do not mean that in this respect the opinion is hypocritical or devious. I mean only that it is incomplete. The highly intellectualized picture so elaborately drawn rests, one suspects, on a more primitive vision or fear.

Think about that cryptic first sentence. Translated into concrete terms, the justices appear to be denying that the right to abortion (presumably the "liberty" referred to) will find protection ("refuge") in the position taken by those who challenge that right (the "jurisprudence of doubt"). But, who, it must be asked, has to be made to understand that a liberty is unlikely to be protected by its critics? As if this question presented no problem for their solemn tone, the justices plunge on in the same baffling direction. The very next sentence complains that "19 years after our holding . . . [in] *Roe v. Wade*, . . . that definition of liberty is still questioned." And then the majority notes that the United States, as amicus curiae, is again asking that the Court overrule *Roe*. So at least as a literal matter, it is clear that this most weighty of judicial opinions opens by developing the thought that the right to abortion will find no protection among those who are asking the Court to abolish the right to abortion.

It is possible, however, to read the first paragraph, not as painfully self-evident, but as evocative. This would be more respectful, and it is also consistent with some specific phrasing. The use of the general word *lib-*

erty implies that much more is at stake than any particular right. Similarly, the threat is said to come not from a specific criticism but from a whole "jurisprudence of doubt." A "refuge" is needed, then, because it is a storm that is raging. This is enough, it might be thought, for an opening paragraph. The nature of the struggle and of the potential calamity can be identified in due course.

These broad considerations are not, however, identified in the next section of the opinion, which explains the Court's determination that the right to abortion is protected by the due process clause. True, this part of the opinion does contain lofty, not to say pretentious, language about the relationship between the right to abortion and the need to define "one's own concept of existence" and even "[t]he destiny of woman." In themselves, these famous passages add only the thought that the liberty threatened by the storm swirling around *Roe* is a highly significant right. Oddly, this claim, which is so strenuously asserted, is undercut by the justices themselves when in the same section they concede not only that "[s]ome of us as individuals find abortion offensive to our most basic principles of morality," but also that there is "weight" to the arguments for overruling *Roe*. But putting all quibbles aside and assuming that the sentiments expressed about the importance of the right to abortion are coherent and heartfelt, these passages do not address the possibility, suggested by that brooding opening paragraph, that much is at risk *beyond* this particular right. The first sentence of the opinion, that is to say, cannot be rescued from vacuousness by being restated to say, "A profoundly significant constitutional right finds no protection among those who deny that it is either morally valuable or constitutionally protected." Indeed, the earlier suggestion that more is under attack than a constitutional right is raised again as the second section concludes: "[T]he reservations any of us may have in reaffirming the central holding of *Roe* are outweighed by the explication of individual liberty we have [just] given *combined with* the force of *stare decisis*."[2] The "liberty" that needs a refuge, it appears, is in significant part whatever liberty is implicated by respect for precedent.

There follow many pages (fully twice as many as are spent justifying the constitutional status of the right to abortion) that explain what is at stake in respecting the precedent represented by a case such as *Roe v. Wade*. In this third section the Court invokes institutional considerations of the highest order. Indeed, at first glance this long discussion seems to redeem fully the portentousness and incompleteness of the opening paragraph of the opinion. The phrase "jurisprudence of doubt" it turns out does, indeed, refer to far more than criticisms of *Roe* or even of the Court's privacy decisions in general. It refers to a dangerous misunderstanding of the subtleties of the doctrine of stare decisis in constitutional cases. Ultimately, it refers to the kind of doubts that are created when the Court overturns decisions under circumstances that create the appearance of "surrender to political pressure." And this jurisprudence of doubt would threaten "liberty" in the broadest sense of that word. By undermining the Court's legitimacy, disregard for the precedent established by certain momentous constitutional decisions, such as *Roe*, would exact a truly "terrible price":

> Like the character of an individual, the legitimacy of the Court must be earned over time. So, indeed, must be the character of a Nation of people who aspire to live according to the rule of law. Their belief in themselves as such a people is not readily separable from their understanding of the Court invested with the authority to decide constitutional cases and speak before all others for their constitutional ideals. If the Court's legitimacy should be undermined, then, so would the country be in its very ability to see itself through its constitutional ideals.[3]

In short, the liberty that is under attack—"under fire"—is nothing short of the liberty to be a part of a political culture that is committed to the rule of law and understands itself through the prism of constitutional values. If in certain crucial circumstances the Supreme Court is seen as surrendering to political pressures, the resulting jurisprudence of doubt will corrode American constitutionalism.

Now, this claim is obviously subject to being criticized as self-important or even grandiose, but it may not seem vulnerable to the charge of incompleteness. I believe, however, that a moment's reflection confirms that even in these stunningly expansive passages, the justices do not fully or precisely describe the vision that drives their decision to reaffirm the essentials of *Roe v. Wade*. Step back for a moment and consider the suspiciously rarified nature of the Court's anguished argument: What is at issue, after all, is the place of stare decisis in a certain class of constitutional cases. Is it even remotely plausible that judicial legitimacy and American commitment to the rule of law depend in any fundamental way on this arcane judicial doctrine? Can it be seriously contended that our devotion to constitutional ideals rides on a juristic norm that most citizens understand only dimly and that even some sophisticated judges and lawyers believe should have no applicability in any constitutional case?

Intellectualizations about fidelity to precedent can be, I know, beautiful to the lawyerly eye.[4] But, as the dissenters indicate,[5] the Court's position depends on answers to some rather mundane empirical and historical questions. For example: To what extent do Americans now believe (and to what extent have they believed in the past) that the Court's constitutional decisions are based on precedent rather than politics? To what extent do they believe these decisions should be based on precedent? Do

Americans in fact understand prominent Supreme Court reversals in the way the *Casey* majority does, as responses to new factual understandings rather than new judgments of principle? If not, has cynicism about the Court's fidelity to stare decisis undermined respect for the rule of law? Would Americans see reversing *Roe* as more political than upholding *Roe*? Would they see judicial abandonment of *Roe's* trimester scheme (which, of course, the plurality in *Casey* supported) as significantly less political than they would abandonment of the right to abortion itself? And even if the Court is right about the immediate effects of reversing *Roe*, what evidence can be found that the harm done to the legitimacy of the Court would be irreparable?

Assume for a moment that stare decisis is essential for judicial legitimacy in the way indicated by the majority and assume further that this legitimacy is tied up with American commitment to the rule of law. Even so, the argument remains empirically ungrounded. Why should anyone believe that these perceptions about the Court are essential for America's constitutional idealism? There are many sources, other than the Supreme Court, of constitutional ideals. In the nineteenth century, opponents of slavery did not derive their understanding of the Constitution from the judiciary. The freedom of speech remained a potent political principle despite judicial nonenforcement throughout that century. And today neither opponents of the death penalty nor advocates of the right to bear arms abandon their constitutional convictions merely because their principles have been rejected repeatedly by the Court. Americans get their constitutional ideals from all sorts of places—from the *Federalist Papers*, from sixth-grade civics, from newspaper editorials, from the Gettysburg Address, from neighbors, from religious institutions, and so on.[6] A legitimate judiciary no doubt contributes to our constitutional self-understanding, but it does not follow that Americans would abandon constitutional ideals if the Court's legitimacy were reduced.

It is, of course, impossible to know just how American constitutionalism would change in response to some increment in public cynicism about the Supreme Court. The *Casey* opinion elides this problem by suggesting vaguely that the elements in the asserted chain of causation—stare decisis, judicial legitimacy, rule of law, constitutional idealism—are indistinguishable or at least "not readily separable." But these concepts are all quite different. Certainly, "legitimacy" in the usual sense of that word does not necessarily involve the capacity to inculcate constitutional ideals. Citizens can accept the prerogative of judges to decide constitutional cases while still believing that Supreme Court justices are capable of serious errors and, therefore, are a fallible source of constitutional ideals. In fact, both beliefs are held by many loyal Americans who honor the judiciary as an institution. (Who, one wonders, *does not* , at least at some level, hold these beliefs?) In short, the Court's capacity to secure compliance and its moral standing as a governmental institution—its legitimacy—can exist quite apart from the grand educative function that is the object of the Court's articulated anxiety.

Moreover, "the rule of law," as venerable a term as that is, does not capture what the members of the majority are concerned about either. It is possible, for instance, to believe that the Court has followed "the law" by following a precedent and still believe that the Court is a highly fallible guide to constitutional ideals. (Indeed, it seems possible that this is a set of views held by those justices in the plurality who had grave doubts about the original holding in *Roe.*) It is also possible to believe that a judicial decision is lawful according to formalistic interpretive criteria but nevertheless is not an enunciation of constitutional ideals according to moral or political standards. And, needless to say, it is possible to believe that a decision is lawful according to realistic criteria but not a faithful reflection of constitutional ideals according to historical or textual sources.

Of course, I do not mean that the plurality's claims make no sense at all. Nor do I mean that the three justices could or should have awaited definitive studies bearing on the causal questions before releasing their torrent of urgent words. I mean only that from a down-to-earth perspective their argument is unlikely. As a matter of idle speculation, yes, it is all possible; but as a ground for an important decision, the claims are at once so tenuous and strident as to approach the hysterical.

Why, then, do thoughtful people, including not only Supreme Court justices but also prominent scholars,[7] accept the argument or at least take it seriously? It could be because constitutional decisions, as well as the commentary about them, tend to produce a certain habituation to improbable factual assertions and loose rhetoric. But I believe it is also because the opinion resonates with an unspoken fear, with a vision of catastrophe that is deeply rooted both in our history and in contemporary debate.

The full scope of this vision can be glimpsed by dwelling for a moment on the end point of the Court's argument, the capacity of the nation "to see itself through its constitutional ideals." The capacity for this kind of collective self-perception is nothing less than the capacity for a national identity. What is at issue, then, is not just the operational integrity of our constitutional system but the existence of the political culture upon which that system rests. What would it mean if the citizens of the United States could not see themselves through their constitutional ideals? A variety of serious observers have said that for Americans to see themselves without constitutional ideals would be for Americans to see themselves without a country.[8] To the extent this is true, losing the capacity for constitutional idealism would convert Americans into a collection of people united by little except geographic proximity. Even the common experience of a shared history could lose its coherence and significance without the sustaining narrative of constitutionalism. Thus, when the justices say that their concern for the Court's legitimacy "is not for the sake of the Court but for the sake of the Nation," it might be that we should take them seriously. It might just be that their underlying fear is the political disintegration of the United States.

I am not claiming that anyone, including the members of the *Casey* majority, believes that stare decisis is necessary for national unity. But the various qualifications in the Court's argument suggest that the authoritativeness and supremacy of the judiciary's interpretive function, not respect for precedent, is the operative concern. Recall that the argument is not that the country's capacity to see itself through constitutional ideals is at risk whenever an important precedent is overruled. The case must involve principled, rather than factual judgments, and even then it must be one of those rare cases where "the Court's interpretation of the Constitution calls the contending sides of a national controversy to end their national division by accepting a common mandate rooted in the Constitution." To abandon precedent under these circumstances would threaten the people's belief that "the Court [is] invested with the authority to . . . speak before all others for their constitutional ideals." All this suggests that just behind the linkages that make up the plurality's explicit argument—that stare decisis sometimes underlies judicial legitimacy, and that judicial legitimacy underlies the rule of law, and that the rule of law underlies constitutional idealism—lies a shadow argument that, if articulated, would go as follows: Stare decisis is sometimes necessary for judicial supremacy, and judicial supremacy is necessary for constitutionalism, and constitutionalism is necessary for nationhood.

Is it possible, you may fairly ask, for sane people to believe, indeed, to believe fervently, that overruling *Roe v. Wade* could threaten the United States as a nation? I think it is possible. Indeed, I think that rather surprising assessments of the fragility of our nation are extremely common and are a significant part of the explanation for what is otherwise a largely inexplicable and obdurate devotion to judicial power.

II

Even if the argument of the *Casey* majority is incomplete and even if aspects of that argument point toward a belief that our national political identity is fragile and significantly dependent on judicial supremacy, concern for nationhood might at first seem an unlikely explanation for the extreme sense of urgency in the opinion. Why not stop with the simpler and more familiar explanation that judges, like everyone else, can become devoted to their own power and consequently enraged at those who resist that power? To insist that *Casey* rests on a deep fear of national disintegration would seem to be, at the least, intellectually uneconomical.

But consider: Almost all of the political "fire" directed at *Roe v. Wade*—the long line of state statutes seeking to roll back that decision as well as the nomination of conservatives to the Court—challenged the substance of a decision but not, strictly speaking, the Court's authority. Indeed, this political activity was aimed at inducing *the Court* to change *its* position.[9] The justices would have been exercising power if they had decided to reverse an earlier Court, and satisfyingly so (one would imagine) for those members of the majority who find abortion morally repugnant and constitutionally questionable. Was Justice Scalia's bitter opinion, which, of course, did call for the overruling of *Roe*, an act of personal or institutional abasement? The urge to power is a reliable law of politics, but, without some supplementation or qualification, it will not explain *Casey*.

Nevertheless, it may seem implausible to attribute a fear of national disintegration to any justices in this modern era. After all, even putting aside that the Articles of Confederation were replaced more than two centuries ago and that it has been over a hundred years since the Civil War ended, the undeniable fact is that a vast consolidation of national power has been under way for fully sixty years. The *Casey* opinion comes at a time when the Court itself recognizes that the serious question domestically is whether the national government has become too powerful. And it comes at a time when internationally the United States is virtually unchallenged as the world's leading nation both militarily and politically.

An apex, however, can feel like a precarious position. This might especially be so in the circumstances of the current successes of American nationalization. Those successes, after all, have coexisted with waves of urban rioting, occasional but horrific acts of terrorism, and the sinister presence of militia organizations. Moreover, the United States is a very young nation. Even the two hundred years since the framing is not such a long time, especially given the extent to which the founders, still so venerated, believed in the natural tendency of subordinate political units "to fly off from the common center."[10] They designed the new Constitution largely in response to the demonstrated capacity of those centrifugal forces to threaten the central government. And it was only a few generations ago that the American experiment stood as a colossal failure, as such forces did pull the nation apart. Finally, the centralization of authority that began with the New Deal is not only historically recent but also intellectually controversial.

Perhaps, then, it is not so surprising that right alongside the apparatus of nationalization can be found signs of deep anxiety about disintegration. Recall just for a moment *National League of Cities v. Usery*, a 1976 case that was limited and distinguished in a series of later decisions and then formally overruled.[11] *Usery* declared that the national government lacked authority to regulate the wages and hours of state employees. Justice William Brennan, whose dissent was joined by two other justices, reacted to this decision by charging that the majority's analysis was "not far different" from the judicial doctrines that had threatened the New Deal. Did this sophisticated jurist really fear, as this comparison (and much of his analysis) suggests, that the Court might soon strip the national government of powers essential to its modern role, even including the power to cope with economic crises? Here are the words he chose to describe the Court's decision: "profoundly pernicious," "alarming," "startling," and "catastrophic." Despite acknowledging that as a practical matter Congress could evade *Usery* by using conditional appropriations rather than commerce power regulations, the dissent depicted the Court's decision as "an ominous portent of disruption of our constitutional structure."

Roughly twenty years later in *U.S. Term Limits v. Thornton*[12] we find virtually the same words, this time in a majority opinion. State-imposed congressional term limits, said the majority, "would effect a fundamental change in the constitutional framework." The Court went on to explain that state qualifications for national office would threaten the understanding that members of Congress "become, when elected, servants of the people of the United States." Or, as the Court also put it, state term limits would conflict with the principle that "representatives owe their allegiance to the people, and not to the States."

Now, as with the issue at stake in *Usery*, the actual operational significance of the constitutional issue in *Thornton* is not so easy to discern. No matter what the result in that case, voters, of course, can and do elect to Congress individuals whose loyalties are in part highly parochial. Our present "constitutional framework"—including the vast powers routinely exercised by the national government—has emerged from laws enacted by congresses made up of such people. Nevertheless, justices feared that term limits would undermine nationhood. Indeed, the majority felt it necessary to deny that this nation is "a collection of states" and that Congress is a "confederation of nations." Justice Kennedy, often described as moderate and thoughtful, went so far as to attack the notion that "the sole political identity of an American is with the State of his or her residence."

Fear of disintegration is expressed more fully in *Usery* and *Thornton* than in most opinions, but the theme is taken up by various justices in a number of intervening decisions. Like rustling in the dark, they hear around them "the spirit of the Articles of Confederation,"[13] and they see lurking behind modern constitutional arguments the position that the United States does not "constitute a nation."[14] I recognize that over-wrought language is a regular aspect of the adjudicative process, especially in constitutional cases. But it will not do to pretend that the particular words repeatedly chosen by the justices reveal nothing at all about their beliefs and fears. These words suggest that informed and intelligent justices fear that our nationhood is contested and fragile. Even as the United States government strides along at the apex of its powers, many justices are beset by a bleak vision of structural disintegration.

While in the sober light of day some specific variations of this fear certainly can sound extreme and improbable, acute anxiety about national unity is commonplace and is not regarded as odd either on or off the bench. The Pulitzer Prize–winning journalist Linda Greenhouse, writing in the *New York Times* about the four justices who had voted to uphold state term limits, declared that "it is only a slight exaggeration to say that . . . the Court [is] a single vote shy of reinstalling the Articles of Confederation."[15] Jeffrey Rosen in the *New Republic* described these same justices as "[h]aving rejected the constitutional legacy of the New Deal . . . [and as being] inclined to question the legacy of Reconstruction as well."[16] In the *Michigan Law Review* Daniel Farber asserted that "new federalists," such as the *Thornton* dissenters, conceive of states as being in some measure "independent nations."[17]

These characterizations were all offered by informed people who did not intend, I think, to engage in propaganda or burlesque. Their lack of embarrassment reveals how acutely and instinctively some people sense the weakness of our constitutional structure. Overstated or not, these kinds of fears are characteristically American. The historian Robert Wiebe has argued that a deep and pervasive pattern of social "segmentation" in the United States has long aroused anxiety about political disintegration.[18] The existence of states as competitors to national power, of course, has been only one part of this complex pattern. Confidence in unity has been undermined by innumerable "small social units—primary circles of identity, values, associations, and goals." These units can be governmental, but they can also be familial, religious, occupational, and ethnic. Of the unease created by this segmentation, Wiebe says: "It was as if each compartment, unable to hear or see clearly what lay beyond its walls, required constant reassurance that it was indeed connected with the next unit and the next and the next in a common, rewarding enterprise."[19] This "longing for cohesion" has, of course, had many kinds of consequences. Wiebe points out, for instance, that it has fueled a series of great national reform movements and that it has helped to create psychological dependence on law, courts, and constitutional myths. "Even a modern elite," says Wiebe, "require[s] the comfort that only an overarching form [can] provide."[20]

Today one of the most familiar manifestations of this longing is the chorus of lamentation over the dangers posed by contemporary "culture wars." The sociologist James Davison Hunter recently followed up his famous book of that title with one called *Before the Shooting Begins*.[21] Perhaps the most acute anxieties have been aroused by multiculturalism. Writing in 1991, under the banner *The Disuniting of America*, Arthur M. Schlesinger Jr. decried a "cult of ethnicity" that puts "in peril" the very idea of "a unifying American identity."[22] He declared: "If separationist tendencies go on unchecked, the result can only be the fragmentation, re-segregation, and tribalization of American life."[23] (As if to prove such claims too tame, the legal scholar Richard Delgado recently weighed in with *The Coming American Race War?*.) The modern ethnic "upsurge," Schlesinger continued, threatens to become "a counter-revolution against the original theory of America as 'one people,' a common culture, a single nation."[24] As if this were not enough, some seven years later Schlesinger added that militant multiculturalism "opposes the idea of a common culture," and he charged that this movement is leading an "assault" on that central tenet of our overarching form, the Bill of Rights.[25]

Inspired in part by Schlesinger, others have voiced their fears. In his best-selling book *The Clash of Civilizations*, Samuel P. Huntington speculated generally about problems of "political disunity in the West."[26] Pointing more specifically at multiculturalism, he said that rejection of the American political creed "means the end of the United States as we have known it."[27] A United States without a cultural core "will not be the United States; it will be the United Nations."[28] Interestingly, something like this outcome was actually embraced (very tentatively) by another eminent expert in international politics, George F. Kennan. Emphasizing the size and remoteness of the government in Washington, D.C. and the range of cultural and ethnic communities that it must accommodate, Kennan wondered whether we might not eventually be better off "if our country, while retaining certain of the rudiments of a federal government, were to be decentralized into something like a dozen constituent republics."[29]

In short, if the members of the *Casey* majority were moved by a vision of national disintegration, they would have been operating as part of a long-standing and currently powerful tradition. For present purposes the key element in this tradition is its focus on the psychological and intellectual bases of nationhood. Even going back to the founding, the significance of the country's size and heterogeneity had to do not only with competing interests but also, ultimately, with divided loyalties.[30] The question then was whether the Union, which Tocqueville later called "an ideal nation which exists only in the mind,"[31] could prevail in the face of American diversity. Current fears about multiculturalism demonstrate that—even with the country effectively so much smaller and enormously more integrated, even with a massive national regulatory apparatus as well as a significant police force and a massive military—intellectual and moral dissensus is still understood to be a threat to nationhood.

In an essay eerily similar to the Court's opinion in *Casey* (but published years earlier), Robert Burt argued exactly that constitutional cases involve clashes among convictions so fundamental as to transcend any "underlying sense of community."[32] Burt thought that in such cases the Court's function is to dramatize "how easily political conflict becomes transformed into diametric opposition . . . and how such opposition can lead . . . to the brink of civil war."[33] Its function, he insisted, is to show "the fragility of communal bonds in democratic theory and practice." That is, by insisting on its own authority and exposing its own weakness, the Court helps to reestablish a new sense of community based on "the listeners' [heightened] sense of their own vulnerability."[34]

Burt's idea is that behind constitutional law in a deeply divided society is fear—fear of breakdown and bloodshed. The radical and arresting corollary to this idea is that constitutional decisions are necessary where law is impossible. "The very purpose of judicial intervention," wrote Burt, "is visibly to call into question the legitimacy of all constituted authority, including the Court's own authority." Brushing in this way up against the possibility of chaos, Americans accept the Court's invalidation of a law because they accept that the underlying moral dispute "cannot be legitimately resolved and that accordingly . . . the legislative enactment that one party has imposed on the other is invalid."[35]

Like the Court in *Casey*, two paradigmatic issues that Burt points to as threatening the social fabric are abortion and school desegregation. For Burt, the Court's decision in *Cooper v. Aaron*, insisting on immediate desegregation in the Little Rock schools despite opposition by state officials and the resulting mob violence, illustrates the restorative judicial function. And in this Burt was echoing the Court's own assessment of the scope and gravity of what was at stake. The opinion begins by explicitly asserting that the case "raises questions of the highest importance to the maintenance of our federal system of government."[36]

The nine justices, according to Burt, dramatized the fragility of their authority by individually signing *Cooper*. Be this as it may, *Cooper* illustrates a more authoritarian aspect to Burt's version of the Court's function. After all, to disagree morally or legally with the Court when the basis of its decision is that common norms do not exist is to risk the very communal disintegration that it is the Court's function to help us escape. And *Cooper* does tend to confirm that at least in the kind of constitutional cases Burt has identified, the justices will view challenges to their authority as anarchic. Thus, the justices felt it necessary in *Cooper* to go beyond what was required to resolve the case to assert as "indispensable" the principle that "the federal judiciary is supreme in the exposition of the law of the Constitution" and, consequently, that "[e]very state legislator and executive and judicial officer is solemnly committed by oath" to support its interpretations.[37] This identification of the judiciary's interpretations with the Constitution itself and the apparent extension of the duty of "support" to state officials who are not parties to any case would, if fully implemented, preclude all official actions predicated on disagreement with the federal courts. That is, the judicial function envisioned by Robert Burt and apparently adopted by the Court in *Cooper v. Aaron* not only requires suspension of the democratic prerogative of morally coercive legislation but also suppression of official dissensus on constitutional interpretation.

That, I think, is the source of what years later in *Casey* the Court called "the rare precedential force" of cases like *Roe*. Because the justices perceived unfettered abortion regulation as threatening the nation's social fabric, they represented the Court's role, beginning in *Roe*, as having been to call "the contending sides of a national controversy to end their national division by accepting a common mandate rooted in the Constitution." To reverse *Roe* would have been to acknowledge the legitimacy of continuing political debate on that mandate. Reversal, therefore, would have risked political disintegration, the very danger that the justices believe gave rise to the Court's authority in the first instance. Here, then, is the *Casey* majority's shadow argument brought out into the light: Stare decisis is necessary for judicial supremacy when that supremacy extends so far as to require suppression of official disagreement with the Court's interpretation; judicial supremacy (taken this far) is necessary for constitutionalism when the Court's interpretation rests on the belief that no common moral norms exist on which to base moral or legal debate; constitutionalism is necessary for nationhood when the issue about which society lacks common moral norms is so central that continuing debate will cause political disintegration.

III

Just as a thought experiment, let us assume for a moment that the shadow argument in *Casey* is overwrought as applied to the issue of abortion. That is, assume that abortion prohibitions could be reintroduced without causing political disintegration. It is, after all, possible that if *Roe* had been reversed, the pro-choice movement would have reacted with no more resistance or violence than the pro-life movement has in fact manifested in reaction to the Court's decision in *Casey*. Some zealots might have carried out shootings and bombings, some intellectual journals might have proposed that the time had come to discuss the possibility of civil disobedience, but the great mass of the pro-choice movement—agonized as it undoubtedly would be—might simply labor on trying to influence state and federal laws, change the composition of the federal courts, and amend the Constitution. Meanwhile, even with its moral fabric strained, the country might continue to go about its business.

While thinking the unthinkable, let us assume that the violent circumstances leading to *Cooper v. Aaron* did not actually threaten the nation. Consider the possibility that, while those events involved ugly threats to the welfare and education of Little Rock schoolchildren, they might not have involved any material threat to nationhood. It is true, of course, that when Governor Faubus ordered the Arkansas National Guard to Central High School, he powerfully evoked associations with the Civil War. But by the time the Supreme Court acted a year later, the president of the United States had ordered units of the 101st Airborne Division to Central High. It bears remembering that this president, the man who had once planned and supervised the Normandy invasion, instructed his attorney general to see that "the force we send [to Little Rock] is strong enough that it will not be challenged."[38] And it was not challenged; the morning after deployment, school integration resumed. Thereafter Eisenhower federalized the National Guardsmen, who, as everyone knows, protected the black students for the remainder of the school year under cruel and chaotic conditions. In short, the overwhelming military power of the national government had been successfully deployed by the time *Cooper* was announced.

Having gone this far, it should be relatively easy to assume that *National League of Cities v. Usery*, had it not been overruled, would not have led to the dismantling of the New Deal and that state-imposed term limits would not have reestablished the Articles of Confederation. While we are at it, we might as well imagine the possibility that multiculturalism, no matter how radical its intellectual underpinnings, is not as a practical matter a threat to the Bill of Rights or to our national identity—no more so than, say, the Communist Party turned out to be.

From this optimistic but not entirely unrealistic perspective, the question that emerges is this: what is the source of the widespread and acute fear of disintegration? One possible answer is that centralization itself may be creating anxiety about nationhood. At the level of regulatory policy, this dynamic is obvious; as Justice Scalia and others have argued, the Supreme Court's decision in *Roe* to centralize abortion policy dramatically raised the moral and political stakes all around, thereby fomenting the very political stridency that eventually produced fears of a culture war. What may not be quite so obvious is that these fears might naturally induce further centralization and, therefore, greater anxiety about disintegration. This implosive cycle would account for the otherwise odd coexistence in the modern case law, as well as in political debate, of the widespread sense that nationhood is precarious alongside the brute facts of successful nationalization.

The dynamic of implosion may be operating not only at the level of policy but also at the level of process. More specifically, our devotion to judicial supremacy, which is the symbolic apex of American nationhood, may be making nationhood seem more precarious than it is and thus inducing ever more nervous reliance on national judicial power. This possibility, I think, can be seen in the shadow argument made by the *Casey* majority.

According to the shadow argument, the function of the Supreme Court in crucial situations does not depend on the justices' assessment of the moral or legal value of the asserted right. Indeed, the justification for the Court's action is that continued discourse about such an assessment would threaten the national political community. The purpose of stare decisis in these situations, as the *Casey* majority makes clear, is to substitute the authority of the Court for further debate, not only for further public debate but also for continuing internal deliberation by those justices who themselves doubt the substantive justifications for the right. One difficulty with this strategy is that it is only natural for debate to be provoked, not precluded, by a judicial opinion that proclaims its own substantive weaknesses. Indeed, much of the reaction to *Casey* demonstrates that the plurality's stubborn adherence to an admittedly questionable constitutional position has infuriated the opposition and, in fact, has begun to produce a radical jurisprudence of doubt.[39]

The lawlessness underlying *Cooper v. Aaron* was less explicit than that underlying *Casey* but no less provocative. While the justices did not announce any reservations about *Brown. v. Board of Education*, they asserted the Court's authority in palpable disregard of the moral and legal underpinning of *Brown*. That underpinning was the determination that segregation laws harmed the hearts and minds of black children. Not one of the nine justices who did think to sign their names to *Cooper* thought to explain how attending Central High School under armed guard would protect the hearts and minds, let alone improve the education, of those brave, beleaguered students. Thus even more starkly (if less explicitly) than in *Casey*, the Court in *Cooper* severed its authority from any constitutional base. True, local resistance subsided and the Little Rock schools were desegregated, but the Court's separation of authority from justification set in motion decades of bitter confrontations throughout the nation. The so-called root-and-branch remedy—that peculiarly un-embarrassed and antiseptic allusion to the vast destruction to be caused by the wrath of God—imposed elaborate plans for student relocation and dispatched fleets of buses and transferred teachers. In these ways it manifested the supreme authority of the federal courts. But the operational assertion of that authority, which evolved without being connected in any believable way to educational equality, did not convince or silence vast segments of the public. Indeed, it infuriated many, thus creating a specter of unruly resistance to judicial authority that no doubt still motivates the drive for ever-greater central authority.[40]

The American republic has been resilient enough to withstand the severe cleavages created by the Court's rulings on abortion and racial balance. But the shadow argument of *Casey* not only predictably elicits severe disagreement but also predictably shapes perceptions of that disagreement. According to the shadow argument, the Court's interpretation must be accepted, not because it is right, but because dissensus on an issue deemed crucial and unresolvable will tear the country apart. Under these circumstances, disagreement with the Court must be perceived as anarchic. Therefore, although the nation has not in fact been destroyed by the political opponents of the Supreme Court, those opponents are viewed by many in the political class, including jurists and scholars, as dangerous subversives rather than as angry citizens. It *appears* that the country cannot withstand the dissenters' anger and their moralism because they dispute judicial interpretations that are premised on the conviction that disagreement is dangerous to the nation. Against the backdrop vision of political breakdown, ordinary dissenters look dangerously lawless.[41]

It will not do ultimately, of course, merely to assume—as I have been assuming in this discussion—that the justices were simply wrong in the circumstances of *Casey* or *Cooper* to fear national disintegration. This fear is self-induced, a product of the brittle psychology of excessive centralization, only if it is true that the nation can withstand more than the justices and their allies believe it can. If, on the other hand, it is true that debate on issues like abortion will destroy the nation, those who insist on challenging the Court's decisions *are* threatening the nation. No one can be sure about the future, but there is a certain calming effect in seeing that this whole matter turns on a question rather than an axiom, that it depends on a difficult prediction rather than a self-evident fact. And there should be a cautionary effect in recognizing that fear of chaos triggers as an instinctive reaction the further centralization of authority, which can itself induce the illusion of chaos. Surely within limits Brandeis was right to believe that strength should create self-confidence and that a self-confident people can afford to tolerate dissent even on fundamentals.

Within those limits it might be said that nationhood finds no refuge in a jurisprudence of fear.

NOTES

1. I am referring in this essay to those sections authored by Justices O'Connor, Kennedy, and Souter, and joined by Justices Blackmun and Stevens. 505 U.S. 833, 843–902.

2. Emphasis added.

3. *Planned Parenthood v. Casey*, 505 U.S. 833, 112 S.Ct. 2791 (1992).

4. For an especially elegant example, see James Boyd White, *Acts of Hope: Creating Authority in Literature, Law, and Politics* (Ann Arbor: University of Michigan Press, 1994), 153–83.

5. See *Planned Parenthood v. Casey*, 998–1000 (Scalia, J., concurring in the judgment in part and dissenting in part).

6. For a full account, see Gunnar Myrdal, *An American Dilemma: The Negro Problem and Modern Democracy* (New York: Harper and Brothers, 1944), chap. 1.

7. See, e.g., White, *Acts of Hope*; and John Hart Ely, *On Constitutional Ground* (Princeton: Princeton University Press, 1996), 304–6.

8. See, e.g., Samuel P. Huntington, *The Clash of Civilizations: Remaking of World Order* (New York: Simon and Schuster, 1996), 305–6; Robert H. Wiebe, *The Segmented Society: An Introduction to the Meaning of America* (Oxford: Oxford University Press, 1975), 149–50; Myrdal, *An American Dilemma*, 3.

9. In the legislative debates over the statute at issue in *Casey*, proponents repeatedly argued that their bill was consistent with judicial precedent and would be upheld by the Court. See, e.g., 77 *Legislative Journal, Commonwealth of Pennsylvania* 2274–2386 (December 8, 1981).

10. *Federalist*, No. 15.

11. *National League of Cities v. Usery*, 426 U.S. 833, was overruled in *Garcia v. San Antonio Metropolitan Transit Authority*, 469 U.S. 528 (1985).

12. *U.S. Term Limits, Inc. v. Thornton*, 514 U.S. 779, 837–38, 820–21 (1995).

13. *EEOC v. Wyoming*, 460 U.S. 226, 248 (Stevens, J., concurring) (1983).

14. *FERC v. Mississippi*, 465 U.S. 742, 761 (1982) (quoting *Testa v. Katt*, 330 U.S. 386, 389 (1947)).

15. Linda Greenhouse, "Focus on Federal Power," *New York Times*, May 24, 1995, at A1.

16. Jeffrey Rosen, "Terminated," *New Republic*, June 12, 1995, at 12.

17. Daniel A. Farber, "The Constitution's Forgotten Cover Letter: An Essay on the New Federalism and the Original Understanding," 94 *Michigan Law Review* 615, 625 (1995).

18. Wiebe, *The Segmented Society*.

19. Ibid., x, 91.

20. Ibid., 125, 149.

21. James Davison Hunter, *Before the Shooting Begins* (New York: Free Press, 1994).

22. Arthur M. Schlesinger Jr., *The Disuniting of America* (New York: Norton, 1992), 16–17.

23. Ibid., 18.

24. Ibid., 43.

25. Arthur M. Schlesinger Jr., *The Disuniting of America: Reflections on Multicultural Society*, rev. ed. (New York: Norton, 1998), 150, 153–54.

26. Huntington, *The Clash of Civilizations*, 304.

27. Ibid., 306–7.

28. Ibid., 306.

29. George F. Kennan, *Around the Cragged Hill: A Personal and Political Philosophy* (New York: Norton, 1993), 149.

30. *Federalist*, Nos. 15, 17.

31. Alexis de Tocqueville, *Democracy in America* (Arlington House ed. 1970), 1:152.

32. Robert A. Burt, "Constitutional Law and the Teaching of the Parables," 93 *Yale Law Journal* 455, 456 (1984).

33. Ibid., 465.

34. Ibid., 465, 469.

35. Ibid., 486, 487.

36. *Cooper v. Aaron*, 358 U.S. 1, 4 (1958).

37. Ibid., 18–20.

38. For an account, see Taylor Branch, *Parting the Waters: America in the King Years, 1954–63* (New York: Simon and Schuster, 1988), 224.

39. See, e.g., Symposium, "The End of Democracy? The Judicial Usurpation of Politics," *First Things*, November 1996.

40. See, e.g., Larry Alexander and Frederick Schauer, "On Extrajudicial Constitutional Interpretation," 110 *Harvard Law Review* 1359, 1362 (1997) (arguing for judicial supremacy "without qualification" on the basis of the need to stabilize constitutional meaning and labeling the chief alternative "anarchy").

41. How odd it is that in a free society Justice Scalia thought it necessary to describe abortion protestors on both sides of the issue as "good people, not lawless ones." *Planned Parenthood v. Casey*, 999.

CHAPTER 3

"Casey at the Bat"—Taking Another Swing at *Planned Parenthood v. Casey*

Michael Zuckert

I

NOT ONLY do the authors of the two previous chapters converge in a consideration of the three-person joint opinion in *Planned Parenthood vs. Casey*, but they emphatically agree that "Mighty Casey has Struck Out." Beyond that they differ in their understanding of what the *Casey* court was trying to do and to some degree in exactly where the Court went wrong.[1]

Gerard Bradley believes *Casey* is built on a deep commitment to a particular substantive right, what he elsewhere calls a *megaright*, in the name of which the Court has stepped forward as a new sort of "superior being" to remodel our common life, most often against the beliefs and commitments of the American people themselves. Robert Nagel, on the other hand, sees *Casey* resting rather in a procedural, or perhaps better "second order" vision. He finds in *Casey* a "shadow argument," built on the Court's recognition that it needed to settle the abortion issue via an assertion of judicial supremacy because there was no "common moral norm" in American society to appeal to on the basis of which it could be otherwise settled. Thus the Court must settle it by fiat or "risk political disintegration." The Court acted in *Casey*, as it has in many other important cases, in terms of a "jurisprudence of fear," fear of national breakdown. According to Bradley, however, the Court acted on something much more affirmative and substantive. As he restates the new covenant they offer: "We will be your Court and you will be our people."[2] His implication, of course, is that the Court sees itself as prophetic guide of the American people, moving us forward into the new moral promised land of personal autonomy. According to Nagel, the Court offers us its own bare authority in place of a moral vision; according to Bradley, the Court offers itself as guide to a new moral vision.

The critiques they mount against the Court are rooted, as might be expected, in their respective analyses. Bradley is not persuaded the Court is composed of "superior beings" (in an earlier essay he compares them to the "humbug" Wizard of Oz), and he thinks they are leading us not to the promised land but to the Waste Land:

> What are the roots that clutch,
> What branches grow
> Out of this stony rubbish?

Devoid of special moral insight, detached from the Constitution as the Court is, Bradley wonders what gives these nine (or five, or three) citizens the special authority to lead us onto a new moral continent? Democracy, says Bradley, is "the default setting" of our common life. Nagel ends up in a very similar place, the issue of the Court's authority, although he gets there via another road. He slashes away at the whole web of fact and conjecture on which he believes the jurisprudence of fear has arisen: Is there as much moral chaos out there as the Court seems to think? And if so, can the Court resolve it? Should the Court resolve it? Nagel, like Bradley, finds the Court at the end of the day standing there, "naked and alone," howling out its ungrounded assertions of authority.

Despite their somewhat different approaches to *Casey*, there are two places where they agree and, moreover, where they are both importantly correct. First, on the significance of *Casey*. Just as they say, *Casey* is especially important, for it articulates in its inchoate way the underlying structure of constitutional understanding that has been moving the Court for lo these many years. (Bradley finds the position articulated in *Casey* to be a "part of the *ratio* of cases . . . since the sixties."[3]) That Casey remains important more than a decade later is evident from the more recent *Lawrence v. Texas*, the 2003 case striking down Texas's antisodomy law. Justice Kennedy, by all accounts the lead author of the *Casey* plurality opinion, wrote the opinion for the Court in *Lawrence*, this time bringing with him a clear majority of the Court. The opinion he wrote clearly depends on *Casey*, but does not extend the analysis beyond what was presented in *Casey*. Thus the *Casey* opinion remains vital in this double sense. Our two authors also agree in seeing *Casey* as a failure, a judgment I concur in, but I think it not a strikeout as they do, but perhaps rather a pop fly to short center field.

My aim in this chapter is thus mainly to supply a different reading of *Casey*—or of the opinion coauthored by Justices O'Connor, Kennedy, and Souter. I will try to show that the opinion, understood as I think it ought to be, is not vulnerable to the critiques Nagel and Bradley mount of it. For all that I do not mean to defend the *Casey* Three, however, for I find their opinion quite unsuccessful even when read more sympathetically.

II

Nagel does much with the opening words of the joint opinion, and only a bonehead could fail to be impressed by his dialectical teasing of meaning out of a sentence he calls "both portentous and elusive." "Liberty," the sentence in question says, "finds no refuge in a jurisprudence of doubt."[4] His reading of this sentence turns out to be an important part of his reading of the opinion as a whole, for it points him toward the discussions of stare decisis and the authority of the Court as central to the joint opinion. That is to say, the difference between his approach to the case and Professor Bradley's is provoked by the great weight and particular meaning he gives to this sentence.

Despite its centrality to his reading of *Casey*, it seems to me that he misses its real point, however, and importantly misses the way it directs us toward other parts of the opinion as equally if not more determinative than the parts he discusses. The motivation behind the opening is available only if we recall the context in which *Casey* was heard and decided. A prior series of decisions had cast doubt on whether a majority of the Court continued to adhere to *Roe*.[5] Many expected (with either hope or fear) that *Casey* would be the end of the road for *Roe*. What would happen in *Casey* was a matter of speculation, however, because in the previous cases the Court had held back from a clear-cut statement either reaffirming or rejecting *Roe*. The Court could, of course, continue to do this very thing, and so long as it did, it would be fair to say that "a jurisprudence of doubt" prevailed, that is, doubt about the status of *Roe*. The joint opinion's opening sentence is merely a declaration that it will not continue on this path: it will make a definitive statement on the central right in dispute. Liberty is better served, the joint opinion says, by issuing a clear statement of this sort. All things equal, and leaving aside for the moment the question of whether this particular liberty is justified or not, it is difficult to contest the joint opinion's contention: liberty will be more secure if there is no doubt as to its existence and as to the commitment to protect it.

Contrary to Nagel's view, the reaffirmation of the abortion right in the so-called 'mystery passage' is not a detour, but a necessary part of the opinion. Nagel finds it significant that this part of the opinion is briefer than some other parts, but really that is no reason to think it less important. *Brown v. Board of Education*, was, after all, very short as court decisions go, but it was undeniably of greater significance than many decisions much greater in girth. Nor is discussion of stare decisis and the role of the Court a sign of debilitating tension or inconsistency in the opinion. As the joint opinion itself says: "the reservations any of us may have in reaffirming the central holding of *Roe* are outweighed by the explication of individual liberty we have given combined with the force of *stare decisis*."[6] It is not said here that concerns for stare decisis or the institutional role of the Court *alone* are decisive. That these considerations figure in the definitiveness of the joint opinion's attempt to put to rest the "jurisprudence of doubt" is neither surprising nor inappropriate. As a court of law, the Supreme Court should follow precedent, all things equal. And that is, by and large, what the Casey Three attempt to show in their survey of whether *Roe* qualifies as the sort of opinion that is justifiably overturned despite the relatively strong presumption the Court invokes in favor of preserving precedent.

The Court's statement on following precedent may seem disingenuous in light of the many precedents the Court in fact overturns in *Casey*: As the *Casey* Three conceded, they "must overrule . . . parts of *Thornburgh* [*v. American College of Obstetricians*][7] and *Akron I* [*v. Akron Center for Reproductive Health, Inc.*]."[8] The joint opinion even overrules, or at least, clearly rejects that part of *Roe v. Wade* which laid out the trimester analysis. The *Casey* Three went out of their way, however, to distinguish those elements of the previous constitutional law of abortion that they were overturning from those they were affirming. The overturned parts had become unviable either because changes in the deep factual context had occurred (e.g. fetal viability now can be dated at twenty-three or twenty-four weeks rather than twenty-eight weeks as assumed in *Roe*'s trimester scheme) or because some subsequent decisions had misapplied elements of *Roe*'s constitutional standard by discounting entirely the state's interest in potential life during the first trimester.[9]

The Court did not, therefore, repair to the view that in order to presume a modicum of order in a society rent by contention, it must stand by its previous decisions no matter what. It did not even entirely hold to its own version of the significance of precedent in a society committed to rule of law. In a line of analysis that has been particularly controversial the *Casey* Three argued the special importance of standing by precedent when that precedent is controversial and the subject of serious, widespread, intense "efforts to overturn it and to thwart its implementation."[10] To reverse precedent under such conditions runs the very high risk of giving the impression that the reversal was merely "a surrender to political pressure."[11] A widespread impression of that sort "would subvert the Court's legitimacy beyond any serious question," for it would suggest the Court's acts are not "grounded truly in principle," but are instead "compromises with social and political pressures," or perhaps even the product of "drives for particular results in the short term."[12] Nagel is surely correct that the *Casey* Three are sensitive to the Count's institutional situation and its ability to maintain its position as oracle of the Constitution, but according to its own testimony its sensitivity to the

Court's vulnerability stems not from a perception of a moral vacuum that it must fill, but rather from an identifiable set of beliefs about the Court that, interestingly enough, are nothing but the staple of most academic teaching about the Court. The *Casey* Three apparently believes that the broad teaching, prevalent among legal realists since before the New Deal and among almost everybody else (law professors, political scientists, journalists) since then, that the "Court is a political institution" poses the gravest threat to the Court as an institution and with that to the commitment of the United States to governance under rule of law. If Court decisions are indeed merely another way of registering political pressures in the society or are purely the outcome of the policy preferences of the justices who happen to constitute the Court majority at the moment, it is difficult to see what might justify the special authority the Supreme Court possesses in American life. This part of the Court's opinion, therefore, might better be seen as the Court versus the professoriate rather than the Court versus society-wide moral anarchy.

Many critics find this line of the *Casey* Three argument particularly outrageous, however, especially as applied to the abortion question. The outrage has two dimensions. In the first place, taking the Court's analysis merely in its own terms, as a foray into the sociology of legitimacy, many wonder whether the Court's persistence in a path that has already estranged large bodies of citizens from it is indeed the avenue down which bolstered legitimacy resides. More importantly, critics argue, persistence in a morally vicious and constitutionally ungrounded line of decision cannot be justifiable even if abandonment of that line of decision might lead some citizens to conclude that the Court does not possess infallible insight into the meaning and mandate of the Constitution. Of course, the critics are correct on this last point; at least in some parts of their opinion the *Casey* Three appear genuinely vulnerable to this kind of attack. At the conclusion of its long discussion of the force of precedent, the joint opinion pronounces that

> A decision to overrule *Roe's* essential holding under the existing circumstances would address error, *if error there was*, at the cost of both profound and unnecessary damage to the Court's legitimacy, and to the Nation's commitment to the rule of law. . . . We conclude that the basic decision in *Roe* was based on a constitutional analysis *which we cannot now repudiate*.[13]

Now, if the Court believes "error there was" on a question as morally significant as abortion, it is difficult to see how it "cannot now repudiate" the error. Can the benefits of maintaining judicial continuity outweigh the consequences of "error" on a matter of this importance?

Despite the language quoted above, the *Casey* Three do not adopt the position that even if *Roe* is wrong it should be adhered to for the sake of judicial legitimacy. The joint opinion does not say that precedent, even when gravely mistaken, should always be followed—this is the point of the extended effort to distinguish the action in *Casey* from that in *Brown* or *West Coast Hotel*, both of which rightly overturned well-established lines of judicial decision. The discussion of precedent follows on and takes as established the first part of the opinion, which involves a reconsideration and reaffirmation of "the fundamental constitutional questions resolved by *Roe*."[14] Only after having done that does the joint opinion turn to "principles of institutional integrity, and the rule of *stare decisis*."[15] The latter considerations obviously have independent weight in leading to the retention of *Roe*, but the context makes clear they do not suffice of themselves to produce the result. The joint opinion's effort to rearticulate the grounds for the basic rights affirmed in *Roe* is thus no detour but is central and stands as prerequisite to the institutional and precedential arguments on which Nagel focuses his critical fire.

III

Bradley attends to the central issue and the central argument; at the center he finds the megaright of contemporary constitutional law, a right of more or less unfettered moral choice possessed by sovereign autonomous selves. The closest he comes to an exact formulation of this megaright is the following: "all value choices are protected, so long as no harm is visited upon nonconsenting third parties."[16] This is a right he finds nowhere to be connected to or derived from the Constitution;[17] nor, I suspect, does he find it to be one that makes much sense in itself. Bradley here is, so to speak, more or less in the same ballpark as the *Casey* Three, but a different reading is possible and, on balance, more plausible. Such a reading modifies his rendition of *Casey* in two ways: (1) it reveals closer connections to the American constitutional tradition than Bradley is willing to admit, and (2) it allows a more constitutionally focused critique of just where the *Casey* Three went wrong.

The place to begin is with Bradley's megaright—it is a right he sees aiming at or growing out of a recognition of a sovereign autonomous self, a "self-determining sovereign chooser."[18] Yet, where the Court speaks (for the most part) of liberty, Bradley speaks (almost entirely) of autonomy. Autonomy is a very foreign sounding, highfalutin sort of thing that even the most high-powered search program will not find in the Constitution. "Autonomy" is an import from German philosophy; liberty is part of the Anglo-American legal and political heritage, the Judeo-Christian religious heritage, a long-standing resident in the moral philosophy of the West, and, for present purposes perhaps most important, an integral part of the Constitution. The Declaration of Independence goes so far as to affirm the securing of the right to liberty as among those rights for the sake of which all legitimate government exists.

The Court, not only in *Casey* but in the whole string of cases leading up to it, speaks of the liberty right as particularly valuable and relevant to fundamental life-shaping decisions, such as whether to marry, whether to have children, and how to educate one's children.[19] At other times the Court has included matters like the right to choose one's occupation in life. Those large, life-shaping decisions, all things equal, ought, under the liberty right, to belong to individuals. The Court appears to be following a line of thought in the Declaration of Independence, which moves from an affirmation of liberty (to do particular acts) to a right to the pursuit of happiness, a larger and more comprehensive thing, something like the right to pursue an overall shape of life. Within American constitutional history there has been much controversy over what bite liberty has over and against democratic decision, and what role the Court has in supplying that bite, but, without rehearsing all that history, it is at least clear that appeals to liberty against legislative interference with it have a long and well-established place in American political culture—and, while not completely uncontested, the judiciary frequently has played an active role in mediating this conflict. So far, then, as the Court can make a plausible case that it is merely acting on behalf of this well-known, time-honored, homegrown liberty-right, it has a good case for doing what it does.

Of course, Bradley denies that the Court's activity can best be described in this way. That is one reason for his employment of that foreign term, autonomy. He appears to have a number of reasons for rejecting the Court's attempt to assimilate the abortion cases to this long-standing liberty tradition of American constitutional and political morality. A revealing passage in an earlier version of his argument is the following: "May the law . . . [not] rule out some truly worthless option, like killing one's unborn son or daughter, leaving a range of available options concerning sexual relationships, marriage, procreation, child rearing?"[20] Implicit here are a number of important rejoinders to the Court's ploy of treating the abortion right as an instance of the traditional liberty right. First, he reminds us that although liberty has been long with us, the abortion right has not. Americans hardly dreamed that they possessed such a right before *Roe*. Second, he also reminds us, on no understanding of liberty is it taken to be an "absolute." The old formula that the rights of others or the common good set legitimate limits to liberty seems to have been jettisoned in the abortion cases. Bradley is not so clear as he might be, however, about what liberty-limiting considerations he is appealing to—the rights of the fetus, the common good, the mutilation of the individuals who engage in practices that are rightly forbidden—these are among possible considerations he mentions in his writings. Perhaps Bradley's vagueness on the reasons that support regulation of abortion results from his notion of where the burden of proof lies. The Court has innovated in this area, and thereby disrupted a long-standing political and moral consensus; it is the Court, therefore, on whom the burden of proof rests. Bradley believes he has done his job if he shows that the Court has no adequate or legitimate reason to support its great innovations in this area—and he believes he has done this by uncovering the megaright and the foreign theory of the autonomous self on which it rests.

Contrary to what I might have suggested, Bradley did not just impose the notion of autonomy on the Court; the joint opinion indeed does speak of "choices central to personal dignity and autonomy" as "central to the liberty protected by the Fourteenth Amendment." Indeed, it is that as well as the most famous sentences in the opinion that prompts Bradley, I think, to conclude that this decision goes far beyond anything conceived as liberty within the Anglo-American legal or the Western moral traditions. "At the heart of liberty," the joint opinion tells us, "is the right to define one's own concept of existence, of meaning, of the universe, and of the mystery of human life. Beliefs about these matters could not define the attributes of personhood were they formed under compulsion of the State."[21] This is the famous "mystery passage," so named both because of its reference to the "mystery of life," and because its meaning is itself a bit of a mystery.

This passage not only dwarfs traditional notions of liberty, but has the capacity to be particularly offensive, not only politically and socially in the very large range of free choice of action it appears to leave to individuals, but, let us say, metaphysically also, in its apparent endorsement of a nihilistic view of the universe—what meaning there is is meaning we supply (each of us) for ourselves. Let us call this view the doctrine of *Nietzschean autonomy*, or, in Bradley's term, *strong autonomy*.[22] Consistent with this approach to the case, Bradley finds that "Casey may mark the high (or low) point of an improbable judicial agnosticism about moral values."[23] The justices, he claims, "articulate a theory of value," and the theory "is a subjectivist one."[24]

Bradley's version of the megaright thus has two defining features, one concerning the source of the right, the other concerning its scope. The source, he maintains, is the theory of Nietzschean autonomy as outlined above. We human beings live in a morally and metaphysically silent universe in which it is both possible and necessary to create and then impose our own meanings. The scope of the right, he believes, is more or less equivalent to John Stuart Mill's famous "harm principle": the state may not interfere with actions that do not harm nonconsenting others. One implication, of course, is that any activities solely between consenting adults are ipso facto legitimate and immunized constitutionally by the megaright against state prohibition or burdensome regulation. Under such a standard the Constitution turns into a support not only for abortion but for such things as homosexual rights and assisted suicide, that is, for practices the moral consensus of the West has for the most part condemned for as long as the memory of man runneth not to the contrary.

As stated, this megaright and the theory on which it is based are exceedingly vulnerable to the criticisms Bradley mounts against it, and to some others as well. We might identify five chief places where the megaright lies open to serious objection. First is the point we have already noticed implicit in Bradley's exposition: this megaright and its accompanying theory have little resonance with the history, text, or theory of the Constitution. Second, the whole construct is contrary to what many Americans believe about the source of meaning, and it is by no means clear the Court has the authority to impose alien first principles on the polity. A Constitution evolving to match the changing moral and metaphysical conceptions of the nation is one thing and is arguably legitimate, but a Constitution evolving to impose exotic ideas on the nation is quite another.

Third, the theory of Nietzschean autonomy does not consist with the requirements of healthy moral and political life. Morality requires an acceptance of obligation, or at least of the rightness of limitations on the desired actions of the self. Morality requires at a minimum the acceptance of the moral claims of others, of the demands of justice. Such claims are hard to derive from the doctrine of Nietzschean autonomy. Alexis de Tocqueville long ago presented a classic form of the argument as it applies to democratic politics. Some notion of an extrinsic source of morality is particularly necessary in a democracy, for a democratic people, even more than democratic individuals, has the potential to confuse its voice with the voice of God. The doctrine of popular sovereignty and the collective strength of the democratic people (as opposed to the individual weakness of democratic individuals) open the collectivity to immoderate acts of self-assertion and injustice, which require a strong commitment to extrinsic sources of intrinsic justice to counter. Tocqueville saw America to be a successful democracy precisely because the American religious heritage supplied the self-limiting basis for respect for the rights of all. Dostoyevsky identified the problem with Nietzschean autonomy as the basis for moral and political life when he brought out the thesis: "If God is dead, then everything is permitted." But no society can operate on the premise that everything is permitted.

Bradley's version of the megaright contains a proviso in favor of the harm principle—everything is permitted except acts that harm nonconsenting third parties. Although Bradley does not bring out the point, it is nonetheless the case that, as Dostoyevsky suggested, it is not clear that Nietzschean autonomy mandates the harm principle: If God is dead, *everything* is permitted. Finally, and perhaps, most far-reachingly, the doctrine of Nietzschean autonomy as Bradley extracts it from the "mystery passage" is thoroughly self-contradictory. It contains an implicit authoritative metastatement about meaning we do not define for ourselves, a definition, moreover, that trumps our own "concepts of existence, of meaning, of the universe." That is, read as a statement of Nietzschean autonomy, the *Casey* Three's position would be saying that we have a right to define concepts of meaning and so on because there isn't any meaning "really out there." But this grounding of the right to define meaning also negates *in advance* any definitions we come up with under it.

IV

The theory of Nietzschean autonomy has its weaknesses, to be sure, and perhaps Bradley is correct to maintain that the *Casey* Three adopted this very weak rationale for its decision. Their language was vague enough, broad enough, brief enough that this (or any number of other theories) might be buried in there. If Bradley errs in attributing Nietzschean autonomy to the *Casey* Three, as I think he does, this is an eminently plausible error, and one for which the *Casey* Three must, in the jargon of the day, "bear full responsibility."

The beginning point for an alternative understanding of the joint opinion can be Bradley's formulation of the megaright—personal autonomy plus the Millian harm principle. Bradley is surely correct to see that Justices O'Connor, Kennedy, and Souter do not mean to affirm personal autonomy *simpliciter*. Without looking outside *Casey* itself, we can see the justices admitting various principles and interests on which state action limiting individual choice may be premised—the state's interest in "potential life," in the health of women, in the life of viable fetuses. In the glare of the "mystery passage" it is easy to forget that *Casey* actually upheld several regulations of the abortion right that had previously been rejected by the Supreme Court.

The *Casey* Three, on Bradley's account, accept limitations on personal autonomy that are not evidently consistent with what Bradley sees to be the underlying theoretical rationale for the megaright. That may mean merely that the authors of the joint opinion are confused, but it may also mean Bradley has incorrectly identified their underlying theory as Nietzschean autonomy. That is the possibility I wish to explore.

If the "mystery passage," as Bradley concedes, cannot be understood to protect anything and everything an autonomous being might choose to do, then what can it be understood to do? What is it about anyway? The best way to understand it is not in terms of Bradley's Nietzschean autonomy, but rather to see it as an expression of what I will call hermeneutic Socratism. As the joint opinion puts it, "At the heart of liberty is the right to define one's own concept of existence, of meaning, of the universe, and of the mystery of human life."[25] The "heart of liberty," according to the joint opinion, is a certain liberty of belief. This seems to have little to do with the issues in *Casey* (or *Roe*, or the other abortion cases), however, for the issue there is not belief, or even the expression (or nonexpression) of belief, but action—may the state prohibit abortions or not? No one doubts the right of individuals to form beliefs about any number of things (e.g. about the optimal speed limit on the interstate highway system, or the rightness of free choice regarding abortion), but this right does not of itself, it seems, translate into a right to act on the belief so formed. Many of us may believe a higher speed limit would be desirable, but our right to believe and even publicly argue for this gives us no constitutional or other right to put our belief into practice so long as there is a law to the contrary. Is the situation any different for abortion?

Does the Court's affirmation of "the heart of liberty" have any relevance at all? I believe the answer is yes, but it is an answer that must unfold in stages. In identifying "the heart of liberty" as it does, the joint-opinion writers are articulating a "hermeneutic" view of human existence: To be human is to live meaningfully, that is, to live in the light of meanings. We are not automata or animals driven by blind instinct or chemical processes. To live in the light of meanings is the glory, the specific dignity of humanity. This is a version or an echo of the Aristotelian view that man is the rational animal. It is intentionally broader and more open-ended, however, because it aims to recognize as fully human orientations around meanings that may not qualify as strictly rational from an Aristotelean perspective—for example, faith commitments. Thus, according to the *Casey* Three's hermeneutic view, we are the beings who live meaningfully, in the light of some understanding of what we are, of what the whole in which we find ourselves is, of what is required of us, of what the best way of life is. For human existence to be hermeneutical is thus for it to be reflexive as well. Our "definitions" of meaning enter into and give shape to our lives. We are "defined" as we define.

Although the *Casey* Three do not endorse anything quite so tailored as the Socratic view of philosophic questioning, there is a definite Socratic dimension to their position. "The unexamined life is not worth living," said Socrates when on trial for raising questions and thereby casting doubts on Athenian received answers to questions about what makes life worth living. It was not enough for Socrates to take over answers to the significant questions about human existence he raised: with the *Casey* Three, he thought that "beliefs about these matters could not define the attributes of personhood were they formed under the compulsion of the state."[26] As Socrates learned to his detriment, however, the state frequently attempts to impose its answers about meaning, and those like Socrates, who do not automatically accept those answers but make them objects of explicit inquiry, suffer.

Hermeneutic Socratism is specially conscious of the tendency of state or society to impose meanings and thus thwart the human vocation of its citizens and members, and in response it attempts to build support for an extensive sphere of free inquiry and an extensive protection for individual belief. Hermeneutic Socratism represents at least a plausible interpretation of the underlying rationale for the First Amendment's protections of speech, and press, and by extension of free inquiry, as well as the amendment's protection of religious freedom and immunity from religious establishment. As meaning-seeking beings, humans have a right to search for meaning, to exchange views about meaning, and to live with their beliefs under the protective shelter of the Constitution.

The Court speaks of "the right to define one's own concept of existence, of meaning, of the universe, and of the mystery of human life" as lying "at the heart of liberty."[27] Bradley and many others take this in a Nietzschean rather than a Socratic way, as suggesting a kind of creative invention of meaning, as though the court endorses the Nietzschean notion that each of us is freely and consciously to *create* our own meaning, as though the world is silent except for our inventions. Since many of us accept meanings that we understand not to be our own invention (as individuals or as a species), the Court would be reading out of the Constitution the views of those who do not see humanity as the source of meaning if it committed to Nietzschean autonomy.

But the Court, I think, means something different, a difference pointed at by its reference here to a "right": it is both our right and perhaps our duty, our glory and perhaps our burden, to live within the light of meanings. It is in any case necessary to living as a human being. There is nothing in this that predisposes to the priority of humanly created meanings over meanings found or given to us. Perhaps the contrary: in a sense our meanings live us. These are meanings not so much that we must *define* (in the active sense of create or make up) as *accept* for ourselves. That may indeed involve accepting not only such views as, say, that we live in a whole possessed of a transcendent source of meaning (God or nature, for examples), but also some view of an immanent source of meaning, an authoritative meaning giver (for instance, the Supreme Court as interpreter of the Constitution, our local rabbi as expounder of Talmud). In the latter case even though the substance of the meaning we accept comes from another agent, we are still the ones who accept this meaning as authoritative. From the *Casey* Three perspective we have still exercised our right vis-à-vis the "concept of existence, of meaning, of the universe" in the light of which we live. The alternative, the Nietzschean view, is subject to the deep self-contradiction alluded to above.

If it were legitimate that meanings simply be imposed rather than freely accepted, then there would be no essential difference between living a human, or hermeneutic, existence and being an automaton. It is thus that an enforced religion is a great affront, even if the imposed religion is the one true religion. Imposed meanings are not lived in a human way, from the inside, so to speak, and thus not meaningfully. This is why nearly all agree that religious freedom is a great good and a fundamental right; the goodness and rightness derive not from an indifference to religion, but from its potentially deep significance to a fully human life.

Hermeneutic Socratism is thus first and foremost a doctrine about free thought and the rights of conscientious conviction. This is the autonomy to which the *Casey* Three first refer. They realize, as they must, that the question of action is a further question. As they say, "[T]hough the abortion decision may originate within the zone of conscience and belief, it is more than a philosophic exercise."[28] We may have some deep right to decide for ourselves how we understand "the meaning of it all," or better put, a right to understand it as we are given to understand it, but surely we have no right to commit any and every act our conception of existence may suggest to us, nor to deny every legal duty that we find uncongenial. What bearing, then, does hermeneutic Socratism have, for example, on the alleged abortion right?

The character of hermeneutic Socratism implies that the distinction between thought or belief and action or conduct as we have so far discussed it is too starkly drawn. If the central thesis of hermeneutic Socratism holds that the human being is the being who lives in the light of meaning, then the doctrine refers not only to beliefs but to living, that is, to acting, and so shaping one's life, "in the light of" these meanings. The *Casey* Three are appealing to this aspect of hermeneutic Socratism when they identify the "matters" involved in the liberty right as applied to the abortion cases: "These matters, involving the most intimate and personal choices a person may make in a lifetime, choices central to personal dignity and autonomy."[29] The choices are not merely matters of belief, but of action that give a character to one's whole life. There is some sort of presumption in favor of translating belief into action, that is, in favor of *living* in the light of one's meanings. But only some sort of presumption; neither the *Casey* Three nor common sense concludes that everyone can or should be free to do "whatever is right in their own eyes." But which actions have a claim to freedom from state interference and which not? Where does the alleged abortion right fall?

To put the question in a relatively stark form: what is the difference between the abortion decision, left free (more or less) under the *Casey* doctrine, and a decision by a woman to abandon or even murder her ten-year-old child so that she might autonomously pursue, say, a new, very self-fulfilling career, free of the encumbrances of child care? Even Bradley grants that the megaright does not extend this far. But why not? The standard or easy answer is the one Bradley incorporates into his megaright: the right to autonomy does not extend to harming innocent others. That is, the presumption of hermeneutic Socratism favoring conduct in conformity with conviction extends only as far as "the other guy's nose." But why does this not apply in a straightforward way to the "rights of the unborn?" This is the issue the Court did not face squarely in *Roe* or any of its progeny, and it is the issue that opponents of abortion find most clear-cut and dispositive. If the fetus is an innocent third party, then even under Bradley's megaright abortion should be illegal. The Court has not given, and the *Casey* Three continue the practice of not giving, this claim a direct answer, but the theory of hermeneutic Socratism represents the best effort yet made in any Supreme Court opinion upholding the abortion right to address this question.

The proscription of abortion, or the desire to proscribe it, the Court believes, is based largely on deeply held views, translated into legislation, regarding "the meaning of procreation [and] also human responsibility and respect for it."[30] One version of such a view "is based on such reverence for the wonder of creation that any pregnancy ought to be welcomed and carried to full term no matter how difficult it will be to provide for the child and ensure its well being."[31] Some at least of the *Casey* Three seem to share this view (or some variant of it) because they speak in various ways, of "reservations" about "reaffirming *Roe*" and even confess to finding abortion "offensive to our most basic principles of morality."[32] That is, the judges, or some of them, do not sign off on "Nietzschean autonomy." But they are saying that if legislation is based on nothing other than these admittedly singularly important deep views about "the mystery of human life," and so forth, then the legislation is not justified under the notions of hermeneutic Socraticism embedded in the Constitution's commitments to liberty and free thought. Each of us has a right to take our views ultraseriously as a guide to our own lives, but none of us has a right per se, and without more, to make others live under the sway of our conscientious convictions. For example, what if a coalition of Jews, Muslims, and vegetarians formed in New York to forbid the sale and consumption of pork? Would not Christians and secularists be within their rights to say that even the most heartfelt and life-shaping convictions about the most significant transhuman phenomena do not justify this law, at least not within the American constitutional order? (It remains a further question whether and under what part of the Constitution the Supreme Court ought to declare it unconstitutional.)

The case of the mother tempted to abandon her ten-year-old son is really quite a different matter, however. Here we do not have a prohibition based alone on an answer to deep questions about the mystery of human existence, and so on, but we have a real rights-bearing person whose rights are threatened by the mother's intended act. Of course, most opponents of *Casey* say that abortion is much more like the example of the woman and the ten-year-old than like the banning of pork. "Unborn children" have rights, just as born children do, Bradley says. Here is a second place where hermeneutic Socratism figures in the joint opinion. Abortion, they say, is deemed by some "nothing short of an act of violence against innocent human life; and, *depending on one's beliefs*, [an act with consequences] for the life or potential life that is aborted."[33] That is, the life, potential life, rights, or claims of the unborn are matters within the sphere of hermeneutic Socratism, unlike the concrete life of the ten-year-old. There is no way independent of the deep definitions of meaning *Casey* affirms to say that the fetus has the rights of personhood. This is different from the case of the ten-year-old. We may differ in our theories of what about us makes us rights bearers, but the reality of the ten-year-old transcends all theories and convictions. The status of the fetus does not. If the status of the fetus were as clear as the status of the ten-year-old, then the question about the abortion right would go away. John Finnis, the distinguished philosopher of law from Oxford and Notre Dame, speaks of "the one real basis of human equality and equality rights, namely the fact that each living being possesses, actually not potentially, the radical capacity to reason, laugh, love, repent, and choose as this unique, personal individual, a capacity which is not some abstract characteristic of a species but rather consists in the unique, individual, organic functioning of the organism which comes into existence as a new substance at the conception of that human being and subsists until his or her death whether ninety minutes, ninety days, or ninety years later."[34] With all due respect to Finnis, however, the *Casey* Three's point is that all these human-making and rights-producing qualities he cites are not evidently and "actually not potentially" present in the fetus—at least not to most observers. And they are present in the ten-year-old.

The *Casey* Three imply, then, that the case has not been made for the claim that the fetus itself has a right to life, which the state under the due process and equal protection clauses is obliged to protect. But if the state is not constitutionally obliged to protect the fetus, why is it not constitutionally permitted to do so? The argument from hermeneutic Socratism would seem to allow such protection, if for no other reason than that the deep meanings of the majority should be as worthy of translation into norms of conduct as those of individuals per se. This is precisely the move that the doctrine of hermeneutic Socratism as developed in the joint opinion does not allow. The very degree to which human beings are hermeneutic is the degree to which deep conceptions of meaning cannot and should not be imposed by society or the state. The centrality and depth of our hermeneutic existence carves out a large sphere of immunity. The Court thus nearly reverses Bradley's formula: democracy is not the default setting when it comes to the largest issues of meaning.

The *Casey* Three argue that the status of the woman's right—to control her body, to act in liberty regarding the major life-shaping decisions of her own life—is more akin to the status of the rights of the ten-year-old boy than to the status of the fetus. "Her (potential) suffering is intimate and personal."[35] It is her own, it belongs to an agent who is, without any possible doubt, an agent *sui juris*. The state, therefore, cannot "insist, *without more*, upon its vision of the woman's role, however dominant that vision has been in the course of our history and our culture."[36] The operative part of this pronouncement is the "without more."

Not only is the legislated bar on abortion based on a set of deeply held beliefs "without more," but these views, the Court suggests, are part of a long-standing cultural complex, a culturally defined "vision of the woman's role" in society. The *Casey* Three obviously mean to suggest a link to the parallel line of cases on gender discrimination, although, like much else in this important opinion, the line is barely hinted at and surely insufficiently developed to be of much use to those of us attempting to interpret its Delphic utterances. Nonetheless, let me try my hand at presenting one of probably several possible ways of interpreting this barely limned connection to the broader range of women's rights cases.

According to the intermediate level analysis the Court deploys in examining laws containing gender classifications, the state is required to produce an "important state interest" as justification for its allegedly discriminatory acts. Sometimes the state has responded with claims to the effect that traditional male roles (e.g. breadwinner) and traditional female roles (e.g. homemaker) serve to justify the gender classification contained in the challenged law. The Court has rejected the use of such conceptions of traditional roles as "stereotypes," as impositions consigning women most often to an inferior position in society and limiting the options for both men and women to make and act on those fundamental life-shaping decisions about one's own way of life that are prima facie protected under the right to liberty.[37] The *Casey* Three, in evoking this line of cases, are suggesting that legislation prohibiting abortion not only proceeds from deep convictions, which, without more, ought not to be the basis for legislation, but that in this case these convictions are part and parcel of a set of beliefs that define the "woman's role" in these stereotypical ways the Court has disallowed. It is not just a set of convictions about the meaning of life, reverence for the unborn, and so on, but a collection of beliefs consigning half the population (at least) to preset patterns of life, which have serious implications for the relative status, power, and liberty of the sexes.

The Court leaves this line of thought undeveloped, and that is just as well, for to develop it would commit the *Casey* Three to many questionable and controversial theories about the significance of abortion restriction. The Court rightly looks away from this line of thought, because a rational and decent person could share the antipathy to abortion and seek to render it illegal quite independently of any of the alleged connections to a long history of the oppression of women. Despite being tempted by the oppression theme, the Court wisely puts its main emphasis on hermeneutic Socratism.

The Court's hermeneutic Socratism, if I have explicated it correctly, is far from the Nietzschean autonomy right Bradley finds in the opinion; that is, from his "right to protection of all value choices so long as no harm is visited upon non-consenting third parties."[38] For one, as I have said, Bradley's understanding of autonomy does not, in any evident way, yield the proviso in favor of nonconsenting third parties—think of Raskolnikov. Second, the Court does not speak on behalf of *all* value choices, but of certain choices that have life-shaping significance. Those merit special regard and some presumption of immunity from state control because the life they shape is, after all, particularly that of the one shaped. Third, the Court is not in fact committed by hermeneutic Socratism to the harm principle alone, as Bradley states it. There is nothing in hermeneutic Socratism to eliminate broad considerations of public good, not reducible in any direct way to the protection of third parties, from being potential limitations on protected liberty.

At bottom, however, the difference between Nietzschean autonomy and hermeneutic Socratism lies in the former's dogmatic commitment regarding the source of meaning (the self, or humanity) and the latter's openness on this question. Correlatively, Nietzschean autonomy identifies the individual's (or the species') role as legislative meaning creating, as source of all value. Hermeneutic Socratism does not posit the human sovereign giver of value, but the searcher, recipient, and appropriator or acceptor of meaning (including but not limited to value).

Let me briefly summarize, then: *Casey* rests on the doctrine of hermeneutic Socratism, a doctrine with roots and bases in the Constitution and in our infraconstitutional traditions. It ties into the First Amendment's affirmations of freedom of speech and free exercise of religion, into the constitution's general concern with protecting liberty, and into the Declaration of Independence's affirmation of the right to pursuit of happiness. Back beyond the American political tradition, it links to, but clearly generalizes the Christian, or at least Protestant commitment to free faith, and the Socratic commitment to the examined life lived out in terms of the truths disclosed in the examination.

V

If I am correct, the *Casey* Three are no more nihilists, or Nietzscheans than they are devotees of traditional Thomistic natural law. To shield them from Bradley's blasts does not, however, in itself imply that their hermeneutic Socratism supplies a sound basis for resolving the abortion dispute within constitutional law. Although a comprehensive critique is not possible here, let me briefly develop several objections to the approach taken in the joint opinion.

First, as a judicial and political action it failed badly in terms of its own goal: it meant to overcome the "jurisprudence of doubt" by supplying a set of reasons for affirming *Roe* that would persuade or at least reconcile the critics of *Roe*. The opinion was so poorly put together, however, that it has mostly had the opposite effect of further angering and galvanizing the opposition. The Court sought a probably impossible goal here, but it failed to rise to the level of exposition its task minimally required. Although the *Casey* Three came closer to facing many of the crucial questions raised by the abortion dispute than earlier cases had, it nonetheless did not develop its answers adequately.

Hermeneutic Socratism, second, is not adequate as a general constitutional theory. Although I have insisted that hermeneutic Socratism has firmer links to the Constitution than Bradley admits, nevertheless it is not the theory of the Constitution, nor is it rooted sufficiently in the Constitution. The Constitution, both in its original form and in its Post–Civil War amended form is rooted in a complex theory of political legitimacy. That theory has some elements in common with the hermeneutic perspective but differs from it in being, first, a theory of rights and, second, an empowerment of governance in order "to secure these rights." The Constitution captures this general theory of legitimacy in the Fourteenth Amendment's due process and equal protection clauses. The two clauses are simply parallel and complementary to each other: the state is not unjustifiably to deprive persons of their rights (if it deprives them with "due process of law," then it is acting justifiably). Nor is the state to deny persons legal protection of their rights. The Constitution represents a relatively complex set of arrangements for carrying into effect this mandate: first, there are institutions, at both state and national levels, empowered to govern; second, there are relatively specific enumerations of rights that immunize (more or less) individuals from governmental authority, or certain sorts of exercises of authority in the sphere of some of these rights; third, there is the Supreme Court, a body in part exercising the power to police the boundaries between various claimants to governmental authority and between authorities and individual claimants to immunity from authority.

Hermeneutic Socratism appears to be a version of the underlying theory, but one that has jettisoned many of the defining features and practices of the Constitution itself. First, the Constitution builds on a notion of natural or human rights; as open-ended as these may appear to be sometimes, they are more precisely etched than anything in the theory of hermeneutic Socratism. The doctrine of rights is an attempt to find a precise rendering of the prima facie claims to both protection and immunity an individual may raise. What is relatively precise in the rights theory is completely open-ended in the hermeneutic theory of the *Casey* Three.

Second, the theory of the Constitution contains a clear recognition that governance not only threatens, but more significantly secures, rights. A decent, stable, and effective legal order is understood as the primary requisite for the exercise of the liberty individuals may exercise. Hermeneutic Socratism is too open-ended to have an articulated understanding of the relation between authority and liberty (or autonomy, or meaningful action).

Finally, despite the fact that the theory of the Constitution leaves a valid and legitimate place for the Supreme Court to patrol the borders between authority and liberty, it does not do so in the vague and open-ended form presented within the theory of hermeneutic Socratism. The latter doctrine violates the constitutional mandate because it inflates the autonomy of courts even more than that of individuals.

The theory of hermeneutic Socratism is no more appropriate for resolving the debate over abortion than for serving as a general theory of the constitutional order. Let us approach the abortion question in the most constitutionally commonsensical manner. (I consider only the central issue—the abortion right, the "right to choose," itself.) Granting a prima facie liberty or immunity claim to pregnant women (perhaps as a part of a general prima facie liberty right to do with our bodies what we wish), the two obvious questions that must be addressed are these: (1) do the rights of the fetus (to life, e.g.) counterbalance the woman's generalized liberty rights? (2) are there other considerations of the public good that counterbalance the woman's generalized liberty right? Both questions inhere in both the theory and text of the Constitution. The problem with hermeneutic Socratism is that it is ill equipped to respond to either question.

As we have seen, hermeneutic Socratism has some resources relative to the first question. These resources do not seem to be adequate, however. The *Casey* Three opinion in effect rests on the differences between the claims of the fetus and those of the woman. Given the uncertain status of the fetus as a rights bearer, the woman's undeniable character as a hermeneutic being in effect trumps. The Court is correct, I think, to resist the easy answer of, for example, Professor Finnis, but it has nonetheless taken what appears to be a lazy response to the question. Admittedly the question of fetal status is a difficult one, both in law and philosophy, but this does not justify refusing to face it or answering it merely by default; that is, by not answering it, the Court negatively determines the status of the fetus. Perhaps the Court implicitly reasons as follows: the claims worthy of legal recognition are hermeneutic claims, and only those. A fetus, whatever it may be, is not an actual hermeneutic being; that is, it is not yet living in the light of meanings, and so on. If this is a theory of rights (of who or what kinds of beings have rights), then the Court needs to argue it out more forcefully than it has done. If that is the Court's view, is it an adequate rights theory? Does it follow from the theory of hermeneutic Socratism that the only beings worthy or requiring legal protection are actual hermeneutic beings? It seems to me that one point of the very open-endedness of the theory is to foreclose any such narrow or precise conclusion.

Finally, hermeneutic Socratism is quite unsatisfactory in addressing the second question. Indeed, a remarkable feature of *Casey*, as well as of the whole line of cases stemming from *Roe*, is how little the Court has addressed this question. Let us say that we (or the Court) remain in a state of uncertainty about the rights status of the fetus itself. Might we not nonetheless justify general prohibition of abortion on the grounds of the general good? Let me pass over interesting but potentially complex issues like abortion regulation in the name of population policy. Might the state not conclude, given the uncertainty over the status of the fetus, and thus of the rights-endowing qualities of persons, that the benefit of the doubt should be given to the fetus not only for its sake, but for the sake of the rights of all persons? That is not the same point as Bradley's "democracy as default setting," for it looks to abortion prohibition (with some specified exceptions, e.g., life of the mother), as a measure in service of general rights protecting. In the face of uncertainties over the status of some, could not the state rationally conclude it is best not to enter into or encourage its citizens to enter into a moral casuistry in this so central matter, but that all actual or potential humans should be considered rights bearers precisely because we lack certainty on the question? I do not mean to say that a thoughtful grappling with the abortion question in the light of rights theory will necessarily produce the answer I just sketched. But it will be open to that answer and would certainly have to take it very seriously. Hermeneutic Socratism, as applied by the *Casey* Three, certainly did no such thing, nor is the doctrine well tailored to do so. It is, I suspect, too open-ended to serve as a constitutional doctrine, and the Court would be well advised to be rid of it, whatever its power and charms.

NOTES

1. Admittedly, Bradley organizes his essay around the testimony of Professor Michael Seidman of Georgetown University in recent Senate hearings. Bradley sees Seidman's position as "adapted" from the three-person opinion in *Casey* ("Is the Constitution What the Winners Say It Is?' in this volume, p. 10). I am going to focus on the original rather than the adaptation, both because it has greater authority, and because it raises more fundamental issues. Looking primarily to *Casey* will also allow me to draw together the Nagel and Bradley statements as well as to draw on some of Bradley's earlier provocative writings on *Casey*.

2. Ibid., p. 18.

3. Ibid., p. 11.

4. *Planned Parenthood v. Casey* (plurality opinion) 505 U.S. 833, 844 (1992).

5. Consider the following from the plurality opinion: "we acknowledge that our decisions after *Roe* cast doubt upon the meaning and reach of its holding. . . . State and federal courts as well as legislatures must have guidance as they seek to address this subject in conformance with the Constitution. Given these premises, we find it imperative to review once more the principles that define the rights of the woman and the legitimate authority of the State respecting the termination of pregnancies by abortion procedures." Ibid., 845. Also see the plurality's reference (at 858) to *Webster v. Reproductive Health Services*, 492 U.S. 490 (1989).

6. *Planned Parenthood v. Casey*, 853.

7. *Thornburgh* v. *American College of Obstetricians* 476 U.S. 747 (1986).

8. *Akron v. Akron Center for Reproductive Health, Inc.* 462 U.S. 416 (1983).

9. *Planned Parenthood vs. Casey*, 860, 875.

10. Ibid., 867.

11. Ibid.

12. Ibid., 867, 865.

13. Ibid., 869; emphasis added.

14. Ibid., 845.

15. Ibid., 845–46.

16. Gerard V. Bradley, "The New Constitutional Covenant," *The World and I*, March 1994, 373.

17. See Bradley, "Is the Constitution What the Winners Say It Is?" p. 16.

18. Bradley, "The New Constitutional Covenant," 373.

19. *Planned Parenthood v. Casey*, 847, 851.

20. Bradley, "The New Constitutional Covenant," 364.

21. *Planned Parenthood v. Casey*, 851.

22. Bradley, "Is the Constitution What the Winners Say It Is?" p. 16.

23. Ibid., p. 11.

24. Ibid., p. 16.

25. *Planned Parenthood v. Casey*, 851.

26. Ibid.

27. Ibid.

28. Ibid., 852.

29. Ibid., 851.

30. Ibid., 853.

31. Ibid.

32. Ibid., 853, 850.

33. Ibid., 852.

34. John Finnis, "Abortion, Natural Law, and Reason," in *Natural Law and Public Reason*, ed. Robert P. George and Christopher Wolfe (Washington, D.C.: Georgetown University Press, 2000), 91.

35. *Planned Parenthood v. Casey*, 852.

36. Ibid.

37. See, e.g., *Orr v. Orr*, 440 U.S. 268 (1979).

38. See Bradley, "The New Constitutional Covenant."

that the question of what constitutes a human being cannot be a "value judgment." Our institutions, marking the "rule of law" and "government by consent," already presuppose a rather precise understanding of the kind of being that is alone, by nature, suited to the teaching and restraint of law. In a curious turn, the judges known these days as "conservative" are willing to regard that question of nature as problematic and put it into the political arena for determination. But most of the other judges seem willing to snatch that question out of the political arena and reserve it to their own hands. In reserving it distinctly for the province of judges, they remove from the arena of public deliberation questions that were once thought to be at the center of our public lives. And so, the question of our laws on homicide—just how far they extend, just who is protected or removed from the protection of the law—these kinds of questions are now withdrawn from the hands of legislatures. As Russell Hittinger has pointed out, that is the equivalent of saying that citizens may no longer join in this community to deliberate together on their laws on homicide. For twenty-five years the judges have taught that this question is no longer part of the legitimate business of our politics, or of our civic life; and we are now seeing the molding of a new generation of people who have been tutored to these lessons. More and more people seem inclined to say that the law should not interfere in these vexing "private" questions involving unborn children, abortion, sexuality, and the ending of lives. But if those questions are not fit for the concerns of our political life, then we are either creating new franchises here, unaffected by the restraints of the law, or we are creating a new regime in which we will be governed in these matters by an oligarchy of men and women in robes.

Several years ago, as I say, some of us sounded the alarm in a symposium on "Judicial Usurpation," and that warning produced an astonishing resonance in the land. Some people thought that, with the issue raised in this way, the judges may have been alerted, and with that alert, jolted into sobriety. But starting in November 1997, a remarkable trend of decisions began to take hold in the lower federal courts, striking down, putting on hold, almost every law on "partial-birth" abortion passed within the separate states. When I wrote on the subject in the spring of 1998, the laws in eleven states had been enjoined by the judges.[2] By the middle of July, the *Washington Post* put the figure up to seventeen. Many interesting things had been revealed in this wave of decisions, and we had seen enough by then to know that the mere sounding of alarms would not do: It had become apparent that for many of the judges, the motor that propelled them in these decisions was a machine that ran of itself, powered by its own convictions, and it would not be readily stilled. In some respects, there is nothing new here: It is not particularly novel that a corps of judges, sharing a similar perspective, come to guard their own power.

Nor is it especially novel that the political class who form the judiciary may manipulate the levers of the law—use language or concepts in a tendentious way—for the sake merely of getting their way. Some of the judges have now been tutored in Critical Legal Studies, alongside of Legal Realism, and they have come to view the law, without illusions, as a device for the wielding of power.

That, as I say, is nothing new. But what is revealed, in this recent wave of decisions, is a curious willingness on the part of judges to absorb premises that were once thought to be quite incompatible with the notion of judging—with that special discipline that affects the exercise of power, in a democracy, by officials unelected. The political story is that the class in charge of the courts have made it clear that they will not have any tinkering with this right to abortion, which they have come to regard more and more as the first freedom or the first right, running to the core of privacy, and more fundamental, perhaps, even than the freedom of speech or the freedom of religion. The judges have made it clear that they will not brook even the slightest restraint on this freedom of abortion. But the remarkable news for the law, and political philosophy, is that, as the judges have incorporated this new ethic, they have absorbed premises that are finally at war with the premises of jurisprudence itself. The judges seem to have entered this rather advanced stage without any awareness that they are doing anything particularly remarkable; and that may be another sign of how deeply the profession, and the public, have been anaesthetized when it comes to the moral premises of judging and the law.

Standing to sue: I must confess that as a young man, in my twenties, beginning the study of constitutional law, I found it a revelation when I was made to understand the moral/political implications that were tucked away in that bloodless phrase "standing to sue." Is there a case in controversy here, is there a real injury that brings this matter before the courts? On the surface it may appear to mark a certain fastidiousness or fixation on procedure—until one realizes that it is bound up with the premises of a constitutional order. The members of the Supreme Court decided at the beginning that the Court would not act as an advisory council, offering advisory opinions. Were the judges to act in that way, the Court would work in effect as a third house of the legislature, lending its opinions or its political judgment to the opinions that took hold in the legislature. The insistence on waiting for a case in controversy marked the critical judgment that power may be left in the hands of other officers, that there is no need for judges to lay hands on any subject right away. In that event, power remains primarily in the hands of officers who bear a more direct responsibility to the American people in the form of elections. The maxim, in other words, is that, in a republic, judges who are not elected must exercise their power only under a certain constraining discipline. They must wait for a case, in which real injuries are manifest—a real case, not a contrived case, for any contrived case virtually turns the issue into a situation in which judges are invited to offer their judgments in the abstract, as though they were legislators. A case allows us to see how a law, necessarily framed in the abstract, actually bears on the real world. And that context of the case also helps to cabin or confine the power exercised by the courts. As Lincoln would later point out, the political officers may be able to respect the judgment rendered by the court by respecting the disposition of the case in regard to the two litigants. But if the political officers are not persuaded by the broader rule of law articulated in the case, it becomes possible to read the case narrowly, to confine its significance to the parties and the case at hand. In that way, even a bad decision might be mercifully confined in its effects, while preserving the form and substance of respect for the law.[3]

But that understanding of a democratic ethics, we might say, behind the laws of standing, seems to have been disregarded with a certain nonchalance or contempt by the judges in the most recent cases. Of course, we have the powers of equity, along with injunctions, because there is an enduring moral rationale for those functions. But they must be used cautiously, sparingly, for the most compelling reasons. In the cases on partial-birth abortion, however, these concerns were flicked aside as matters of no consequence. In seventeen states, judges had to agree to enjoin the law, or strike it down on its face, and in taking that move, they had to confirm, in their own judgment, that the surgeons and clinics that offered abortion would have been chilled in their legitimate activities: they would have been threatened with prosecutions simply for doing their "normal" work—simply for carrying out the abortions that they routinely perform much earlier in the pregnancy. In accepting the plausibility of this argument, the judges kept crediting the claim that there was a "vagueness" to these statutes, which made them constitutionally suspect. And so the court of appeals in Ohio found something too hazy, apparently, too hard to grasp, in the definition of the "D and X" procedure (dilation and extraction), the procedure that marks the partial-birth abortion:

> The termination of a human pregnancy by purposely inserting a suction device into the skull of a fetus to remove the brain. "Dilation and extraction" procedure does not include the suction curettage procedure of abortion or the suction aspiration procedure of abortion.

This language was evidently meant to concentrate the bill on the kind of abortion that was performed at the point of birth, not by cutting up the child or vacuuming out its parts. Later on, in the opinion, Judge Barbara Kennedy described the D & X procedure, with lines that might have been taken from Dr. Martin Haskell, the man who gave the world this novel procedure:

> Finally, the physician removes the scissors, inserts a suction catheter into the hole, and removes the skull contents. The head will then compress, enabling the physician to remove the fetus completely from the woman.[4]

Now, where is the vagueness in any of this? But of course the judges did not exactly mean that the statute was unintelligible. What they really meant was that the statute still could not establish a clear barrier between the abortions that were permitted and the abortions that were forbidden. As Judge Kennedy pleaded, the D & X abortion might not always be so easy to distinguish from the D & E (dilatation and evacuation) abortion, where the child (or rather "fetus") is being cut up. For in that procedure, too, the surgeon may have to use clamps to compress the head. And in some cases, as she pointed out, "some physicians compress the head by using suction to remove the intracranial contents" (i.e., brains).[5]

The problem of "vagueness," then, is not in the language, or the clarity of the statute. It lies rather in the claim that there is no clear way of distinguishing the killing done on the child near birth with the killing routinely done in other abortions, even grislier. But one of the clearest things that had to be known about the drafting and the politics of the bills on partial-birth abortion was that the framers of the bills were working on the strategy of engaging the issue of abortion on the terrain of the hardest cases for the partisans of abortion, the abortions that took place at the point of birth. The framers of these bills made it their object to concentrate on the abortions at the end of a full pregnancy, at the point of what anyone of common sense would refer to as "birth." The drafters were trying to avoid any attempt to confound what they were doing with the regulation of abortion. They were trying, that is, to deal with abortion at a point where even the most adamant defender of abortion could not look at the emerging infant and describe it as anything other than a child. The legislators went out of their way, then, to insist that they were not presuming to reach that vast mass of abortions now permitted under the law. They were concentrating, as they made clear, on this one type of abortion, with the baby turned around, so that the feet emerged first instead of the head, and with the abortion performed when only the head of the child remained in the birth canal.

Judge Richard Bilby in Arizona acknowledged this point when he noted that the framers of the bill in that state had meant to "erect a firm barrier against infanticide."[6] The remarkable thing in these cases, so remarkable because it has not been remarked upon, is that judges, like Bilby, have gone on, in language suitably muffled, to argue that the legislators may not do this anymore: They may not erect a barrier against outright infanticide if that legal proscription would have the effect of chilling, or inhibiting, the performing of abortions anywhere else in the stages of pregnancy. And yet, why should it? Why should the law have this chilling or inhibiting effect, apart from anything it might do to awaken the practitioners, suddenly, to the fact that they are dismembering human beings? Apart from that, however, there could be a chilling effect from the law only if there was a serious prospect that the legislators, or the administrators of the law, meant to use this statute in an uncontained way, to prosecute surgeons who are performing other kinds of abortions. But that is exactly what is tested through the requirement of a case in controversy: We wait to see exactly how this statute is being applied in practice. In these cases, the very rationales of the statutes, along with their political strategies, converged in placing the focus, quite narrowly, on those procedures performed on a child "partially" born, partially extruded from the birth canal. The proper judicial stance, anchored in principle, fortified by tradition, was to hold back and wait for a case: Let the authorities enforce the law, let us see whether the law was indeed focused on its declared object, or whether it was used as a lever against other kinds of abortions.

Instead, the judges were willing to enjoin the enforcement of these laws before they had any evidence about the character of that enforcement. The judges seemed to be acting then as another political chamber, to which a faction may appeal when it has lost in the other political chambers, of the legislature and the executive. In breaking, in this way, from the traditional constraints, the judges had to accept a "facial challenge" to these laws that ran beyond the rules that must usually inform facial challenges. The Supreme Court restated the logic of the matter in 1987, in *United States v. Salerno*:[7]

> [A] facial challenge to a legislative Act [said the Court] is, of course, the most difficult challenge to mount successfully, since the challenger must establish that no set of circumstances exists under which the Act would be valid. The fact that [an Act] might operate unconstitutionally under some conceivable set of circumstances is insufficient to render it wholly invalid, since we have not recognized an "overbreadth" doctrine outside the limited context of the First Amendment.[8]

But when it came to the matter of abortion, the operating rule of the judges now seemed to be just the reverse: A law was presumed to be unconstitutional if there was any conceivable set of circumstances in which it might be applied in an unconstitutional way. This was not a change that the judges were inclined to install in general, or in principle; it was a rule apparently carved out to apply, as part of a special regime, for this enclave of the law dealing with abortion. Judge Kennedy in the court of appeals in Ohio explained that this was not something struck off by the inventiveness of her colleagues. But rather, that it was installed by the Supreme Court itself in *Planned Parenthood v. Casey*[9] in 1992. The Court, in that case, held that a law on abortion could be held unconstitutional on its face if "in a large fraction of the cases in which [the law] is relevant, it will operate as a substantial obstacle to a woman's choice to undergo an abortion."[10] From this perspective, it does not matter at all that the cases be few, or the numbers insignificant, when set against the vast scale of things. The question is whether the law works a substantial inhibition or restriction, and that, after all, is the purpose of a law—not to offer an exhortation, but to forbid and restrain something wrongful. For the person restrained, that law must always be "relevant," and the inhibition "substantial." In other words, to complete the translation, any law in the field of abortion, any law that imposes a serious restriction on the freedom to perform abortions, no matter how circumscribed and modest, must be open to a facial challenge precisely because it does restrict this freedom, apparently given its standing now as something like a "first freedom."

Judge Kennedy, in Ohio, pointed out that Chief Justice Rehnquist had raised objections on this issue in his dissent in the *Casey* case; a show of argument that worked, as she thought, to confirm her own point. That point was confirmed yet again when the Supreme Court refused, in 1998, to take certiorari in reviewing the judgment of Judge Kennedy and her colleagues in the Sixth Circuit. In refusing to review the judgment, the Court left unchallenged this reading offered by Judge Kennedy about the new rules over facial challenges and abortion, the new rules that were put in place by *Planned Parenthood v. Casey*. Justice Thomas registered his own protest here, joined by Justice Scalia and Chief Justice Rehnquist—that there was a need to settle this matter and decide whether the traditional rules, restated in *Salerno*, had been superseded now and replaced by a new regime, created in *Planned Parenthood v. Casey*.[11]

But until that sense of things is dislodged, the right to abortion has been made the object of a special protection by the federal judges, using new regimes of rules, tailored solely to the needs of that "abortion liberty." Yet, more than that: The judges had now prepared the ground for striking down a federal law on partial-birth abortion if it were passed again during the next Congress and signed into law by the president (instead of being vetoed, as it was, by President Clinton). For the courts had now set in place layers of argument to establish that a law addressing partial-birth abortions would be unconstitutional, and that sense of things would be confirmed even more deeply two years later, with the decision of the Supreme Court in *Stenberg v. Carhart*. On that case, more later. But that case, combined with the others, offered this brute fact: The same doctors and clinics who claim to be threatened or "chilled" by the laws passed, say, in Illinois and Michigan, would presumably claim to be quite as chilled and threatened by any comparable law passed at the national level. The same plaintiffs, then, will go into courts again—the same courts presided over by the same, friendly federal judges—and they will no doubt produce the same result.

And yet this new, advanced state of things, attained by the judges, can be sustained mainly by the willingness of the judges to employ the levers of the law, and their lawyers' wit, to tie up any legislation that seeks to impose even the mildest restraints on abortion. That wit seems to become ever more necessary, when the judges, in the sweep of their advocacy, find themselves asserting, with conviction, arguments that stand in conflict with one another. And so, on the one hand, it became critical to the argument of "vagueness" that the doctors cannot tell the difference between partial-birth abortions, proscribed by the law, and the abortions that they themselves performed. But on the other hand, it was part of Judge Payne's insistence, in the district court in Virginia, that this procedure of the "D & X" was notably safer for the pregnant woman than other kinds of abortion so late in the pregnancy. By removing the fetus substantially intact, the surgery would avoid the risks of laceration and infection that are present when the fetus is being dismembered in the womb and parts are floating about in the birth canal. To bar the D & X, then, said Judge Payne, was to bar a procedure that was distinctly safer to the mother. That ban could not be compatible then with any law that gave a decisive weight to the interests and health of the pregnant woman.[12] But if this procedure were distinctly, and knowably, safer, then the procedure itself must be knowable and distinct. As Judge Michael Luttig would later point out in the court of appeals in Virginia, the American Medical Association had opposed this procedure on partial-birth abortion, and when it weighed in on this issue, the AMA did not seem to have any trouble in identifying, with exactness, the procedure it was condemning. "The procedure called 'partial birth abortion,'" said the AMA, "is medically known as intact dilation and extraction."[13] As Judge Luttig noted, that procedure was defined by four features: (1) the deliberate dilatation of the cervix, usually over a sequence of days; (2) the conversion of the fetus to a footling breech; (3) the extraction of the body except for the head; and (4) the "partial evacuation of the intracranial contents of a living fetus to effect vaginal delivery of a dead but otherwise intact fetus."[14] It was plain that the statute was never meant to cover abortions by suction curettage or by dilation and evacuation. Contrary to the imaginings of Judge Payne, the law could not really encompass a procedure in which an umbilical cord, or any part of a fetus, happened to be dragged through the birth canal on the way out. The fetus may be killed, he may be dismembered, but as Luttig sought to explain, these abortions are not performed with the intention of bringing a fetus "through the vagina for the purpose of killing it there, but only to complete the removal" of a fetus, or its parts, after the killing has taken place.[15]

Throughout the controversy over partial-birth abortion, the media had shown an inclination, quite at odds with the rules traditionally taught in journalism: to incorporate in the opening paragraph the "what" of the story—in this case, "what" *is* the procedure thought to be so awful, "what" is being forbidden? Instead, the media have usually told listeners and readers first that the procedure is highly "rare," performed late in pregnancy. But if the procedure is rare, it must be quite distinct; and if it is rare, how do we know that it is so safe? How could there have been enough cases to support a claim of statistical significance? Judge Payne acknowledged the point made by one expert witness for the defense (Dr. Boehm), that "there have never been any studies comparing the trauma caused to a woman's cervix, uterus, or other vital organs depending on the different procedures used."[16] The claim that the procedure was safer than others could not be an empirical claim, resting on evidence collected in a systematic way. The judge thought it was reasonable however to conjecture that "there is less risk of leaving fetal tissue behind or of sharp fetal fragments puncturing the uterus [in this kind of abortion], and thus it 'might be safer for the woman.' "[17] The AMA had testified, in Congress, that there were virtually no conditions under which this surgery advanced the health of the woman in any physical sense. Payne's speculations might prove accurate in any instance, but it was not based on any procedures that satisfied the properties of an experiment. It was a species of conceptual reasoning, which might have been right or wrong, as I say, but it *depended critically on the assumption that this class of abortions was quite distinct conceptually from the variety of other abortions.* But once that predicate was in place, Judge Payne would have dissolved the very ground on which he claimed that the statute was vague in its object, hazy in what it proscribed, and the source then of serious threats to surgeons throughout the land, who might find themselves performing one of these surgeries without quite knowing it.

If Judge Payne held to his claim that the distinctions among these surgeries were defectively "vague," then Dr. Philip Stubblefield in Boston would have been in serious jeopardy himself, for charges of fraud. Stubblefield has been the chairman of Obstetrics and Gynecology at the Boston University School of Medicine, and he testified on the side of the plaintiff before the federal court in Nebraska. In defending the procedure, Stubblefield told the court that the D & X procedure was so familiar, so precise in its definition and its surgical advantages, that he was adding a section on this operation to the chapter he regularly contributes to the reference known as *Dr. Nichols's Text-book of Gynecologic Surgery.* He also planned to teach the procedure at his teaching hospital.[18] But Dr. Stubblefield would surely be guilty of a certain confidence game if he offered to teach, for remuneration, a medical procedure that could not be distinguished from other kinds of procedures.

When these strands of reasoning are collected from the opinions, it becomes clear that reason is not exactly their defining feature or their animating force. What comes through, rather, is a certain steadfastness on the part of judges, a willingness to persist even with arguments that—to take a line from George Eliot—are "not strenuously correct." What we sense in these cases is the steeliness of the judges, their remarkable obduracy in standing their ground, as a measure of their determination simply to prevail. "Do I contradict myself? Well, then, so be it; I am a man, or a judge, of many parts." And this too is not new under the sun; this too we have seen before. Yet, not quite. Something is, perforce, different; something was compelled to be different as a consequence of that original strategy that brought forth the bill on partial-birth abortion, the strategy of taking modest first steps, and beginning at the simplest level. The object was to begin at the point of birth, where even the partisans of abortion could not claim, with a straight face, that they had doubts about the species, or the human standing, of that small being who was killed. Part of the purpose was to convey the news to the public that abortions could be performed throughout the entire length of the pregnancy, that the age of the child mattered not at all with the fundamental premises of abortion. For the child at no age was invested with an intrinsic dignity or significance, unaffected by the interests of anyone else. And that sense of things would be brought out as the tables were turned now, and the partisans of abortion were compelled to defend abortion on the terrain of their hard cases—not the cases of rape and incest, of which we hear every time, but the cases at the point of birth. The judges may have shown, in these cases, a remarkable steadfastness, but in preserving their commitment to abortion unimpaired, unqualified, they have been compelled to say things that judges, or cultivated men, could not have said in public in another age.

And so, in Nebraska, federal judge Kopf, in the district court, insisted that if the drafters of the law had meant to ban only "D & X" abortions, they had done a clumsy job, because, as Kopf put it, the doctors who perform abortions "routinely 'deliberately and intentionally' deliver 'vaginally' a 'substantial portion' of a living fetus in order to kill it when performing a D&E." Consider, as he said, the work of Dr. Leroy Carhart, that public-spirited surgeon who challenged in the court the statute in Nebraska. Consider how Dr. Carhart spends one of his typical working days, revealed in this transcript, which Judge Kopf recalled for the record:

Q. When you are doing D & E that involves dismemberment, where does the dismemberment occur; in other words, do you insert instruments into the uterus and dismember the fetus inside the uterus, or do you dismember it in some other way?

A. Well, we insert one instrument inside the uterus, grab a portion of the fetus and put it through the cervical os. The dismemberment occurs between the traction of . . . my instrument and the counter-traction of the internal os of the cervix. . . .

Q. So the dismemberment occurs after you pulled a part of the fetus through the cervix, is that correct?

A. Exactly. Because you're using—The cervix has two strictures or two rings, the internal os and the eternal os, and you have—that's what's actually doing the dismembering. . . . I don't know of any way that one could go in and intentionally dismember the fetus in the uterus. If you grab an extremity and twist it, you can watch the whole fetus just twist. It takes something that restricts the motion of the fetus against what you're doing before you're going to get dismemberment.

Q. When you pull out of a piece of the fetus, let's say, an arm or a leg and remove that, at the time just prior to removal of the portion of the fetus, is the fetus alive?

A. Very often, yes sir.[19]

Ah, there is the cunning of it all, don't you see? The legislature pretends to be confining its focus very tightly, but in reality it is not confined at all, for the daily practice of abortion involves these good, workmanlike practitioners hacking up, dismembering, living human beings. You might say, Dismemberment "Я"Us. That is what we *do*; that is what this surgery, and the life of the clinic, has as its object.

In case anyone happened to miss the implications of the dialogue, Judge Kopf pointed out that the surgeon, in his ordinary work here, "deliberately intends to shear the 'partially-delivered' intact limb from the fetal body."[20] Now I realize that I may betray here a certain nostalgia for the 1940s and 1950s, and it may be that I look upon that era of my boyhood with a tint rosier than the character of our people really warranted. But my own serious hunch is that any jurist—or any person, for that matter—would have been embarrassed, or at least affected with a certain awkwardness—if he had to explain in public that we must protect the freedom of professionals and honest workmen, whose work happens to involve the dismembering of live, innocent human beings, and especially babies. That was not something, in an earlier day, that would have been looked on as ordinary work. Nor was it likely to be seen as work affected with a deep constitutional protection because it was somehow bound up with a constitutional right and with something that stands now as one of our "first freedoms."

The strategy of "the modest first step" was designed in part to shift the landscape, or force the proponents of abortion to defend abortion, as I say, on the terrain of their hardest cases. Some of us thought that we would begin with the most modest first step of all: that we would propose simply to preserve the life of the child who survived the abortion. After all, abortion involves the termination of a pregnancy, or the separation of a child from the mother who does not wish to bear that child. But it does not necessarily imply, or entail, the destruction of the child, if the pregnancy can be ended while the child is saved. And yet, in fact, we know that abortion is animated by the passion that would be expressed in this way: "I cannot give away what is my own, or what I can see, clearly, as a child. If I could give up a child of my own, I could as readily carry the pregnancy to term, and give up the child for adoption." Strictly speaking, *Roe v. Wade* does not entail the destruction of the child, and in theory then it might be compatible with Roe to require every pregnancy to be carried at least to the point at which a child could be preserved outside the womb. And yet, as we know, the Court has ruled out any restriction of that kind, including measures far more modest as the mandate of procedures more likely to bring the child through the abortion alive.[21] The right articulated in *Roe v. Wade* has been understood as a right that encompasses a right, in effect, to destroy the child. Or, to put it another way, no restriction on the killing of the child could be suffered if it could work a serious inhibition on the freedom of a woman to elect an abortion.

Judge Clement Haynsworth was not, then, winging it on his own in 1977, in the celebrated case of *Floyd v. Anders*. In that case a child had survived an abortion for twenty days, undergone a surgery, and died. The question was raised as to whether there was an obligation to preserve the life of the child, and the answer tendered by Judge Haynsworth was no: As Haynsworth explained, the mother had decided on abortion, and therefore, "the fetus in this case was not a person whose life state law could protect."[22] Ordinarily, a child born alive is protected under the laws of a state, but now we had a new constitutional right, a right to abortion, and that new right worked its effects simply by shifting the labels: That child born alive was not a child, or a person, protected by the laws of homicide; that being was merely a "fetus," marked for termination. In effect, the right to abortion was interpreted as the right to an "effective abortion" or a dead child.

Several years later, in *Planned Parenthood v. Ashcroft*, Justice Powell would take notice, in a footnote, of a doctor who made, explicitly, this macabre argument that the right to an abortion is the right to an "effective" abortion. Powell pronounced that argument at the time as "re-markable."[23] From this observation, cast up in passing, many pro-life leaders have drawn the inference that the Court had rejected this claim, and the whole corpus of premises that would stand behind it. And yet, from that comment, cast off in passing, in a footnote, we can draw no such inferences. To say that an argument is "remarkable" is not exactly the same as saying that it is wrong; and still less is it to explain wherein its wrongness lies. The brute fact is that the Court has never proclaimed this understanding to be wrong—and filled in the premises that established, and explained, its wrongness. That omission cannot be charged merely to inadvertence: To explain why that claim is wrong, to explain why the child bears an intrinsic dignity, is to put in place the premises that would finally undercut, or dissolve, the "right to abortion" and all of the jurisprudence built upon that slogan.

And yet, many pro-life lawyers have insisted that there is no need to make this move, that the law already incorporates the understanding that the child who survives the abortion is protected by the laws of the state. But I'm afraid that these pro-life lawyers have permitted themselves to sail in the currents of an unwarranted serenity, and this recent wave of decisions on partial-birth abortion should have the effect of jolting them out of their beamish slumber. The judges in the lower federal courts were compelled to defend abortion at the point where there was no chance to feign skepticism about the human standing of the offspring. They would encounter abortion at the point where it was indistinguishable from infanticide. Our conjecture, years ago, was that even the Christine Todd Whitmans in the Republican Party would not throw a tantrum and threaten to walk out of a party that rejects infanticide. We took it as a given that even the party of abortion would not endorse infanticide made plain. But in these recent decisions, the judges have stepped up to the issue of infanticide, and it can be reported that they have not shrunk from it.

To be sure, they have not quite endorsed it in a full-throated way or proclaimed infanticide as a positive good. Yet they have made it clear, in a chilling way, that they will not be put off, or distracted, from the defense of abortion, even in the cases where abortion merges with outright infanticide. And so, in the case in Arizona, Judge Richard Bilby noted that the framers of the bill had been willing to leave untouched, unthreatened with restraint, the vast volume of abortions. They had been determined to proscribe only this small, confined class of abortions, in which the killing was especially gruesome. As Bilby said, the framers had meant to "erect a firm barrier against infanticide."[24] But now, as I noted earlier, Bilby went on to explain that the legislators cannot really do that any longer. In so many words, he went on to argue that the right to abortion has a trumping effect, and this attempt to cast up a barrier against infanticide cannot be accepted so casually if it has the effect of inhibiting other abortions, which remain legitimate in the eyes of the law.

Several months earlier, Judge Kopf had found a fatal defect in the law on partial-birth abortions in Nebraska: As Kopf noted, that law made no provisions for the health of the mother. The framers of the law did not evidently think that such provisions were necessary, because the procedure of D & X abortions had nothing to recommend them in serving the health of the mother—except for some expanded notion of mental health: that is, that a woman might suffer acute distress, or mental anguish, if she were barred from having one. But even if there were some risk to the health of the mother, the framers could have been forgiven for wondering just what danger any mother would have to face before she would find an apt remedy in crushing the skull of her unborn child and suctioning out his brains. The defenders of the law were disposed, then, to argue that the issue of harm was largely beside the point—and indeed that even *Roe v. Wade* and *Planned Parenthood v. Casey* were beside the point—because, as they put it, "the Supreme Court has never recognized a constitutional right to kill a partially born human being."[25] Their insistence, in other words, was that the right to abortion cannot entail the right to kill the child, the child at the point of birth, or the child in the midst of birth. I find it quite telling, then, that the court, faced with the assertion of this principle, treated it as a matter of no consequence. If the defenders were right, then that simple line should have been dispositive (that there has never been "a constitutional right to kill a partially born human being"). That line should have said enough to ward off the objections of the court and supplied a sufficient explanation of why a legislature would protect the life of a child at birth. But in turning that argument aside, in treating it as a matter of no consequence, the judge was in effect revealing something that even pro-life lawyers had sought to deny to themselves: namely, that Judge Haynsworth's notorious dictum in *Floyd v. Anders* was not only quite conceivable; the premises, the understanding, contained in that opinion, were being absorbed now by judges scattered throughout the federal courts.[26]

Burke once remarked that the seasoned political man, "who could read the political sky will see a hurricane in a cloud no bigger than a hand at the very edge of the horizon, and will run into the first harbor."[27] What I have set down up to now were the conjectures I had offered at the time, in the summer of 1998, as I read the landscape, as well as the political sky. Those conjectures did not seem to me to depend on high powers of prediction. There would be no surprise, and no delight of comprehension, when these anticipations were confirmed in the most jarring way just two years later, in the summer of 2000, when the Supreme Court came down with its decision in *Stenberg v. Carhart*.[28] The Court, in a narrow vote of five to four, struck down the law on partial-birth abortion in Nebraska, and by inference, in the thirty other states that had passed a law of this kind. I had been present at the oral argument in the case in April, and it had been evident at the time, even to the dimmest observer, that Justice Sandra Day O'Connor would be the swing vote. The question was whether O'Connor would be willing simply to sustain the conservative party on this issue through the simple—and conservative— expedient of having the Court hold back its hand. The properly conservative and judicial response would have been: Let us wait and see if there is such a case. There was, after all, a rationale for courts working under the discipline of waiting for real cases in controversy: Let us see whether the attorney general of Nebraska, armed with this new statute, uses it to launch prosecutions against doctors performing abortions that were never proscribed in this legislation.

But during the oral argument, Justice O'Connor's silence was telling. Her usual concern for procedure had vanished. From O'Connor there was not the slightest intimation that she was willing to settle the case on decorously conservative grounds, by insisting on the rules of standing, and sending the case back. The inference seemed inescapable that O'Connor would be folded in with the liberal bloc, to strike down the law in Nebraska. Two months later that inference was confirmed, and Justice O'Connor did indeed become the "swing" vote. In this case, that meant swinging away entirely from the Reagan-Bush appointees, including Justice Kennedy, who had been her partner in defection, along with Justice Souter, in the plurality opinion in *Planned Parenthood v. Casey*, eight years earlier. As Kennedy made plain now, in tones of injury and disbelief, O'Connor had staged a defection from a defection: In order to align herself with the liberal bloc in this case, she had to repudiate that carefully crafted middle course that Kennedy thought he had signed onto in *Casey*.

In Kennedy's version now, the Court in *Casey* had built on the *Webster* case in 1989, in insisting that the state had to be conceded an ample measure of authority to act on behalf of the unborn child, as life worthy of respect. In Kennedy's reading of *Casey*, a woman might be conceded a critical autonomy in making decisions on abortion, and yet "the State's constitutional position in the realm of promoting respect for life is more than marginal."[29] In this case Nebraska "deprived no woman of a safe abortion and therefore did not impose a substantial obstacle on the rights of any woman."[30] O'Connor herself was now intimating that Nebraska might salvage its law if it merely permitted the D & X to be performed when "the procedure, in appropriate medical judgment, is necessary to preserve the health of the mother." The judgment, that is, of Dr. Carhart. But as Kennedy remarked, it should have been as plain then to Justice O'Connor, as to anyone else, that "the assurance is meaningless. . . . A ban which depends on the 'appropriate medical judgment' of Dr. Carhart is no ban at all."[31]

That critical point, directed against the central pretense in the case, was echoed also by Justice Thomas, in the main dissenting opinion, the opinion read from the bench: "Justice O'Connor's assurance that the constitutional failings of Nebraska's statute can be easily fixed . . . is illusory. The majority's insistence on a health exception is a fig leaf barely covering its hostility to any abortion regulation by the States—a hostility that Casey purported to reject."[32] It was O'Connor's thin strand of justification, in her concurring opinion, that the law in Nebraska might have been sustained if the legislators had only been far more fastidious in marking off the lines of their definitions, so that the ban on abortion would not spill over to affect the D & E procedures.[33] But as Thomas and Kennedy argued, there was virtually no chance that any functional person could have mistaken the D & E for the procedure of killing a child at the point of delivery. With the D & E, as Dr. Carhart had testified, the surgeon used the traction created by the opening between the uterus and the vagina to tear the parts of the child from the rest of the body. And so, what the abortionist was left with at the end, he said, in a memorable phrase, was "a tray full of pieces."[34] "No one," then, said Thomas, "including the majority, understands the act of pulling off a part of a fetus to be a 'delivery.' "[35] Therefore, no ordinary citizen—let alone doctors or lawyers—would have suffered any confusion as to what exactly the law had meant to forbid.

For Justice Scalia, holding back in wry detachment, it seemed curious that so much outrage should be vented, so much forensic effort should be expended, in mapping Justice O'Connor's betrayal of the settlement in the Casey case. To Scalia, it was merely the shedding of self-delusion. The outcome in the Stenberg case was not, as Kennedy claimed, "a regrettable misapplication of Casey." But rather, as Scalia argued, it was "Casey's logical and entirely predictable consequence." Kennedy had apparently found, in that decision, an intricate weave, designed by the most refined jural minds. Scalia looked past the contrived phrasing, with its airs of subtlety finely worked, and he saw, beyond the artifice, a principle of action far more elementary: namely, "the Court's inclination to bend the rules when any effort to limit abortion, or even to speak in opposition to abortion, is at issue."[36]

When the case was viewed with the eyes of the common man, one could see, as Scalia said, a "method of killing a human child . . . so horrible that even the most clinical description of it evokes a shudder of revulsion."[37] But for Justice Breyer and the majority, it was not apparently possible to restrict even this egregious form of abortion without imperiling the whole corpus of "abortion rights." That was plainly the meaning of the concern, expressed by Breyer and O'Connor, that the law could spill over and affect even D & E abortions, the most common form of abortions performed in the second trimester and beyond.

As Breyer himself conceded, there were "no reliable data on the number of D & X abortions performed annually," and therefore there were no reliable studies to confirm that this procedure was safer for most patients, or for any particular patient. Breyer found himself fashioning then a judgment of this kind: If the attending doctor thinks that the surgery might be safer for his patient, then the withholding of the procedure for that patient could indeed be a threat to her life or health. He could also lean on Dr. Carhart in extracting some possibilities that could conceivably arise in principle. And so, with this reasoning, the alternative procedure of D & E carried grave risks, which could be avoided by the D & X:

> The use of instruments within the uterus creates a danger of accidental perforation and damage to neighboring organs. Sharp fetal bone fragments create similar dangers. And fetal tissue accidentally left behind can cause infection and various other complications.[38]

But with that style of argument, Breyer was taking a radical step, nowhere acknowledged in his argument. The method used quite typically in performing late abortions was now seen as far more hazardous in principle than this novel form of abortion, as gruesome as it was. For the sake of gaining that speculative advantage for the pregnant woman, it was now thought legitimate to kill a child with about 70 percent of its body dangling from the birth canal. Would the implication not be obvious? On the same premises, would it not be even safer to deliver the child whole and simply let it die? For the doctor could then wholly avoid the insertion of instruments into the uterus. Or he could avoid the dismembering that would allow fetal parts to be left behind, where they could be the cause of infection. With these steps, the Court had backed into the acceptance of the method known as "live birth abortion," the form of abortion that had been brought to light recently at Christ Hospital in Oak Lawn, Illinois: A baby is delivered live from the mother and simply put aside, unclad, and left to die. With the opinion in *Stenberg*, Breyer and his colleagues brought themselves to the threshold of accepting infanticide outright, and it takes but the shortest step to cross that threshold. Whether it was the design of the judges or not, the decision in *Stenberg* did indeed form a design, and the effect of that design was to prepare the public mind for an acceptance of infanticide, unfolding in the gentlest way, step by step.

This decision in *Stenberg* could not have been surprising for anyone with eyes to see what the federal courts had put in place over the preceding two years. Nevertheless, the decision delivered a blow of sobriety, for it revealed now even more clearly what the highest court in the country was willing to do in protecting the right to abortion, even when it moves over the edge into evident forms of infanticide. That blow was sufficient to jolt even the legislative directors at the National Right to Life Committee, who had been moving with inertia, clinging to the bill they had invented, the bill on partial-birth abortion. The handwriting had been on the wall, so to speak, for two years, but the Right to Life Committee seemed to be frozen, not knowing what to do, distrusting every alternative, and finally just hoping that the Supreme Court would somehow refuse to uphold those decisions, mounting in the federal courts. But the shock of the decision in *Stenberg* finally moved the legislative directors to consider a measure they had rejected years earlier as far too modest. That was the measure billed as the "most modest first step" of all on abortion, the proposal simply to preserve the life of the child who had *survived* the abortion. During the litigation over partial-birth abortion in Wisconsin, Judge Richard Posner, in the federal Seventh Circuit, had twitted the drafters of the bill: The state had never claimed the authority to reach directly, to protect the child in the womb. In that case, he observed, "the statute cannot discourage abortions—cannot save any fetuses—but can merely shift their locus from the birth canal to the uterus." He could ask then quite plausibly just why the state could claim an interest in making that shift.[39] For all of their advantages in teaching, the bills on partial-birth abortion had never filled in that critical premise: that the child marked for an abortion was an entity that came within the protection of the law. That was precisely the premise that this most modest bill of all would fill in. In the aftermath of the decision in *Stenberg*, that measure would be brought back again and introduced in the House as the Born-Alive Infants Protection Act. It would be introduced again in 2001; it would be thrust to the side after the events of September 11; and yet it would be brought to the floor of both houses in the spring and summer of 2002, and passed unanimously.

The rationale of that bill, and the adventures of steering it through Congress, form a story I have told now, in proper length, in another place.[40] But just around the time that bill was introduced, in July 2001, there was felt a second jolt, or an aftershock, from the *Stenberg* case, which confirmed even more forcefully the rationale for proceeding with that bill. A panel of the federal appellate court in the Third Circuit struck down the law on partial-birth abortion in New Jersey. Coming, as it did, after the *Stenberg* case at the end of June, the decision in *Planned Parenthood v. Farmer* had become a foregone conclusion. But the opinion, written by Judge Maryanne Trump Barry, displayed a strikingly different temper. Judge Barry suggested that the decision would have come out in the same way, even if the appellate court had not been given direction by the Supreme Court. For Barry, the right to abortion took on the quality of a touchstone: the terms of the law would have to be recast, and even the meaning of words altered, if they somehow got in the way of that cardinal right. And so, with language rather colored, Judge Barry expressed her contempt for the effort to draw a line between the child in the womb and the child at the point of birth. The willingness to draw that distinction here, she thought, involved "semantic machinations, irrational line-drawing, and an obvious attempt to inflame public opinion":

> [T]he Legislature would have us accept, and the public believe, that during a "partial-birth abortion" the fetus is in the process of being "born" at the time of its demise. It is not. A woman seeking an abortion is plainly not seeking to give birth.[41]

If there was ever a decision that embodied the very vices it was decrying, this must surely have been it. For the argument now was that it was all, in the end, a matter of perceptions, of "semantics" and "line-drawing": There were no objective facts—no birth, no "child" being killed at the point of birth, because the mother, after all, had elected an abortion. Once she had made that fateful choice, there was no child to be killed, no birth to take place. For as Judge Barry said, the pregnant woman was "plainly not seeking to give birth." This decision must mark the emergence of a kind of "postmodern" jurisprudence: What the judge "saw" in the case would depend entirely on the theories she was willing to install. But it also confirmed what even many pro-life lawyers had refused to believe: Judge Haynsworth's opinion in *Floyd v. Anders* was not an anomaly or an aberration; it was being established now as the reigning orthodoxy among many federal judges.

As federal judges have moved along this path, or described this trajectory, they have backed into doctrines that would have shocked an earlier generation of statesmen and jurists. And yet more than that: they have detached themselves, step by step, from the moral premises of the American regime in "natural rights," and from the premises of jurisprudence itself.[42] If we return for a moment to the beginning of the American law, or to that new beginning under the Constitution, we can hardly do better than to look to the lessons taught by that first generation of jurists—by men such as John Marshall or James Wilson—who seemed to recognize that the arts of statesmanship at the founding were bound up with the obligation to teach. James Wilson was part of the first Supreme Court appointed by George Washington, and in the presence of the president and vice president, he took up his chair of jurisprudence at the University of Pennsylvania, in Philadelphia, in 1790. In his opening lecture on jurisprudence, Wilson took matters to the root: The very purpose of the government was not to create new rights, but to secure and enlarge the rights we already possessed by nature. But if we are the bearers of natural rights, the question might be posed, When did we come into possession of them? The question was apt, and the answer, tendered by Wilson, followed a direct path: Natural rights inhere in human beings; they are not conferred simply by positive law; and therefore, those natural rights had to come into existence for us when any of us simply began to be:

> In the contemplation of law, [wrote Wilson] life begins when the infant is first able to stir in the womb. By the law, life is protected not only from immediate destruction, but from every degree of actual violence, and, in some cases, from every degree of danger.[43]

Wilson, recalled the practice, running back to ancient Greece, of exposing newborn infants, or confirming to their fathers the power of life or death. But the common law, he said, marked off a radically different tradition: "With consistency, beautiful and undeviating, human life, from its commencement to its close, is protected by the common law."

Several years later, in the redoubtable case of *Chisholm v. Georgia*, Wilson and his colleagues would produce the first set of opinions in a case before the Supreme Court. Wilson would take this occasion, at a kind of beginning of the American law, to return to the root of the law in the principles of general jurisprudence, and, even beyond that, to what he described as the "principles of mind." Wilson insisted that the law in America would be planted on an entirely different foundation from that of the law in England. That law in England, made familiar by Blackstone, began with the notion of a sovereign issuing commands. But the law in America, said Wilson, would begin "with another principle, very different in its nature and operations":

> [L]aws derived from the pure source of equality and justice must be founded on the consent of those, whose obedience they require. The sovereign, when traced to his source, must be found in the *man*.[44]

I cite these passages for the sake of pointing to the notable shift in the mind of the judges from Wilson, on the one hand, to Payne, Bilby, Kopf, on the other. It used to be understood that the protection of life, or the unjustified taking of life, stood at the center of the commitments of the law. The right not to suffer an unjustified assault on one's life stood as a natural right, a right that began as soon as we ourselves began to be. The judges now seem to tell us that infanticide, or the taking of life, is no longer so momentous. But if the rejection of homicide stood as the first, or the central, commitment of the law, that commitment had to begin with the very notion of the kind of being who is the subject, or object, of the law. The notion of government by consent implies an understanding of the kind of creature who alone is capable of weighing the things that are good and bad, and tendering his consent. It surely could not be squared with this understanding of the polity and law that we could evade the defining commitments of the polity, or ignore the objects of protection, through the simple device of changing labels: That is not a human being, but a "gvork." It is not a "snark" but a "bojum." "That is not a human or a person protected by the law; it is merely, as Judge Haynsworth said, a 'fetus,' marked for 'termination.' " This is not merely a shift in labels; it is a decision, freighted with moral significance, to remove a whole class of beings from the class of rights-bearing beings, who have a claim to the protection of the law. That kind of shift cannot be carried through on the strength of mere assertion, or stipulated, as a gesture of the positive law, by people who have the authority to issue commands. That kind of a shift must bear the heaviest burdens of justification.

But the judges tell us now that infanticide is no longer, as we used to say, a big deal, and yet that can be the case only if homicide itself has ceased to be such a big deal. That, in turn, would have to imply that there is something less portentous about the taking of human life—perhaps that we do not attach the same reverence to the notion of a "man." There would seem to be, then, a subtle but sharp break with the understanding of the founders, for we could no longer take that notion of "man" as the very core, or ground, of our jurisprudence. But if "man" is not, any longer, the ground of our jurisprudence, it may be because (*a*) we are no longer as clear, or as certain as we used to be, as to what constitutes "nature" and human beings. Or (*b*) even if we thought we understood what is a human being, we think that our judgment here may be a matter of opinion or convention—or even a certain tribal preference for our own species—and so we are content to leave to the decision of the community, or the political process, the authority to determine just who is a human being. But that is to say, (*c*) we must assume that there is no intrinsic meaning or dignity that attaches to the notion of a human being. The judgment must be then a matter dependent wholly on the positive law. And by that we mean that we depend on the positive law to settle the matter because we see no other source of understanding, no other ground of judgment, apart from the will or opinion of people in authority.

In other words, to add everything up, we might assert the decisive place of authority because we think there is no standard of judgment apart from authority, and no standard that can guide authority apart from opinion. Since there is no human nature, there is no intrinsic dignity in human beings, which can be the source in turn of intrinsic rights that do not depend on the positive law. Everything begins to point to the positive law, everything begins to find its resolution there: brute positive law, a positive law whose exercise cannot be tested any longer by any standards of right and wrong, by any principles of judgment, outside itself. Under these conditions, power is indeed the source of its own justification.

By the time we have followed this chain of reasoning, we will have discovered that there has been nothing short of a transformation of our jurisprudence, an alteration in the character of the thing. Justice Scalia, in his spirited and yet sober reasonings, has alerted us to a class of rights or claims so exquisite, so powerful as claims, that they virtually work to extinguish themselves. And so, for example, let us suppose that "expression" may be found and protected when we find emphatic gestures or acts, even when they are unaccompanied by words and arguments. Let us suppose, for example, that people who pitch tents in LaFayette Park, near the White House are really engaged in a form of expression. And so, too, then are those people who sought to give themselves more fully to the arts by engaging in nude dancing. They too, we were told, were engaged in acts of "expression," and we were told this with a conviction so earnest that the argument was carried all the way to the Supreme Court with a claim under the First Amendment.[45] As Justice Scalia pointed out, every bodily gesture could be translated or converted, then, into an act of expression. Pitching tents outside the White House may be taken as a kind of "statement" of concern for people who seem to be "homeless," set against the callousness or indifference of the community. Then, too, a willingness to drive through traffic lights blazing red may be taken as a gesture of opposition to lights that are overly long, or even the restraints that impede the liberty of travel. If we assign to rights of the First Amendment a first standing, a preeminent place, within the scheme of the Constitution, then we may assign a certain trumping power to these claims of rights. But in that event, the people who mass on the town common to protest, or to speak against their government, may be overborne by another crowd, far less literate perhaps, but even more passionate in their determination to press their views and silence the demonstrators. But the crowd that now summons an overpowering force is itself engaged in an act of expression. If that expression is to be honored, not repressed, then it has the effect of quashing into insignificance the first act of expression, on the part of the demonstrators. To put it another way, an attempt on the part of the authorities to protect the right to speech and expression may be offset by other acts of expression; and in that way, the fundamental right to speak becomes a right that cannot practicably be vindicated. In our willingness to assert rights to a degree of unparalleled refinement, to squeeze out rights so pure that they never yield to restraints or offsetting duties, we back into a set of rights that finally have the quality of extinguishing themselves.

In the case of the courts, and the recent decisions on partial-birth abortion, I would suggest that the aggressiveness of the judges has entered a comparable stage. It is not merely that judges are spirited in their willingness to challenge legislatures, for that is implicit in the office and the function, and if the task of judging is done at all, it should be done in a vigorous, spirited way. What is striking now about the performance of the judges, and the mark of a new stage, is that the judges have been compelled to offer a defense of abortion that is explicit, unshaded, unaffected by apologies or qualifications. As they have done that, they have put in place premises that are ultimately at odds with the grounds of their own authority, for they are at war with jurisprudence itself. The law is no longer committed, as part of its central mission, to the protection of human life, for it is no longer clear that there is a body of natural rights that forms the grounds of our rights, and our jurisprudence. Nor is it taken for granted any longer that there are human beings, with a distinct nature as moral agents, which fits them distinctly for law and political life. Under these conditions, the question of human life, of what is a human life, is a question for political authority, and the decision will have to be made without the consultation of any standards of moral judgment outside of the opinions held by those who exercise power.

James Wilson observed that the American law began by incorporating the revolutionary premise that there could be an illegitimate law: That was the case only because the American law began by rejecting positivism as the source of law, and recognizing an independent standard of right and wrong outside the positive law. To displace or extinguish that sense of things is to remove what Wilson and the founders thought was distinct to the American law. But American law was making more explicit here the premises, or the moral understandings, that were necessary to law in the strictest sense; and so the overturning of those premises was nothing less than the eradication of law itself at its moral root.

The new jurisprudence reaches its completion by detaching itself, then, from every premise necessary to the notion of lawfulness. It rejects the logic of natural rights; it denies that any of us has rights of intrinsic dignity because it denies that there is any such intrinsic dignity attaching to any human being, as the subject and object of the law. For it denies that human beings have a standing or existence in nature, or any jural standing, then, apart from the positive law. We have left all of the trappings of office, we have men in robes sitting in offices of dignity; we have elaborate procedures and forms, and schools to instruct people in the forms; but we have, with full solemnity, the forms without the substance of law. A mature profession has a title for every occasion, and we might say then that the judges have given us a full-blown articulated jurisprudence, but a jurisprudence without its substance. We have attained in fact the state of antijural jurisprudence.

In his debates with Stephen Douglas, Abraham Lincoln would refer pointedly to Senator Pettit of Indiana, who had pronounced the self-evident truth of the Declaration a "self-evident lie."[46] Pointedly, because of the grim implication contained in the example. Pettit denied what Lincoln regarded as the "proposition" on which the American republic was founded, "All men are created equal." Lincoln regarded that axiom as "the father of all moral principle" among us, because it established the ground for the inference that the only rightful government over human beings depended on the consent of the governed. Without that premise, we could not have established, coherently, the republic built upon that premise; the republic that arranged itself in institutions containing a legislature with the office of senators and congressmen. Senator Pettit could exercise the authority of his high office only on the strength of that proposition he treated with contempt. The example of Senator Pettit made it clear that a large portion of the American political class no longer respected the moral premises on which its own authority rested. Without much contrivance, that state of affairs explained quite plainly just why these men were willing to use their authority to extend the reach of slavery and to break down the restrictions on slavery that were thought critical at the time of the founding.

I mention all of this for the sake of pointing out that, in this commentary on antijural jurisprudence, I am not waxing metaphoric; I mean to be literal. The example of Pettit shows, as clearly as any example can show, that it is quite possible to have, in a polity, the exercise of authority on the part of officers who are hostile to the moral premises on which their own offices depend.

It was not too much to say of these men, during our grave "crisis of the house divided," that they were guilty of treason to the republic. They were enemies of the republic at its moral root. In classic terms, running back to Aristotle, this was an example of the "corruption" of the polis, the perversion in the nature of the thing. This was nothing new, then, and as Lincoln and the classics understood, it is not something that will diminish over time, as our species makes progress in politics. Nothing Hegelian here; no laws of history moving us inexorably in one direction. Things may be cyclical; polities may improve or fall into corruption, at any stage of technology or material welfare. And so there should be nothing surprising or bizarre in suggesting that we may be encountering, in the case of the judges, something we have seen quite strikingly before: In this case, men and women exercising the authority of judicial office back into premises that are utterly incompatible with the premises on which their own offices, and their own authority, ultimately rest. It is a form of corruption at its deepest level, well beyond graft. We have seen it before, and we will certainly see it again—which is precisely why the founders thought it necessary that people, in a republic, be tutored constantly in the first principles of their own freedom. But we would rescue ourselves from a benign haze if we could steel ourselves to see what is plainly before us—if we stop concealing what is taking place by telling ourselves fairy tales or applying happy labels. And the first step in recognizing what is before us is to call it by its proper name.

NOTES

1. See the Symposium "The End of Democracy? The Judicial Usurpation of Politics," *First Things*, November 1996.

2. See "Slouching towards Infanticide," *Weekly Standard*, May 25, 1998, 26–29.

3. For a fuller statement of this understanding, see my own book, *First Things* (Princeton: Princeton University Press, 1986), 418–22. For Lincoln's understanding, see the debate with Stephen Douglas at Quincy, Illinois, October 13, 1858, in *The Collected Works of Abraham Lincoln*, ed. Roy P. Basler (New Brunswick, N.J.: Rutgers University Press, 1953), 3:255, and First Inaugural Address, March 4, 1861, in *Collected Works*, 4:268.

4. *Women's Medical Professional Corp. v. Voinovich*, 130 F.3d 187, 199 (1997).

5. Ibid., 198.

6. *Planned Parenthood v. Woods*, 982 F.Supp. 1369, 1377 (U.S. District Court for Arizona) [1997].

7. 481 U.S. 739.

8. Ibid., 745.

9. 505 U.S. 833.

10. Ibid., 895.

11. See *Voinovich v. Women's Medical Professional Corp.*, 149 L.Ed. 2d 496 (March 1998).

12. See *Richmond Medical Center v. Gilmore*, 11 F.Supp. 2d 795 (1998), at 824–25.

13. Cited by Judge Michael Luttig in *Richmond Medical Center v. Gilmore*, overriding the judgment issued by Judge Payne in the district court, 144 F. 3d 326, at 327.

14. Ibid., 328.

15. Ibid., 329.

16. Payne, *supra*, note 12, at 825.

17. Ibid.

18. See *Carhart v. Stenberg*, U.S. District Court in Nebraska, 11 F.Supp. 2d 1099, 1112 (1998).

19. Ibid., 1104.

20. Ibid., 1130.

21. See *Planned Parenthood of Kansas City v. Ashcroft*, 462 U.S. 476, 483 (1983).

22. *Floyd v. Anders*, 444 F.Supp. 535, 539 (1977).

23. See *Planned Parenthood of Kansas City v. Ashcroft*, 485 n. 7.

24. *Planned Parenthood of Southern Arizona v. Woods*, U.S. District Court for Arizona 982 F.Supp. 1369; 1377 (1997).

25. *Carhart v. Stenberg*, 972 F.Supp. 507, 529 (D. Neb. 1997).

26. The reader may consider whether the same operative premise is not also at work in the opinion handed down by Judge Charles Kocoras in February, striking down the law on partial-birth abortions in Illinois:

In those rare instances when the fetus is still "alive," cutting the cord may cause its death within six to ten minutes. In completing the delivery during this time period, the physician may have "partially vaginally delivered" a living fetus. . . . In addition, in cases where a woman spontaneously aborts, it may be in her best interests for the physician to complete the abortion. (*Hope Clinic v. Ryan* [N. Dist., Illinois], 995 F.Supp. 847, 855 [1998].

27. Edmund Burke, "Thoughts on the Cause of the Present Discontents," in *Selected Writings and Speeches*, ed. Peter J. Stanlis (New York: Anchor Books, 1963), 123.

28. 530 U.S. 914.

29. Ibid., 964. "Casey made it quite evident . . . that the State has substantial concerns for childbirth and the life of the unborn and may enact laws 'which in no real sense deprive women of the ultimate decision.' 505 U.S. at 875 (joint opinion of O'CONNOR, KENNEDY, and SOUTER, JJ.). Laws having the 'purpose or effect of placing a substantial obstacle in the path of a woman seeking an abortion of a nonviable fetus' are prohibited. 505 U.S. at 877. Nebraska's law does not have this purpose or effect." Ibid., 965.

30. Ibid.

31. Ibid.

32. Ibid., 1013.

33. Ibid., 947–51.

34. Quoted by Kennedy in ibid., 959.

35. Ibid., 991.

36. Scalia, dissenting opinion in *Stenberg v. Carhart*, ibid., 953–56, at 954.

37. Scalia, in ibid., 953.

38. Ibid., 926.

39. 162 F. 3d 463, U.S. Court of Appeals, Seventh Circuit (November 3, 1998), at 470. For my own commentary, see "Courts Strike Down Laws against Partial-Birth Abortion," *Wall Street Journal*, December 7, 1998.

40. And I hope the reader will then see my book, *Natural Rights and the Right to Choose* (Cambridge: Cambridge University Press, 2002). The essay here had been incorporated in different parts of that book, but I am adding here, to the essay, from other parts of the book as well. The experience of arguing, in Congress, for the Born-Alive Infants Protection Act is told as a kind of epilogue and memoir in the book, chap. 8, 234–94.

41. *Planned Parenthood v. Farmer*, 220 F. 3d 127, 143 (July, 26, 2000).

42. That argument is made at length, as the central argument, in Arkes, *Natural Rights*.

43. James Wilson, "Of the Natural Rights of Individuals," in *The Works of James Wilson* (Cambridge: Harvard University Press, 1967), 2:585–610.

44. 2 Dallas 419, 458 (1793).

45. See *Barnes v. Glen Theatres*, 115 L.Ed. 2d 504 (1991).

46. See Lincoln in the debate at Alton, Illinois, October 15, 1858, in *Collected Works*, 3:301–2.

CHAPTER 5

Judicial Power and the Withering of Civil Society

George W. Liebmann

THIS ESSAY is about the effect of judicial interference on subordinate and mediating institutions, and what should be done about it. I hope, however, to avoid both the usual lamentations and the usual remedies.

Thus I shall not emphasize the courts' establishment clause jurisprudence, the flaws in which are well recognized, nor the recent speeches before the American Law Institute by Justice Margaret Marshall of the Supreme Judicial Court of Massachusetts[1] and President Gerhard Casper of Stanford.[2] Nor shall I examine the various remedial efforts, usually in the form of narrowly conceived statutes and constitutional amendments that have been proposed as remedies. I hope to discuss some problems and ideas that are less familiar, not all of them judicial in origin, but to whose exaggeration the courts have contributed.

THE PROGRESSIVE AMENDMENTS

As respects state government, I do not view Fourteenth Amendment jurisprudence as the sole central problem, nor the Tenth Amendment and a curtailed commerce power as the logical remedy.

There have been a number of periods of centralization in American history, including that of Hamilton and Marshall, Civil War and Reconstruction, the Progressive Era, the New Deal and World War II, and the Great Society and Warren Court, but in terms of constitutional structure the Progressive reforms have been both the least discussed and the most enduring. Little attention has been paid to the delayed effect of the Sixteenth (income tax) and Seventeenth (direct election of Senators) Amendments, which reduced the states' roles in the choices of federal officers[3] and all but preempted the major revenue source. It is true that the states retain for themselves sales and property taxes, and that their monopoly of the latter is the subject of a constitutional guarantee.[4] It is also true, however, that nowhere in modern democracies outside the United States and Canada are sales and excise taxes deemed suitable revenue sources for subnational governments,[5] and that land taxation is of reduced value in a service economy. If state initiative and authority are to be restored, there is need for updated guaranties of fiscal federalism such as those provided in Article 106 of the German Basic Law, which prescribes the shares of federal, länder, and municipal governments in income and excise taxes,[6] and similar changes in France as a result of the Mitterrand decentralization reforms.[7] The Sixteenth Amendment would not by itself have such deleterious effects on federalism but for the federal conditional spending power, which has gone unchecked since Justice Stone's famous declaration to Frances Perkins: "The spending power, my dear, the spending power is all you need." The German constitutional court has effectively barred conditions on grants-in-aid;[8] only recently have some American courts begun inching in the same direction, most notably in the plurality opinion of Judge Luttig for the Fourth Circuit in *Virginia Department of Education v. Riley*.[9]

The direct election of senators in important ways eliminated the political safeguards of federalism celebrated by Professor Wechsler,[10] and more recently the reconstitution of national political conventions in deference to the primary system has further reduced the direct influence of state officers on federal policy and appointments.

We need to be reminded of the wisdom of James Madison's principle of "filtering," which would lead to greater dominance over political conventions by elected state and federal officeholders and those they select. We are far from a condition like that in Germany, in which half the members of the Constitutional Court are directly appointed by and responsible to the länder.

Judicial Centralization

In our system, federal district judges serve for life, have vast powers in constitutional cases, are readily rendered the beneficiaries of judge-shopping, and in all but rare instances are appointed on recommendation of a single senator on the basis of qualifications that have little to do with their capacity to decide constitutional issues. The remedy commonly proposed for this appears to me ineffectual. Three-judge courts merely remove the power exercised by a single district judge to a single circuit judge, who outranks and overawes his colleagues and acts on a less adequate trial record.[11] A lesson can perhaps be taken from the British Labor Government's proposed legislation domesticating the European Convention on Human Rights in which only the three highest British courts, acting en banc, are empowered to declare parliamentary legislation to be inconsistent with Community law, subject to legislative override, and from provisions in Germany and France reserving judicial review of legislation to the highest court. A similar approach here would reserve the power to enjoin the operation of statutes at least to the courts of appeal, acting en banc.

The Supreme Court has imposed a number of unappreciated constraints on state policy. Thanks to *Shapiro v. Thompson,*[12] invalidating state durational residence requirements for welfare benefits, states are no longer the "insulated chambers" celebrated by Justice Brandeis, but are subject to invasion by freeloaders if they adopt generous social programs. This restriction was reaffirmed in *Saenz v. Roe,*[13] even after Congress, by enacting the Welfare Reform Act of 1996, had undertaken expressly to validate such restrictions. Restrictive liability and damage rules are apt to be undermined by application of "modern" conflict-of-laws rules of a highly discretionary nature. The principles of the *Williams v. North Carolina* cases decided as long ago as 1942, holding that the state of a married couple's domicile was powerless to prevent them from obtaining divorces elsewhere, have undermined state control of marriage and divorce, despite Justice Jackson's eloquent protest: "people are entitled to rules of law that will enable individuals to tell whether they are married and, if so, to whom."[14] The famous "race of laxity" said to result from state corporation laws is similarly a result of the failure of Congress to act under the full faith and credit clause to define the minimum contacts required for a state's legislation to be applied.[15] The potentialities of federal legislation under the full faith and credit clause and of interstate compacts as coordinating mechanisms, and of federal credits for state taxes as fund-sharing devices (the basis of the unemployment compensation system) have been neglected since the death of Justice Brandeis, and any serious revival of federalism will require renewed attention to those devices as well as closer restriction of the dormant commerce clause to legislation that is truly discriminatory.[16]

The Lost World of Local Government

I turn from states to municipalities, the stepchildren of American government. Nothing has changed since the time of Lord Bryce, who declared that "the government of cities is the one conspicuous failure of the United States."[17] The reason for this is not wholly constitutional in nature but derives, ironically, from the one area in which municipalities enjoy effective independence: provision of their own auditors. This "anarchy of local autonomy" in the audit process, in which municipal auditors are generally appointed by or elected on the same ticket with those whom they audit, was said by the Webbs to have given America "the worst local government of any nation claiming to be civilized."[18] It remains true now as was said also in the time of ancient Athens, that "a position that must be surrendered after a year and under a strict rendering of accounts was no good foundation for personal power."[19]

Not all the wounds of American municipalities are self-inflicted, however. The application of the reapportionment decisions to local governments has rendered difficult the organization of municipalities as federations of neighborhoods, as proposed by some writers, and has even been invoked to prevent parents from electing members of the boards of their local school.[20] Nor have municipalities been accorded the last word on any subject, a fact that itself demoralizes them and discourages public participation in their governance. Until the early years of this century some scholars not implausibly asserted that there was an inherent right to self-government. That notion was exploded in *Hunter v. Pittsburgh*,[21] a case decided by Justice Holmes in 1907, which is taken to stand for the infinite destructibility of municipal governments. Just why the *Dartmouth College* case limiting the power of state legislatures to impair corporate charters where the right to do so was not reserved, does not apply to municipal charters as well as those of private corporations is unclear.[22] Not only are municipal powers defeasible, but, under a principle known as Dillon's rule applied by the courts of most states, they are to be severely construed.[23] Nor is there any reason to dispute Bryce's conclusion that "the transfer of the control of the municipal resources from the localities to the state had no other effect then to cause a like transfer of the methods and arts of corruption."[24]

While state home rule amendments confer a sort of concurrent police power on municipalities, subject to preemption by statewide law, in no sense, fiscal or regulatory, are they masters of their destiny. They also are subject to the full force of the constitutional constraints that bind states: the state action doctrine confines municipal corporations in ways it does not confine private corporations. Functionally, this frequently makes little sense. The functions of municipalities are heavily property-related; a property franchise for such functions and a parental franchise for schools is thus easy to justify. Yet, under Supreme Court doctrine, only special-purpose districts are allowed a property franchise.[25] Citizens of municipalities possess opportunities for exit and voice not as fully available to citizens of states, rendering political and economic checks on local abuse arguably more adequate even if there is greater danger of rule by a faction. As Professor Hayek cogently observed:

To re-entrust the management of most service activities of government to smaller units would probably lead to the revival of a communal spirit which has largely been suffocated by centralization. The widely felt inhumanity of the modern society is not so much the result of the impersonal character of the economic process, in which modern man of necessity works largely for aims of which he is ignorant, but of the fact that political centralization has deprived him of the chance to have a say in shaping the environment which he knows.[26]

The effect of constitutional constraints has been the atrophy and gradual privatization of municipal government, through proliferation of quasi-private authorities and business improvement districts and voucherized and charter schools.

While many urban boundaries are obsolete—apparently determined, as H. G. Wells said, "by mapping out the wanderings of an intoxicated excursionist"[27]—unlike the position in rural areas, once a municipality has been created, the creation of any public submunicipal body requires the assent of the state legislature. This has made impossible or difficult the creation of new special districts, with functional boundaries, in response to felt need. Except in subdivisions created since the 1960s in which there are private residential community associations, there is thus a lack of community-level agencies of governance. Nor has there been interest in legislative authorization of new units of organization such as privatized streets or *woonerven*[28] or land readjustment associations for city blocks.[29]

THE COURTS AND THE PROFESSIONALS

The impact of judicial decisions on the professions need scarcely be labored. *Goldberg v. Kelly*[30] and its progeny, requiring full-blown administrative hearings to condition or withdraw state credits or impose serious school discipline, served as a full employment act for lawyers by delegalizing the exercise of administrative discretion. Our culture today is one in which, as we are reminded each evening by what poses for entertainment on television, the only legitimate decisions are jury verdicts, when affirmed by courts of last resort. Legal services are now a commodity, by reason of commercial speech decisions exalting market values over professional ones. The proposition that professional relationships are healthier when initiated by the client rather than the lawyer has gone by the board, and liberalized class action[31] and fee award[32] rules have also dispensed with the notion that litigation should be brought for the benefit of clients rather than lawyers. Divorce and bankruptcy are now actively promoted, and lawyers are sellers of indulgences rather than transmitters of values. Organized lawyers are the chief enemies of discovery reform and alternative methods of resolving disputes. The expansion of constitutional doctrine has caused the legal to displace the political process, all controversies now being cast in terms of absolutes.

As with law, so with medicine. Medical advertising aggrandizes costs. Constitutionalizing the abortion controversy eliminated the advice of family physicians as a restraint on sexual behavior. Consumer and bureaucratic interests, rather than professional and public health interests have driven changes in medical care, and have bureaucratized the profession; the only reforms now being discussed involve more "rights talk" and more litigation.

Social work was largely destroyed by the judicialization of welfare rights and the related elimination of bureaucratic discretion. Discipline in public schools has been subordinated to the rights of the handicapped, including the emotionally handicapped.[33] Transportation and financing mandates insure that schools no longer are governed by and serve localities and are no longer funded by them.

The mass media have been freed from public control by the commercial speech doctrine, as well as condemnation of efforts to control broadcast obscenity and in the 1950 *Winters v. New York* case, broadcast violence.[34] The forgotten dissent of Justices Frankfurter, Jackson, and Burton in that case reads very well today, but you will not find it in any law school casebook.

ACTIVIST STATUTORY CONSTRUCTION AND ECONOMIC UNITS

Nor is constitutional litigation the sole cause of the destruction of subordinate institutions. Judicial activism in the construction of statutes has played its role. The protection of labor unions has been diluted by a series of court decisions relating to permanent replacement of strikers and political contributions by unions difficult to reconcile with statutory purpose. The fair trade laws limiting price cutting of branded goods of manufacturers preferring a decentralized distribution system,[35] the Robinson Patman Act barring price discrimination against smaller retailers,[36] the Glass-Steagall Act separating commercial and investment banking,[37] the Celler-Kefauver Act purporting to tighten merger standards,[38] the Bank Merger Act, the Public Utility Holding Company Act,[39] and state regulations of branch banking and secondary mortgage and consumer credit abuses[40] all were destroyed or evaded by judicial decisions reflecting free market values at the expense of honest construction of the statutes concerned, while the restrictions on bank and media mergers once thought to have been imposed by the antitrust laws have similarly succumbed to judicial revision. The decision in *United States v. Associated Press,* with its declarations about the importance of a diverse and decentralized mass media,[41] to select one random example, is all but forgotten.

The Courts and the Family

The degree to which judicial decisions have extolled the individual rights of family members above interests of family solidarity need scarcely be labored: the demise of permanent alimony, of the maternal preference rule in custody cases, and of secrecy in adoption proceedings, the perverse effects of liberalized abortion on sexual mores and the illegitimacy rate, all supply examples. Female emancipation is sought through an agenda based on radical autonomy, at the expense of such mundane concerns as tax exemptions and thresholds, family allowances, reform of outmoded zoning laws, and fostering of cooperative mechanisms for child care.[42] The recent *Lawrence v. Texas* case potentially threatens the tax and other benefits provided to married couples in recognition of their role as parents, actual or potential.

Underlying Causes

To what may one attribute the willingness of the American political classes to sweep away all institutions beneath the national state? Principally to a fixation by both Right and Left on the economic; in important ways, American politics has resolved itself into a competition between rival materialist philosophies that uneasily coexist in separate parts of society. But the society that makes markets possible rests in part on precapitalist foundations. Complete dominance by the national government is likewise no way to realize equality.

The enthusiasm for destruction of mediating structures has been hastened by the cause of attaining racial equality. But the consequences of forty years of action has not been the elevation of deprived blacks to meaningful citizenship but the effective transformation of an underclass from peons to wards of the state. The weakening of the institutions that have sustained other groups in their rise in society has conferred only limited benefits on the dispossessed, who have been disserved by the devaluation of standards of personal behavior. The fostering of an ideology of extreme individualism in both morals and economics has been destructive of social capital. American slums are not poor. Their diet and housing stock compare favorably to those of even advanced Asian nations. They suffer from a culture of family breakdown, social isolation of households, a lack of mechanisms for civic cooperation, and a lack of mutual trust. The dominant judicial logic has been that satirized by Professor Philip Kurland in his critique of the Warren Court: "equality of rules is inconsistent with a multiplicity of rule-makers."

Agenda for Reform

A sensible agenda for national government would demand that it first do no harm. Although the original premise of income taxation as stated in Mill's *Principles of Political Economy*[43] was that the tax was fairly applied only to income beyond that necessary for subsistence, exemptions have been allowed to wither. Correction of this should supply the appropriate egalitarian agenda. For the rest, government cannot provide equality: As Hume wrote two centuries before the collapse of communism, "So much authority must soon degenerate into tyranny, and be exercised with great partialities."

The road away from our present discontents is found not in invention of new "rights" but in respect for what was once thought to be a distinctive American value, what Justice Black called "the right of each man to participate in the self government of his society." As the much-maligned Judge Bork pertinently observed, "The Constitution assures the liberties of self-government, not merely those liberties that consist of being free of government. The freedom to govern is enormously important to the individuals who make up a community, for it is freedom to control the environment—physical, aesthetic and moral—in which they and their families live."

The renewal of our institutions requires a willingness not only to honor these principles, but to look the facts of decline in their face. A surprising number of the needed reforms entail only gradual repudiation of invented judicial doctrines or return to the original constitutional design. The Gorbachevs and Havels, raised under a totalitarian system, perceived the need for reconstruction of their civil societies, as did the American military when confronted with its wreckage following the Vietnam War. There are indeed dangers in a condition in which the military has reason to conceive of itself as the only American institution that has yet faced facts.

To this I would add a Brandeisian emphasis, foreign to the rhetoric of Judge Bork and to judges who consider themselves licensed to impose "law and economics" principles, on "the participation of the unknown many in the responsibilities and determination of business" as being "essential to the maintenance of liberty."

I am of the school that believes that Alexis de Tocqueville wrote a great book about the contemporary United States. That book, however, is not, as commonly believed, *Democracy in America*. Rather I recall his reflections on the French Economists, the Thatcherites of their time, in *The Old Regime and the French Revolution*:

> They were very favorable to the free exchange of commodities, to laissez faire and laisser passer in commerce and industry, but as to political liberties prop-

erly so called they did not dream of them. No grades in society, no classes distinct, no fixed ranks, a people composed of individuals almost alike and wholly equal. This confused mass recognized as the only legitimate sovereign, but carefully deprived of all the means which would enable it to direct or even to superintend its own government.[44]

Their program produced two decades of prosperity before the French Revolution by providing "a government which though ceasing to be despotic remained very powerful and maintained order everywhere and a nation in which every man could get rich in his own way and keep his wealth once acquired."[45] Tocqueville notes that

> [i]f the French had continued to busy themselves daily in the administration of the country in the provincial assembles, they would certainly never have let themselves be influenced, as they then were, by the ideas of the writers; they would have kept a touch on practical business which would have saved them from pure theory. As the general liberties perished dragging with them in their van local liberties, the townsman and the gentleman ceased to have contact in public life. These two men never met except by mere chance in private life. The two classes were not only rivals, they were enemies. Thus Paris had become the master of France, and the army, that was to make of itself mistress of Paris, was already assembling.[46]

The prejudice against local discretion that we identify with the Jacobins was, Tocqueville reminds us, shared by the Economists, and our contemporary justices, also, have been too prone to conflate economic theory and political wisdom.

> What already characterized the administration in France was the violent hatred by which it was inspired by all those, whether nobles or bourgeois, who wished independently of itself to concern themselves with public affairs. The smallest independent body which seemed desirous of establishing itself without its concurrence made it afraid; the smallest free association, whatever its object, caused it annoyance, it only allowed those to exist which had been arbitrarily composed and presided over by itself.[47]

The result was that

> [i]n France the political world was, so to speak, divided into two separate and disconnected provinces. One set of people did the actual administration, another set down the abstract principles on which all administration ought to be founded, one set took the particular measures indicated by routine; the other set proclaimed general laws without ever thinking of the means to apply them; one set had the conduct of affairs; the other set, the control of mind.[48]

And so, "[I]t is impossible to imagine the contempt into which the law finally fell even in the minds of those who applied it, when there were no longer political associations nor newspapers to mitigate the capricious activity and limit the arbitrary and changing humor of ministers and their offices."[49]

That is the stage, with our centralized government and increasingly concentrated and vacuous mass media, which we are rapidly approaching now.

NOTES

1. American Law Institute, *Remarks and Addresses at the 74th Annual Meeting* (1997), 75.

2. American Law Institute, *Remarks and Addresses at the 75th Annual Meeting* (1998), 65.

3. Jay S. Bybee, "Ulysses at the Mast: Democracy, Federalism, and the Seventeenth Amendment," 91 *Northwestern Law Review* 500 (1996).

4. Art. 1, Sec. 9, Cl. 4.

5. Ken Messere, Flip de Kam, and Christopher Heady, *Tax Policy: Theory and Practice in OECD Countries* (Oxford: Oxford University Press, 1993), 208.

6. See Carl-Christaphe Schweitzer et al., eds., *Politics and Government in the Federal Republic of Germany: Basic Documents* (Leamington Spa, Worwickshire: Berg, 1984), 173–75.

7. See the authorities cited in George W. Liebmann, *The Little Platoons* (Westport, Conn.: Praeger, 1995), 37 n. 31.

8. See H. Uppendahl, "Intergovernmental Relations in the Federal Republic of Germany," in *The Present and Future Role of Local Government in Great Britain and the Federal Republic of Germany*, ed. Alan Norton (London: Anglo-German Foundation, 1985), 35–48.

9. 106 F. 3d 559 (4th Cir. 1997); see McCoy and Friedman, "Conditional Spending: Federalism's Trojan Horse," 1989 *Supreme Court Review* 85–125.

10. Ralph A. Rossum, *Federalism, the Supreme Court, and the Seventeenth Amendment: The Irony of Constitutional Democracy* (Lanham, Md.: Lexington Books, 2001). See *So. Dakota v. Dole* 483 U.S. 203 (1987).

11. David P. Currie, "The Three Judge Court in Constitutional Litigation," 32 *University of Chicago Law Review* 1 (1964).

12. 394 U.S. 618 (1969); see *Memorial Hospital v. Maricopa*, 415 U.S. 250 (1974); *Zobel v. Williams*, 457 U.S. 55 (1982).

13. *Saenz v. Roe*, 526 U.S. 489 (1999).

14. *Estin v. Estin*, 334 U.S. 541 (Jackson, J. dissenting); see *Williams v. North Carolina*, 317 U.S. 287 (1942) (Jackson, J. dissenting).

15. George W. Liebmann, "Conflict of Laws and Federal Minimum Standards and Federal Chartering," in 1 ALI-ABA, Regional Symposium on the Structure and Governance of Corporations (May 1978), 185.

16. Michael A. Lawrence, "Toward a More Coherent Dormant Commerce Clause," 21 *Harvard Journal of Law and Public Policy* 395 (1998).

17. James Bryce, *American Commonwealth*, 3d ed. (New York: Macmillan, 1985), 1:637.

18. Sidney Webb, *Grants in Aid* (London: Fabian Society, 1911), 4–5.

19. Victor Ehrenburg. *The Greek State* (New York: Barnes and Noble, 1960), 691.

20. *Fumarolo v. Chicago Bd. of Educ.*, 142 Ill. 2d 54, 566, N.E. 2d. 1283 (1990), criticized in J. Evans, "Let Our Parents Run," 19 *Hastings Constitutional Law Quarterly* 963 (1992); and R. Briffault, "Who Rules at Home: One Man One Vote and Local Governments," 60 *University of Chicago Law Review* 339 (1993). On the background of the Chicago proposal, see Carnegie Foundation for the Advancement of Teaching, *An Impeded Generation* (1988), chap. 2; Mary Anne Raywid, "Evolving Effort to Improve Schools," 72 *Phi Beta Kappan* 139 (1990).

The Fumarolo case was limited by a later Chicago scheme in which teacher representatives were appointed and parent representatives were chosen by vote, upheld in *Pittman v. Chicago Bd. of Ed.*, 64 F. 3d 1098 (7th Cir. 1995).

21. 207 U.S. 161 (1907).

22. Jerry Frug, "The City as a Legal Concept," 93 *Harvard Law Review* 1057 (1980).

23. Cf. Clark Gillette, "In Partial Praise of Dillon's Rule," 67 *Chicago-Kent Law Review* 959 (1991).

24. Bryce, *American Commonwealth*, 1:642.

25. *Ball v. James*, 451 U.S. 355 (1971); *Salyer v. Tulare Lake District*, 410 U.S. 719 (1973).

26. Friedrich A. Hayek, *Law, Legislation, and Liberty* (Chicago: University of Chicago Press, 1982), 3:146.

27. H. G. Wells, *Mankind in the Making* (London: Chapman and Hall, 1959), 45.

28. George W. Liebmann, *The Gallows in the Grove* (Westport, Conn.: Praeger, 1997), 224–26.

29. Ibid., 222–24; see George W. Liebmann, "Land Readjustment for America: A Proposal for a Statute," Lincoln Institute of Land Policy Working Paper WP98GL1.

30. 397 U.S. 254 (1970).

31. FRCP 23, as amended in 1966.

32. Civil Rights Attorneys' Fee Act, 42 U.S.C. §1988.

33. *Goss v. Lopez*, 419 U.S. 565 (1975) (5–4 decision).

34. *Winters v. New York*, 333 U.S. 507 (1948) (Frankfurter, Jackson, and Burton, JJ., dissenting).

35. *Schwegmann Bros. v. Calvert Distillers*, 341 U.S. 384 (1951) (Frankfurter, Black, and Burton, JJ., dissenting); *U.S. v. McKesson & Robbins*, 351 U.S. 305 (1951) (Harlan, Frankfurter, and Burton, JJ., dissenting).

36. *Great A&P Tea Co. v. FTC*, 440 U.S. 69 (1979) (White and Marshall, JJ., dissenting). See Herbert Hovenkamp, *Federal Antitrust Policy* (St. Paul: West, 1994), 523.

37. E.g. *Board of Governors v. Investment Company Institute*, 450 U.S. 46 (1981).

38. See *Cargill v. Monfort of Colorado*, 479 U.S. 104 (1986) (Stevens and White, JJ., dissenting).

39. See the annotations to 15 U.S.C. 79j.

40. *Marquette Natl. Bank v. First of Omaha Corp.*, 439 U.S. 299 (1978) (Brennan, J.), a unanimous decision purporting to apply the National Bank Act of 1864, is at the root of today's consumer credit abuses.

41. 326 U.S. 1 (1945).

42. Liebmann, *Gallows in the Grove*, x, 229–31.

43. John Stuart Mill, *Principles of Political Economy*, rev. ed. (New York: Colonial Press, 1900), 829.

44. Alexis de Tocqueville, *Ancient Regime* (Oxford: Blackwell, 1947).

45. Ibid., 183–84.

46. Ibid., 149–50, 92, 82.

47. Ibid., 69–70.

48. Ibid., 155.

49. Ibid., 72.

CHAPTER 6

The Academy, the Courts, and the Culture of Rationalism

Steven D. Smith

LAW PROFESSORS naturally find it pleasant to suppose that we are shaping the law—that judges and especially justices are looking to the academy for guidance as they decide cases and devise doctrines. But is this self-conception realistic, or merely a gratifying delusion?

In this essay I want to consider three aspects of that question. First, I will briefly discuss some of the most obvious ways in which law professors might exercise what we could call "result-specific" influence over judges, and then speculate about the efficacy—or, as seems more likely, the inefficacy—of these modes of influence. Then I will discuss what seems to me the more powerful but also more diffuse form of influence emanating from the academy—the inculcation within the judiciary of a culture of rationalism.[1]

Finally, I want to address a corollary issue that presents what seems to me a puzzling aspect of the problem that is the central concern of the essays collected in this volume. The problem is judicial imperialism, which seems a manifestation of judicial arrogance. The puzzle arises from a lack of correlation between what we might call professional and personal arrogance. A justice who seems quite overbearing in person may be highly deferential in his decisions; conversely, justices who are personally modest can act in very intrusive ways.

Justice Brennan—always a favorite in the academy—may provide an example. Probably no justice in modern times has been as consistently or aggressively willing to brush aside established traditions and to impose his own judgments on the nation. Yet Abner Mikva reports: "Those who knew Justice Brennan personally found it hard to square the charges that he was some kind of officious federal meddler with the persona of this warm, generous, sensitive human being."[2]

The celebrated joint opinion in *Planned Parenthood v. Casey* can also serve to illustrate the puzzle. Probably there is no more blatant manifestation in modern constitutional law of judicial arrogance, rising at times to almost pathological delusions of grandeur.[3] What are we to make of justices who imagine themselves heroically "call[ing] the contending sides of a national controversy to end their national division"—and who fancy that even citizens who disagree (because, for example, they believe that abortion is morally equivalent to murder) will "nevertheless struggle to accept [the Court's judgment]" and will indeed expect the Court not to correct its error but rather to "remain steadfast" and not "br[eak] its faith with the people"?[4] Do people with this sort of self-conception live in the same world as the rest of us? And yet, this outpouring of presumption came from justices who as individuals seem not exceptionally arrogant. Although I cannot claim to know any of the joint opinion's authors personally, my impression from hearsay and distant observation is that these justices have egos no more athletic than those of many other high government officials—including justices such as, for example, the author of the dissenting opinion in *Casey* that was most vigorous in urging deference to the state legislature. Professor Glendon acknowledges this disparity in referring to "the open hubris displayed by the Court's least flamboyant members,"[5] and the discrepancy leads her to wonder: "How did it come about that 'conservative,' 'moderate' justices on today's Supreme Court are often more assertive and arrogant in their exercise of judicial power than the members of the 'liberal,' 'activist' Warren Court?"[6]

The puzzle, in short, is what we might call the "hubris of humility" reflected in apologetically aggressive Supreme Court decisions rendered by very decent individuals who in private may show few signs of the megalomania that their actions and opinions seem to exhibit. I propose that we view this puzzle in terms of the internal dynamics of modern rationalism. And if I am right that the legal academy in recent generations has exerted itself to inculcate and reinforce this sort of rationalism, then this proposition might go some way toward explaining how even (or perhaps especially) a justice who is quite cognizant of his or her considerable limitations might nonetheless be beguiled out of moderation and good sense, thereby becoming (as Bob Nagel has written) a "lumbering bully" apt to "disrupt social norms and practices at its pleasure."[7]

The Result-Specific Modes of Academic Influence

Suppose you are a law professor who wants to influence the courts to move in a particular direction on some specific issue like abortion or capital punishment or religious freedom. How might you try to exert your influence?

Probably the most straightforward approach would be to find a way to get involved in actual litigation, perhaps by representing a party or writing an amicus brief. This approach would be tempting because it might not only advance what you think is a good cause; it might have other more immediate and pecuniary rewards as well. So of course some law professors do regularly participate in litigation; Laurence Tribe is probably the most prominent example. And I suppose that law professors might influence the courts in this way. I am not going to say more about this mode of influence, though, because I think it falls outside of my topic. When law professors write actual briefs or do oral arguments, that is, they are acting as *lawyers*, not as *law professors*. There is no distinctive *academic* influence at work here.

So how might an academic try to influence the courts *while acting as a law professor?* Probably the most obvious and common method is to write scholarly articles or books advocating particular positions. Law professors turn out scholarship calculated to influence the courts in a variety of ways—through *ex ante* prescription regarding legal questions that the courts have not yet answered (or perhaps even thought of),[8] through *post hoc* consolidation and rationalization that tries to entrench results or principles the courts have already approved,[9] and through "spin doctoring" that tries to mitigate the damages from unfavorable decisions—or even to turn apparent judicial defeats into victories. Thus, the unsophisticated observer might have thought that a pair of nine-to-zero Supreme Court decisions reversing circuit court rulings that had invalidated state "assisted suicide" laws would be a crushing defeat for "right to die" jurisprudence;[10] only after listening to or reading Laurence Tribe or Ronald Dworkin would one realize that those decisions actually contain all the seeds that might shortly bear fruit in judicial recognition of the claimed right.[11]

A second possible method of influence is to supply the courts with law clerks freshly trained to see the law the way the professor sees it. Though less direct (because here the professor must speak to the judges through an independent intermediary), this method has the advantage of providing daily personal contact with the judges over a long period of time. Of course, this mode of influence is less widely available than the first: Anyone can write a law review article, but only a few professors at the elite schools can expect to send law clerks to the highest courts on a regular basis.

How effective are these methods of influence? We can only speculate—and indeed, even the judges themselves are probably not fully conscious of all the factors that affect their decisions.[12] My own speculation is not entitled to much deference; unlike some law professors I am not much of a "Court watcher," and the nearest I have come to a Supreme Court justice has been in occasionally sharing a table at moot court banquets or law school luncheons. For what it's worth, though, my view is that these familiar forms of result-specific influence probably have far less force than law professors would like to believe.

It is true that law professors often take their responsibilities for shaping the law in these ways very seriously. I recall a faculty colloquium in which a professor from one of the nation's two most prestigious law schools was presenting an article soon to be published in the journal of the other of the two most prestigious law schools. Asked why he was being conspicuously coy about a controversial implication of the article's thesis, the presenter explained—with endearing candor—that he needed to pin down Chief Justice Rehnquist on the central principle before proceeding to elaborate the full (and to Rehnquist, he assumed, unwelcome) extension of that principle. In addition, I have heard at both first and second hand about how seriously some professors at elite schools regard the business of recommending students for Supreme Court clerkships.

Still, my guess is that the law professor who earnestly engages in these activities with the expectation of guiding the Court is like the child with a toy steering wheel who thinks he is directing the car. Take legal scholarship. This seems a poor vehicle for influencing judges for at least three interconnected reasons.[13] First, advocacy scholarship, at least in the field of constitutional law, is hardly ever very persuasive.[14] Second, on any given issue it is likely that law professors will publish competent articles purporting to show that the law requires different or opposite results; thus, law review articles will tend to cancel each other out. Finally, indications are that the justices hardly ever read academic legal literature anyway.[15]

It is more likely, I admit, that justices' law clerks might read or remember law review articles; they might also be more impressionable, and thus more easily persuaded. My own observations as a law clerk at the circuit court level, however, would suggest that although law clerks *do* often read law review literature, they read it mostly to gain a quick overview of an issue or area of law, and perhaps to collect relevant authorities and citations. It is less likely that a law clerk will feel compelled to draw a particular conclusion by the *argument* of a law review article. And it is less likely still that the law clerk will convey that argument to the judge so as to persuade the judge to adopt a position that he or she would not otherwise have favored.

To be sure, there are reports from time to time of law clerks exerting a powerful influence over the justices, or at least over certain justices.[16] It is even reported off the record that an occasional justice has effectively turned over his office and functions to his clerks. But if this sort of situation occurs at all, it is surely anomalous. For myself, I find it difficult to believe that law clerks as a class have any very significant systemic ability to affect the outcomes of cases—though they may have significant responsibility for *selecting* the cases heard by the Supreme Court. After all, judges (and especially Supreme Court justices) will nearly always have had long careers in law and government. And they will naturally be ambitious, assertive, probably opinionated people; shrinking violets do not often end up in high public office. Moreover, a good deal in the daily practices of a judge seems calculated to enhance the judge's sense of importance or even to nurture whatever authoritarian habits of mind the judge might happen to have.[17] Who else gets to go around saying peremptory things like "I rule that . . ." or "It is so ordered" on a daily basis, not only within his own organization but to the society in general? It seems far-fetched to suppose that someone with these qualities and in this position would be vulnerable to the influence of an inexperienced, short-term employee, usually in his or her twenties, fresh out of school.

It is significant, I think, that the reports of law clerk influence are likely to emanate from law clerks, or former law clerks.[18] I know that when I was a law clerk I sometimes enjoyed thinking I had some influence over the judge's decisions. This pleasant illusion was fed by the fact that the judge sometimes praised my draft opinions, and published some of them with barely any changes. I was emboldened by this positive reinforcement to try writing an opinion significantly different from the one the judge had asked me to write. This experiment did to my assumption of influence what the Michelson-Morley experiment is said to have done to the theory of the universal ether.

Judges are human beings, of course, and no doubt they are affected by the opinions and experiences of other human beings, especially those close to them, such as spouses, children, and friends. In some cases, a trusted law clerk might achieve this status. For example, it seems that Ronald Dworkin the law clerk enjoyed this kind of relationship with his boss, Judge Learned Hand; or at least Dworkin so reports.[19] My suggestion is only that there is little reason to believe that law clerks as a class have much ability to influence judges to go where they were not already going anyway—and even less reason to believe that law professors, who are one step removed, have much influence over judges via law clerks.

If these two modes of influence—writing legal scholarship, and recommending students for clerkships—nonetheless seem more important than I give them credit for, I suggest that this is because they are closely linked to a different mode of influence that is less direct and visible but also, I suspect, more potent. Legal academics *do* have considerable power, that is, to dispense praise and blame within the legal culture, and thus to regulate a judge's current reputation and enduring legacy. Sometimes they exercise this power by consulting with more popular media, passing the word (and the academy's judgment) on to reporters who may understand few of the intricacies of Supreme Court opinions. Thus, the informed public is told that Justice Souter (who was *expected to be* "conservative") is, to everyone's surprise, an intellectual force to be reckoned with, while

Justice Thomas (who *is* "conservative") is not. Don't ask me to justify these appraisals; I cannot, and so confine myself to reporting that they are widely held in the legal academy. Prospective and beginning law professors may themselves inherit these judgments as part of the job.

The academy's power is also exercised through legal scholarship; but here we need to distinguish between scholarship as *a vehicle for rational argument* and scholarship as a *medium for bestowing praise and blame*, or at least (as with casebooks) for conferring attention. We also need to distinguish between law clerks *as law clerks* and law clerks as future leaders of the profession and, in many cases, *prospective law professors*. My point is simply that the legal academy controls to a large degree whether a judge will be perceived today as sagacious, or hopelessly pedestrian, or wickedly reactionary; and the academy also determines whether in the long run a justice will ascend into that select group of jurists who receive continuing admiration—the Holmeses, Brandeises, Warrens—or will qualify for the group deemed worthy of attention or at least respectful disagreement—the Fields, Blacks, Sutherlands, Frankfurters—or instead will be banished to the oblivion occupied by judges who sat on the nation's most lofty tribunal but whose names nonetheless draw blank stares even from the typical constitutional law professor—the Matthewses, Millers, Mintons, Moodys, and Moores. And the judges likely to be favored, of course, are those who render decisions that endear them to the academy.

So how great an influence does this power of praise and blame give the academy over judges' decisions? Again, I can only speculate, and I am also sure that judges differ greatly in their sensitivity to praise and blame from the academy.[20] My hunch is that judges who are especially strong-minded (like Justice Scalia) or who have a healthy and justified self-esteem based on a career of solid achievement even before being appointed to the bench (like Justice White) are relatively immune to this sort of influence, and that judges of more meager gifts and accomplishments are likely to be more susceptible.[21] Perhaps the *Casey* joint opinion should be considered in this light.

But in any case, it seems plausible to suppose that some judges and especially justices would be vulnerable to this sort of influence, and would thus be anxious to cultivate the good opinion of the academy. After all, human beings usually value, and sometimes crave, the respect and affection of their fellows; and there is no reason to suppose that judges as a class would be less sensitive to these considerations than other people. Moreover, as a quick glance at the names of academic buildings should attest, it is common for successful people to want to leave some kind of legacy, or to be venerated after they die. Carl Becker showed some decades ago how within an "Enlightenment" ethos, the anticipated approval of posterity can effectively displace heaven and deity as motivating concerns.[22] So why should judges be free from such motivations? Indeed, the lure of reputation and legacy might be especially powerful for Supreme Court justices, both because the possibility of achieving fame (or notoriety) is considerable and because most of the usual competing incentives have been eliminated by the nature of the office.[23] A justice's performance will not affect either her salary or her chances of promotion; reputation and legacy represent the principal forms of variable compensation still available to a judge.

But even judges who are strongly motivated by the desire to cultivate a good reputation still have to make risky calculations about how to achieve that objective. In some cases the calculation would be quite easy. Thus, I think Justice White could have been virtually certain, if he had cared, that his decision and opinion in *Bowers v. Hardwick*[24] would be unlikely to reap bushels of praise from the legal academy. Conversely, Justice Blackmun could make a safe bet that his decision in *Roe v. Wade* would earn him a measure of approval, even if most of his supporters regarded his opinion as an embarrassment. Ditto for Justice Kennedy in *Romer v. Evans.*[25]

Many other situations, though, would present more difficult calculations. Even at the time of decision, the academy might be divided on an issue. And there is always a chance that what one generation regards as a wise or prudent decision—*Plessy v. Ferguson,*[26] maybe—will be reviled by a later generation as wrongheaded or even deeply wicked.

What this means, I think, is that although the academy holds a stout club in its ability to bestow praise and blame, that hammer is also an unwieldy one; it will strike haphazardly, or often not at all. So without discounting the force of this kind of influence, I want to turn to what I think is a more regular and pervasive kind of influence emanating from the academy.

The Academy and the Culture of Rationalism

Despite political and jurisprudential differences, virtually all academics in this country have agreed that, as Henry Hart put it, "reason is the life of the law."[27] Mary Ann Glendon concludes a recent wide-ranging critique of much modern legal thought by reaffirming the fundamental faith: " 'Reason' say the ancient voices. 'Reason, now and always, the life of the law.' "[28] Of course, academicians differ considerably in what they mean by reason (and some of us are simply hazy on the subject). I will return shortly to the question of what "reason" means in legal discourse. For the moment, the important point is that virtually everyone in the academy agrees that "reason," whatever it is, is the lifeblood of the law.

The Legal Academy as the Inculcator of Rationalism

I don't expect to provoke much dissent in saying that the law schools have a dominant role in nurturing this respect for "reason." The process begins with legal education, as students are taught to "think like a lawyer." Just what "thinking like a lawyer" entails is itself a contestable matter, of course, but at least it means being able to support one's views with whatever the legal culture currently counts as reasons. Thus, I recall my first law school course: Professor Lipson confronting students with his formidable intellect, forcing us to justify opinions, never content with "I think" or "I feel," dismissing assertions right and left with an amused or perhaps indignant, "Ah, but that's just a conclusion." Though Lipson was an unusually skilled practitioner of the art, law teachers generally try for something similar. The preferred method is usually described as "So-cratic," named after the person commonly thought to be the first great exemplar of the "life of reason." I remember feeling baffled by this exercise at first—I could not understand why certain assertions *did* and other assertions *did not* qualify as "reasons"—but over time I along with my classmates naturally became acculturated into the prevailing rationalism.

If legal education inculcates a rationalist mind-set, legal scholarship helps to maintain it by sponsoring an ongoing practice of exchanging arguments about legal decisions. Of course, the practice of law does this too. But in practice institutional constraints severely limit the character, length, and depth of the exchange. Oral arguments are short; briefs are subject to page limits; and "res judicata," "That's the law," and "Get on with it, counselor" are familiar refrains. Legal scholarship knows none of these limits; there the argument can go on forever, and the proliferation of footnotes (which add so much to the rationalist aura) is as likely to be regarded as a virtue as a defect.

The academy's mission in promoting rationalism is especially successful because it seems so nonpartisan. A law student might not understand—or might consciously reject—a professor's substantive legal or political views, yet still emerge from a class with an ingrained assumption that the professor's *rationalist approach* to law—and perhaps, by extension, to life—is admirable and desirable. Indeed, it might become difficult for the student even to conceive of any alternative, except perhaps to do the same thing badly. The only options, it may seem, are rationalism and *irrationality*. In this way, even the prospective lawyer or judge who is a self-styled maverick or rebel will in fact be a true disciple after all.

The Dimensions of Reason in Constitutional Discourse

But how does this methodically inculcated rationalism actually work in legal argument and judicial decision-making? What *is* rationalism, and what does it entail? Reason and rationalism can mean very different things, of course, but for present purposes, I suggest that reason in constitutional discourse has three dimensions.

In its most visible aspect, constitutional law presents reason in instrumentalist or "means-end" terms. Scholars have pointed out that most of the doctrinal formulas articulated by the Court, whether under the First Amendment or the Fourteenth or the commerce clause, are presented in essentially the same monotonously instrumentalist terms.[29] So laws are viewed as means to social ends, and a law's constitutionality is said to depend on how important the law's ends are and how effective and necessary the law is as a means to achieving those ends. In this way, constitutional decisions are tied to the dominant modern conception of reason.[30]

In an important respect, though, constitutional discourse deviates from the instrumentalist model. A familiar tenet of instrumentalist thought holds that reason can only study the relation of means to ends but cannot assess the merits of the ends themselves; these are supposed to be just *given*—probably in human needs, desires, and "interests" (which, as Charles Lindblom observes, are sometimes treated as if they were "objective attributes of human beings" much like "a person's metabolic rate").[31] In this vein, Richard Posner maintains that "there is no profitable reasoning over ends."[32] But in fact constitutional argument seems deeply and even primarily concerned with the legitimacy of *ends*. Scholars like John Ely and Cass Sunstein have shown that even when courts appear to be examining the instrumental efficacy of a law as a means to a supposed end, in reality this examination is mainly calculated to "flush out" the real ends, as opposed to more presentable but inauthentic ends that may have been concocted for public or litigation purposes.[33] The real quest is to determine the actual objective of the law, and the law will then stand or fall depending on the perceived value or legitimacy of that end.

So how is a court to assess the value of an end, if instrumental rationality is by its own admission incompetent to address that question? Here I think we see a second dimension of what reason means in constitutional discourse. Now reason becomes the label for a set of dichotomies or oppositions that are inherited from "Enlightenment" thinking; in each dichotomy reason is one term set in opposition to a different term denoting something that is not reason. I would list three such oppositions:

Reason vs. Tradition
Reason vs. Faith
Reason vs. Emotion[34]

So in this dimension of constitutional discourse, asking if a law is based on reason entails an examination to see whether the law is in reality motivated by one of the supposed antitheses of reason: that is, by tradition, or faith, or emotion. Opponents of a law will try to argue that the law reflects traditional stereotypes, or that it has a religious rather than a secular objective, or that it is based on prejudice or hatred or "animus." If it is, then the law is invalid as contrary to reason. Gender discrimination cases under the equal protection clause are perhaps the best example of the first kind of objection; establishment clause cases illustrate the second kind; and other equal protection cases like *Romer, Cleburne*,[35] and race discrimination cases are clear examples of the third.

But there are severe difficulties in this kind of reasoning. For one thing, the instrumentalist dimension of modern reason conflicts with this "Enlightenment" dimension: as noted, instrumentalism insists that ends or goals are by their nature arbitrary or simply given, and thus impervious to rational assessment, while "Enlightenment" reason tries to perform just that impossible assessment. In addition, the oppositions central to the "Enlightenment" approach are by now highly dubious, to put the point charitably. Thus, a good deal of modern thinking suggests that reason can operate *only* within a tradition, and only on the basis of commitments and constraints that are more a matter of faith and feeling than of rational demonstration.[36] In other words, the "Enlightenment" view of reason itself is difficult to defend on the basis of reason; the inherited dichotomies pitting "reason" against tradition, faith, and feeling themselves manage by now to subsist mostly on tradition, faith, and feeling. Finally, the "Enlightenment" oppositions are notoriously manipulable, so that virtually any view can be shown to be either in accord with reason or an expression of unenlightened prejudice. "One person's 'prejudice,'" Bruce Ackerman remarks, "is, notoriously, another's 'principle.'"[37]

So then what exactly *does* determine the outcome of the Enlightenment examination? Here I think we must acknowledge the third dimension of "reason" as it operates in constitutional discourse: "Reason" refers to the way "reasonable people" think, or to the views that "reasonable people" hold. To put it differently, "reason" is simply an honorific label used to designate the views and positions commonly held by people associated by education or position with leading academic institutions. Indeed, sometimes "reason" is actually presented—seemingly without embarrassment—almost in these terms: A position is asserted without any pretense of demonstration but rather with the confident certification that this is a view that "reasonable persons" hold. Rawls's celebrated abortion footnote is a good example.[38] More generally, Stanley Fish observes that academic judgments approving some positions as "reasonable" and discarding others as "radically implausible" typically reflect "[d]evices for elevating the decorum of academic dinner parties to the status of discourse universals."[39] So the academy teaches the judges to be rationalists, and then (indirectly and in a largely nonrational way) the academy supplies the substantive content of that rationalism.

Let me summarize the argument thus far. My contention is that the academy influences judges not so much in the result-specific ways discussed earlier, but rather by inculcating a culture of rationalism. This rationalism has three principal components: a discourse that clings to the vocabulary of instrumental rationality; a perpetual roving commission that seeks to ferret out views or decisions based on tradition, faith, and emotion; and, finally and most decisively, an attitude of deference to the opinions prevalent among an educated class of citizens. This is the culture within which judges live and move and have their being: It largely sets the boundaries of what they can and cannot think and can and cannot say, and hence determines what the lawyers who address judges can and cannot think and say.

The Consequences of Rationalism

The observation that judges operate in a rationalist culture may seem thoroughly unremarkable, in part for reasons that I have already briefly noticed. If the academy is as successful as I have suggested in inculcating the mind-set of rationalism, then the culture of rationalism may come to seem inevitable—simply a component of what law just is; and someone who points out the phenomenon will seem like the lackluster student who exclaims with an air of discovery, "You know what? I've observed that mathematicians are always talking about *numbers*." Moreover, if the only alternatives are to be careful, good reasoners or sloppy, bad reasoners, then declaiming against rationalism will seem truly perverse.

The answer to this objection, I think, is that rationalism of the modern variety is *not* the only way to live, or to make decisions, or even to think. As Bob Nagel has pointed out, "[R]ationalism is not a synonym for all methods of moral and intellectual inquiry. It is not the same as insight, creativity, wisdom, vision, instinct, or empathy."[40] Recently, an occasional scholar who has grown disenchanted with aspects of modern rationalism will offer *tradition,* or traditionalism, as the principal alternative.[41] Or it might be possible to develop a "jurisprudence of faith"—with "faith" *not* being understood as the antithesis of "reason."[42]

In any event, most of us (I suspect all of us) routinely rely on nonrationalist—though not necessarily irrational—modes of cognition and decision. Probably we have no choice; it is doubtful that pure rationalism has the resources needed to live a sane or satisfactory life. The effect of rationalism, however, is to suppress or marginalize these vital dimensions of our experience. And one consequence of that suppression within legal culture is a constitutional discourse that is impoverished, sterile, and artificial.

At this point I can hardly do better than incorporate by reference, with only the barest summary, Bob Nagel's work, which graphically charts the unfortunate effects of this imposed artificiality in legal discourse and Supreme Court decisions. One consequence is that laws or practices are debated in terms that have almost nothing to do with the real concerns motivating either the supporters or opponents of those laws or practices, so that "[l]ike a cracked mirror, the Court reflects back to the public a weirdly distorted view of its laws and policies."[43] For example, a city ordinance requiring visual barriers around drive-in movie theaters that display nudity[44] generates a discussion not of the moral, aesthetic, cultural, and local identity concerns that underlie the requirement, but rather of the probabilities that distracted drivers might run off the road. "In its relentless search for external justifications," Nagel observes,

> the Court was too grave to notice the comic aspects of its own discussion. The foolishness of the community's asserted justification, however, did not demonstrate that the ordinance was wrong, but only that its defenders had been driven to silliness by the Court's inapposite demands for derivative justifications.[45]

More recently, as Nagel has explained, the Court's opinion on Colorado's Amendment 2 seems simply obtuse regarding the complex motivations and perceptions that drove the human beings who fought over the law.[46]

In addition, a rationalist discourse operates to exclude from the discussion the numerous citizens who lack the ability or the will to master the artificial vocabulary in which the law is discussed. These citizens cannot participate directly in the debate because it has been removed from the forums accessible to them and because they do not know the language of the alien judicial forum;[47] and they cannot be effectively represented because their ways of thinking and deciding are systematically filtered out of the prevailing discourse. Moreover, even those citizens who *do* trouble themselves to master the discourse—in other words, lawyers—are in an important sense excluded, since the rationalist discourse works to disguise or conceal the real bases of decision.[48]

Finally, and ironically, the prevailing rationalism in fact promotes an ad hominem variety of advocacy in which opponents try to cast their adversaries as prejudiced or hateful or unthinking. Although this sort of mean-spirited argumentation might seem to be just the opposite of rational discourse, in fact it is not a lamentable deviation from the prevailing rationalist model; rather, it is just what the logic of that model demands. As I have said, to a significant extent "reason" in modern discourse simply *means* not based on prejudice or emotion or tradition; so the only way to show that a law is not in accord with reason is to show that its supporters are acting from hatred or unthinking prejudice.[49] In this vein, Nagel explains that to a remarkable extent our courts have become places where the name-calling and exaggeration that mark the lower depths of our political debate are simply given a more acceptable, authoritative form. The mainstream in legal academia has been so busy applauding the judiciary's theoretical capacity for elevated dialogue and sensitive moral decisionmaking that it has not much noticed the tenor of much of what the judges have actually had to say.[50]

So the culture of rationalism underwritten by the legal academy has significant consequences for legal *discourse*. Still, does rationalism actually change legal *decisions*? This is a more complicated question than it might seem, I think, but the quick answer is that decisions are in part a product of discourse.[51] It is true that rationalism per se probably does not either mandate or forbid any specific results. The whole spectrum of positions and opinions that people might be inclined to defend *can* be defended in rationalist terms. But a culture of rationalism will tend over time to produce people attuned to some concerns and apathetic toward others. Rationalism helps make us who we are, in short, and who we are affects what we decide.

The Hubris of Humility

This observation brings me to the puzzle I noted at the outset: How is it that people who *as individuals* may be very decent and modest can *as judges* act in such arrogant fashion (and perhaps, sometimes, vice versa)? The answer is no doubt complex, but I want to suggest that part of the explanation lies in the internal dynamics of modern rationalism. In their curious combination of hubris and humility, I think, judges like those in the *Casey* plurality are an example in miniature—and to some extent a product of—the peculiar constitution of modern rationalism.

My thinking here is heavily dependent on analyses by Michael Oakeshott and Friedrich Hayek, but it also departs in one respect from their diagnoses. Both men were trenchant critics of what Oakeshott sometimes called "rationalism" and what Hayek sometimes called "scientism."[52] And both described the root error as a sort of *epistemological* mistake. Oakeshott argued that "technical knowledge," which he regarded as necessary and valuable, had displaced "practical" or "traditional knowledge," which he regarded as also necessary and valuable. "Rationalism," he said, "is the assertion that what I have called practical knowledge is not knowledge at all, the assertion that, properly speaking, there is no knowledge which is not technical knowledge."[53] Hayek—who in Oakeshott's view, incidentally, was part of the problem[54]—thought that the social sciences had mistakenly adopted the assumptions and methods proper to the natural sciences.

Of course both men were ultimately concerned with the political consequences of these mistakes, and both discussed the political conditions that had nurtured them. But for both Oakeshott and Hayek, there is an identifiable, fully formed error about how to achieve *knowledge* that is then imported into the domain of politics. The mistake I have in mind is slightly different in character: It is not an epistemological mistake per se, but rather a mistake that arises when a particular *ethical* proposition that is itself true and valuable is joined (with the help of an equivocation) to an *epistemological* proposition that is also true and valuable to produce a conclusion that is fallacious, and that may be practically disastrous.

Start with the ethical proposition. The proposition might be stated in this way: *Act always on the basis of good reasons.* This is an ethical admonition, not an epistemological claim, because it does not speak to the question of what counts as a good reason; it does not say, for example, whether tradition or intuition or faith can provide good reasons for acting—or even for believing. The ethical proposition merely urges us to act on the basis of whatever we regard as good reasons, rather than on some other basis. You might say that this admonition is a mere truism, and you would be right: *Of course* we should act on the basis of good reasons (as opposed to *bad* reasons, or *no* reasons). You might also say that the admonition is pointless, but here you would be wrong. The admonition is a response to the fact that due to temptation or weakness of will or infirmities of the flesh, we often act in ways that we ourselves understand to be contrary to good reasons. ("I really shouldn't eat this, but . . ." "I know I'll regret this tomorrow, but . . .") Philosophers sometimes call this the problem of *akrasia*.[55] The ethical proposition—"Act always on the basis of good reasons"—urges that we exert ourselves to avoid this common failing.

By contrast, the epistemological proposition does not on its face tell us how to live or act, but it *does* assert that knowledge or understanding of a certain kind or quality can be obtained only if we regularly follow particular prescribed methods, which are called "reason." The methods might be logical, or empirical, or some combination of these, as with the elusive "scientific method"; proponents of "reason" have differed about just what the appropriate methods are. But whatever they are, the epistemological proposition asserts that if we depart from them—from the methods of "reason"—we will not obtain knowledge or understanding of the same kind or quality. This proposition also seems plainly correct: Different methods of investigation and examination naturally *will* produce different levels or qualities of knowledge.

Notice that this epistemological proposition is not necessarily presumptuous, or even very optimistic, about the possible reach of human understanding. On the contrary, with proponents of reason like Locke or Kant the proposition is typically offered—initially, at least—as an *antidote* for overconfidence in our rational capacities, or as a homily on the limitations in human cognition.[56] We need to recognize, the proposition suggests, that there is so much that we can never know, and then to limit our claims of *knowledge* to an appropriately modest realm. So people who are conscious of significant limitations in their own cognitive capacities might be especially receptive to the epistemological proposition.

Notice also that the epistemological proposition does not necessarily disparage other dimensions of human experience and understanding that do not conform to the prescribed methods called "reason." To say that a particular kind or quality of knowledge about some matters is available through the scientific method, for example, is not to deny either the validity or the necessity of relying on tradition or educated opinion or intuition or faith in other matters where the methods of science are unsuitable. Thus, while advocating a method for achieving certainty that involved setting aside tradition and convention, Descartes understood that reason would not answer most questions anytime soon; in the meantime he resolved to live according to the laws and customs of his country and the religion of his childhood. In addition, Descartes insisted that "we must believe all that God has revealed, even though it is above the range of our capacities."[57] In a similar vein, Locke was hopeful that a system of morality might eventually be founded on reason, but he suggested that developing such a system was not urgent because Christian revelation had already provided an adequate basis for moral living.[58]

In sum, both the ethical and the epistemological propositions seem to be basically sound—almost self-evident, one might say—and neither in itself denigrates any dimension of human experience. But suppose we were to superimpose the epistemological proposition onto the ethical one by interpreting the ethical proposition's "good reasons" to mean the same thing as the epistemological proposition's "reason." From this illicit union (illicit because it cheats on the meaning of "reason") we might get a sort of general orientation toward life; we could call that orientation the "life of reason," or simply "rationalism." And that orientation *would* disparage tradition, faith, and intuition as sources of decision, or as modes of living. It would presuppose that the same faculties of conscious cognition we deploy in, say, determining the gravitational force between planets or in calculating the angles in a parallelogram are adequate to deal with pressing questions about life and death and their meaning—and hence that there is no need or excuse for relying on anything outside our "reason" as we confront those questions. In that sense, rationalism would display a kind of arrogance. But it would do so, ironically, on the basis of an acknowledgment of the *limits* of human understanding; this humble confession would be converted by means of an equivocation about the meaning of "reason" into the hubris of rationalism.

Kant might serve as an example of just this conversion. Much of his work is calculated to show the limited scope and capacity of human reason. We can never know the nature of things-in-themselves, he teaches, but only of phenomena as they present themselves to us. So it seems the pretensions of reason are drastically reined in. And indeed, Kant says as much, using a homely metaphor to distinguish himself from more pretentious philosophers: "[I]t turned out," he explains, "that although we had in mind a tower that would reach the heavens, yet the stock of materials was only enough for a dwelling house."[59]

Combine this endearing modesty, though, with Kant's familiar exhortation to be enlightened by "thinking for yourself."[60] Taken literally, this counsel is also unobjectionable, and even truistic. Although I know that some people think better than I do, I cannot really ask them to do *my* thinking any more than I can ask them to do my digesting. But the significance is in the connotations. What Kant intends, as a modern commentator enthusiastically explains, is *living* in accordance with reason, and this entails "autonomy in thinking *and in acting*," which in turn implies a refusal to submit to "state, church, majority, tradition, or dictator" or to act on bases that are "rationally ungrounded," such as "the teachings of a church."[61] In short, the invincible limitations in human understanding lead Kant, or at least his disciples, to a conclusion just opposite that reached by, say, Pascal or Joseph Butler. And in wisely renouncing the project of constructing a "tower that would reach the heavens" we find we have inadvertently renounced the heavens as well—or at least any sort of guidance from the heavens—so that in place of the tower we end up with a sort of defiantly self-sufficient, imperial shanty.

The mistake I have been trying to describe—the mistake by which two true ideas are combined by means of an equivocation to transform humility into arrogance—is unfortunately not one that only philosophers can make. Actually, whatever understanding I have managed to gain regarding this conversion has come not from reading Kant (which is something I hardly ever do), but more from thinking about a close relative's anguished and I think sincere explanation during a tense family gathering of why he felt compelled to abandon the life of faith that he had been brought up in. More generally, the orientation of rationalism that results from this equivocation has come to dominate the academy, I think, including the legal academy, and through the academy it shapes the culture within which lawyers argue and justices deliberate about the constitutionality of laws.

CONCLUSION

I think we can see the conversion I have described at work in cases like *Romer* and *VMI*.[62] "Say what you will," one can almost hear the moderates on the Court saying, "we really *don't* believe that we're endowed with any superhuman wisdom. And we have no desire to be philosopher-kings—or philosopher-queens. We're only trying to do what our oath of office requires—protect and enforce the Constitution. But the Constitution *does* require that a law have a rational basis, doesn't it?" (Notice here the ethical proposition.) "And mere tradition or moral sentiment or disapproval can't count as rational bases, can they?" (Here we see the epistemological proposition.) "So what choice do we have but to invalidate this law?"

Thus two valid propositions are joined by means of an equivocation, and justices who may be every bit as modest as you or I become aggressive intermeddlers in the social order. Rationalism has its way. And the modern legal academy, naturally, can only offer its reinforcing applause.

NOTES

1. Especially in this part of my discussion I am entering an area that for Bob Nagel has been virtually a life's work, and I will rely heavily on some of his writings.

2. Abner J. Mikva, "Keynote Address," 33 *Harvard Civil Rights–Civil L. Law Review* 325, 330 (1998).

3. See Robert F. Nagel, *Judicial Power and American Character* (Oxford: Oxford University Press, 1994), 138; Mary Ann Glendon, *A Nation under Lawyers* (New York: Farrar, Straus and Giroux, 1994), 4–5.

4. *Planned Parenthood v. Casey*, 505 U.S. 833, 867–68 (1992).

5. Glendon, *A Nation under Lawyers*, 5.

6. Ibid., 117.

7. Robert F. Nagel, *Constitutional Cultures* (Berkeley and Los Angeles: University of California Press, 1989), 147.

8. The famous Tribe and Michelman articles arguing for a constitutional right to welfare would be dramatic example of this sort of advocacy. See Laurence Tribe, "Unraveling National League of Cities: The New Federalism and Affirmative Rights to Essential Government Services," 90 *Harvard Law Review* 1065 (1977); Frank Michelman, "Foreword: On Protecting the Poor through the Fourteenth Amendment," 83 *Harvard Law Review* 7 (1969).

9. The vast literature on *Brown* and *Roe* is a good example of this sort of scholarship.

10. *Washington v. Glucksberg*, 521 U.S. 702 (1997); *Vacco v. Quill*, 521 U.S. 793 (1997).

11. See, e.g., Ronald Dworkin, *Sovereign Virtue* (Cambridge: Harvard University Press, 2000), 465–73.

12. Cf. Linda Ross Meyer, "Is Practical Reason Mindless?" 86 *Georgetown Law Journal* 647, 650–51 (1998) ("Indeed, both Karl Llewellyn and Benjamin Cardozo concluded that judges themselves have no idea how they do what they do") (footnote omitted).

13. The futility of writing legal scholarship in an effort to persuade judges is a theme well developed by Pierre Schlag. See, e.g., "Normativity and the Politics of Form," in Paul F. Campos et al., *Against the Law* (Durham, N.C.: Duke University Press, 1996), 29; "Writing for Judges," 63 *University of Colorado Law Review* 419 (1992).

14. Given the palpably sophistical and manipulable nature of modern constitutional discourse, it is hard to imagine how such scholarship *could* be persuasive to anyone even moderately familiar with the genre. See Steven D. Smith, *The Constitution and the Pride of Reason* (Oxford: Oxford University Press, 1998), 121–27.

15. See Patrick J. Schiltz, "Legal Ethics in Decline: The Elite Law Firm, the Elite Law School, and the Moral Formation of the Novice Attorney," 82 *Minnesota Law Review* 705, 768 n. 254 (1998). In a conversation with the law faculty at the University of Colorado, where I used to teach, Justice Scalia said in essence that he rarely if ever reads law review literature; and although a counter-inference is possible, it seems likely that if a justice who was once a law professor does not read law reviews, then other justices would be even less likely to turn to that source. Indeed, it seems that law professors themselves increasingly find legal scholarship almost unreadable. See ibid., 789–90.

16. See, e.g., Edward P. Lazarus, *Closed Chambers* (New York: Times Books, 1998), 262–75, 314–15, 321–22 (ascribing considerable influence to a group of conservative law clerks called "the Cabal" who were the author's own self-described adversaries when he was a law clerk to Justice Blackmun); Bernard Schwartz, *The Ascent of Pragmatism: The Burger Court in Action* (Reading, Mass.: Addison-Wesley, 1990), 35–39.

17. For a discussion, see Nagel, *Constitutional Cultures*, 54–55.

18. Cf. Susan Low Bloch and Thomas G. Krattenmaker, *Supreme Court Politics: The Institution and Its Procedures* (St. Paul: West, 1994), 502 ("Our experience has been that law clerks, in describing themselves, often inflate their importance and power").

19. See Ronald F. Dworkin, *Freedom's Law* (Cambridge: Harvard University Press, 1996), 332, 347.

20. Cf. Jonathan R. Macey, "Judicial Preference, Public Choice, and the Rules of Procedure," 23 *Journal of Legal Studies* 627, 629 (1994) ("Individual judges will have widely varying preferences. Some will want . . . to maximize their own prestige among some subgroups such as lawyers, legal academics, or liberal or conservative groups").

21. Cf. Robert F. Nagel, "Liberal and Balancing," 63 *Colorado Law Review* 319, 323–34 (1992) (hypothesizing that "less intellectually distinguished" Justices like Souter and Kennedy will be "most under the influence of the academic litigator").

22. Carl Becker, *The Heavenly City of the Eighteenth Century Philosophers* (New Haven: Yale University Press, 1932), 119–54.

23. See Janet Cooper Alexander, "Judges' Self-Interest and Procedural Rules: Comment on Macey," 23 *Journal of Legal Studies* 647, 647–48 (1994).

24. 478 U.S. 186 (1986) (upholding Georgia sodomy law against constitutional challenge).

25. 517 U.S. 620 (1996) (striking down Colorado law denying "protected status" on basis of sexual orientation).

26. 163 U.S. 537 (1896) (approving racial segregation under "separate but equal" doctrine).

27. Henry M. Hart Jr., "The Supreme Court 1958 Term—Forward: The Time Chart of the Justices," 78 *Harvard Law Review* 24, 125 (1957).

28. Glendon, *A Nation under Lawyers*, 294. For my own more skeptical view, see *Pride of Reason* and "Missing Persons," 2 *Nevada Law Journal* 590 (2002).

29. Robert F. Nagel, "Rationalism in Constitutional Law," 4 *Constitutional Commentary* 9, 9–12 (1987).

30. Charles Lindblom explains: "In contemporary Western cultures, when people are called upon to give reasons—even to themselves—for choosing a volition, they often find it difficult to maintain sustained thought about it other than by exploring connections between it regarded as a means and some other volition as end. Often they cannot think, cannot analyze, cannot debate except about means to assumed ends. If, at the end of the line, they consider a possible volition as an end only and cannot cast it as means to a still further end, their minds stop working on the issue; they fall silent, have nothing to say or think. Their analysis, even if incomplete, terminates. Even sophisticated intellects often cannot define rational thought other than as thought that appropriately connects means to ends." *Inquiry and Change* (New Haven: Yale University Press, 1990), 41.

31. Ibid., 19.

32. Richard A. Posner, "Reply to Critics of *The Problematics of Moral and Legal Theory*," 111 *Harvard Law Review* 1796, 1803 (1998).

33. See Cass R. Sunstein, "Naked Preferences and the Constitution," 84 *Columbia Law Review* 1689 (1984); John Hart Ely, *Democracy and Distrust* (Cambridge: Harvard University Press, 1980), 145–46. For further discussion, see Smith, *Pride of Reason*, 101–4.

34. If citations are needed to document these oppositions, see, e.g., Ernest Gellner, *Reason and Culture* (Cambridge, Mass.: Basil Blackwood, 1992), 58–59 (reason versus tradition); Suzanna Sherry, "The Sleep of Reason," 84 *Georgetown Law Journal* 453, 462–63 (1996) (reason versus faith); Stephen Toulmin, *Cosmopolis: The Hidden Agenda of Modernity* (New York: Free Press, 1990), 115 (reason versus emotion).

35. *Cleburne v. Cleburne Living Center*, 473 U.S. 432 (1985) (invalidating city's denial of permit for group home for mentally retarded in residential area).

36. For influential expressions of this sort of criticism, see, e.g., Alasdair MacIntyre, *Whose Justice? Which Rationality?* (Notre Dame: University of Notre Dame Press, 1988); Thomas S. Kuhn, *The Structure of Scientific Revolutions* (Chicago: University of Chicago Press, 1962); Michael Polanyi, *Personal Knowledge* (Chicago: University of Chicago Press, 1958).

37. Bruce A. Ackerman, "Beyond *Carolene Products*," 98 *Harvard Law Review* 713, 737 (1985). For a lengthier discussion of this problem, see Smith, *Pride of Reason*, 109–24.

38. See John Rawls, *Political Liberalism* (New York: Columbia University Press, 1993), 243 n. 32.

39. Stanley Fish, "Boutique Multiculturalism," in *Multiculturalism and American Democracy*, ed. Arthur M. Melzer, Jerry Weinberger, and M. Richard Zinman (Lawrence: University Press of Kansas, 1998), 69, 80–83. In a similar vein, Richard Posner remarks caustically that "[p]hilosophers are never so parochial as when they are placing beyond the pale of the 'reasonable' the moral claims of people who do not belong to their social set." Richard A. Posner, "The Problematics and Moral and Legal Theory," 111 *Harvard Law Review* 1637, 1678 (1998).

40. Nagel, "Rationalism in Constitutional Law," 13.

41. See, e.g., Glendon, *A Nation under Lawyers*; Anthony Kronman, "Precedent and Tradition," 99 *Yale Law Journal* 1029 (1990). For my own effort in this vein, see Steven D. Smith, "Separation as a Tradition, 18 *Journal of Law and Politics* 215 (2002).

42. For a preliminary effort, see Steven D. Smith, "Believing Like a Lawyer," 40 *Boston College Law Review* 1041 (1999).

43. Nagel, "Rationalism in Constitutional Law," 16.

44. See *Erznoznik v. City of Jacksonville*, 422 U.S. 205 (1975).

45. Nagel, "Rationalism in Constitutional Law," 16.

46. See Robert F. Nagel, "Playing Defense," 6 *William and Mary Bill of Rights Journal* 167 (1997).

47. Cf. Nagel, "Rationalism in Constitutional Law," 20 (arguing that "the Court's approach belittles political dialogue and participation").

48. See Robert F. Nagel, "The Formulaic Constitution," 84 *Michigan Law Review* 165, 182 (1985) (explaining that constitutional discourse has the effect of "excluding the general public from the Court's audience") and at 195 (explaining that "[t]he use of tests that cannot mean what they say does not necessarily foreclose useful judicial inquiry, but it does involve indirection and artificiality that exclude the reader").

49. For further development of this point in the context of free exercise jurisprudence, see Steven D. Smith, *Getting Over Equality: A Critical Diagnosis of Religious Freedom in America* (New York: New York University Press, 2001), 113–39.

50. Nagel, *Judicial Power*, 129.

51. Cf. Nagel, "The Formulaic Constitution," 171: "One need not believe that form and substance are identical to understand that ways of talking about the Constitution must influence patterns of thought. Because analysis and explanation are not entirely separate processes, the form of the opinion must be expressive of the intellectual habits that shape the Court's conclusions."

52. See Michael Oakeshott, "Rationalism and Politics," in *Rationalism in Politics and Other Essays*, 2d ed. (Indianapolis: Liberty Press, 1991); F. A. Hayek, *The Counter-revolution of Science: Studies on the Abuse of Reason*, 2d ed. (Indianapolis: Liberty Fund, 1979).

53. Oakeshott, "Rationalism and Politics," 15.

54. Ibid., 26.

55. See Martha C. Nussbaum, *The Fragility of Goodness* (Cambridge: Cambridge University Press, 1986), 113–17.

56. See, e.g., Nicholas Wolterstorff, *John Locke and the Ethics of Belief* (Cambridge: Cambridge University Press, 1996), 9, 29.

57. See the *Discourse on Method*, part 3 (custom and religion); *The Principles of Philosophy*, pt. 1, Principle 25 (revelation).

58. Wolterstorff, *John Locke*, 146.

59. Quoted in Onora O'Neill, "Vindicating Reason," in *The Cambridge Companion to Kant*, ed. Paul Guyer (Cambridge: Cambridge University Press, 1992), 289.

60. " 'Have courage to use your own reason!'—that is the motto of enlightenment." Immanuel Kant, *Metaphysics of Morals and What Is Enlightenment?* trans. Lewis White Beck, 2d ed. (New York: Macmillan, 1990), 83.

61. O'Neill, "Vindicating Reason," 299, 305, 298 (emphasis added).

62. *United States v. Virginia*, 518 U.S. 515 (1996) (ruling that Virginia violated Constitution by maintaining male-only military academy).

CHAPTER 7

Judicial Moral Expertise and Real-World Constraints on Judicial Moral Reasoning

Jack Wade Nowlin

DO FEDERAL judges have a special power of moral insight compared to voters and legislators? Perhaps, our first question ought rather to be: Why would it matter? What difference does the question of comparative judicial moral expertise make to our perennial debates about judicial power? The answer to *that* question will become clear once we embark self-consciously on a critical project one might call *taking judicial power seriously*.[1] What does this project entail? In brief, it involves the task of attempting to determine the proper constitutional scope of the federal judicial power by testing various conceptions of the judicial role for structural "fit" and structural "justification" in light of the overarching American constitutional design and competing core constitutional and political values—such as popular sovereignty, representative democracy, the separation of powers, and federalism.[2] This project requires one to take seriously both the overall structure of the Constitution and the evolving democratic political ethos that constitutes an important part of the American constitutional tradition.

Further, the project of taking judicial power seriously also requires one to recognize the *constitutional* nature of the limits on the authority of the federal judiciary: The Constitution established the Supreme Court; the Constitution grants to the Court the "judicial power of the United States"; and the Constitution *limits* that judicial power, as it does powers of the federal executive and legislative branches. For instance, Article 3 places express constitutional limits on the original and appellate jurisdiction of the Court and limits the Court to the resolution of cases or controversies, thus prohibiting advisory opinions. In addition to express constitutional limits on the power of the Court, implied constitutional limits likely exist as well. Notably, the power of judicial review is an implicit rather than explicit grant of power to the Supreme Court, and it is widely viewed as derived from structural constitutional arguments related to the separation of powers and the essential function of the judicial branch—in conjunction with the principle of constitutional supremacy.[3] There is every reason to suppose that this implied constitutional grant of the power of judicial review has concomitant implied constitutional limits (also related to the separation of powers, the essence of the judicial function, and the supremacy of the Constitution) and that these limits may have important implications for questions of judicial interpretive methodology and judicial deference to political actors.[4] In short, one must recognize that judicial authority to interpret the Constitution is in fact itself *derived* from the Constitution and *limited* by the Constitution, and therefore that the interpretive authority of judges does *not* elevate them above the Constitution or free them from the force of the constitutional constraints of Article 3 read against the structural background of the Constitution's design for self-government.

The chief concern, then, of the project of taking judicial power seriously is what we might call a broad interpretive *structural* or *design* question: "What scope of authority does the American constitutional design allocate to the federal judiciary?" The project of taking judicial power seriously requires that the answer to the broader question of "judicial power allocation or role," a structural question, govern the answer to narrower questions of judicial power such as that of how federal judges should interpret the Bill of Rights.[5] In short, whatever interpretive authority judges lay claim to must be consistent with the constitutional limits of the judicial power and therefore must be justified in light of the structure of the Constitution and the competing constitutional values that may be thought to limit the judicial power. Obviously, federal judges may not exercise power beyond that allocated to them by the Constitution.

What then is the relationship of the question of comparative judicial moral expertise to the project of taking judicial power seriously? Several theorists in recent decades have advocated what can be called a "moral" reading of the Constitution. Among these theorists are Ronald Dworkin, Michael Moore, Sotirios Barber, and Stephen Macedo.[6] The "moral" reading of the Constitution demands that judges resolve civil liberties cases on broader *moral* and *political* grounds rather than on narrower grounds related to traditional legal materials, such as text, original understanding, and long-standing legal traditions.[7] The Supreme Court in recent decades has often appeared to engage in such "moral" readings of the Constitution, even though the justices are typically less than forthcoming about the political basis of their decisions.[8]

Is the assertion of an expansive judicial power to engage in broad "moral" readings of rights provisions of the Constitution consistent with a proper understanding of the judicial role under the Constitution? Taking judicial power seriously requires that we test this conception of the judicial role for structural "fit" and "justification" in light of the constitutional design. There is a substantial basis for thinking that such a sweeping conception of judicial power is precluded as a serious interpretation of the American constitutional design by its evident lack of fit with the traditional legal materials establishing the structure of the Constitution. If this view is correct, an assertion of this expansive power by the Supreme Court exceeds the scope of the Court's authority under Article 3 and is thus a violation of the Constitution.[9] Still, in the alternative, if this broad view of judicial authority under the Constitution were thought to meet a threshold requirement of structural fit, a proponent of taking judicial power seriously would then ask an additional question of structural justification: "Why is a reading of the structure of the Constitution in favor of expansive judicial power a morally or politically attractive reading?"

As an answer to this question and as a structural moral justification for expansive judicial power, a facially plausible argument can be made that (1) judges are quite sophisticated moral reasoners in comparison to ordinary voters and legislators and that (2) sophisticated moral reasoners tend to reach the right answers to difficult moral questions, providing at least *one* structural moral-political reason for granting judges such a sweeping degree of power: the promise of moral accuracy in the resolution of contested questions of individual rights and thus the avoidance of violations of the rights of the individual. This chapter will examine that line of argument in some detail, concluding that it has insuperable theoretical and practical difficulties. In particular, it will argue that in practice the inevitable prudential, felt-normative, and conventional constraints on judicial moral reasoning severely limit the ability of judges to engage in sophisticated moral analysis. Thus judicial moral reasoning and analysis is seriously flawed in a number of respects: It is typically understated as the basis for decision in judicial opinions, incompletely theorized or conclusory in nature, and significantly distorted by the argumentative force of legal materials. This point in turn suggests that any contrast between the moral reasoning of federal judges and ordinary political actors in favor of the judiciary is likely significantly overdrawn by the proponents of expansive judicial power. This chapter will conclude, in short, that judges do not possess any attribute approaching a special power of moral insight and, as a result, the justificatory arguments in favor of sweeping judicial power cannot depend upon the putative heightened moral insight of federal judges.

The Meaning of Moral Expertise

Do judges in practice possess some special power of moral insight that might make them better epistemic authorities than legislators or voters?

This question will be approached here as a question concerning the actual moral insight of actual judges under the actual conditions that typically obtain in the judicial process. We shall not discuss what powers of moral insight judges might possess under different or ideal circumstances. A practical focus will allow us to bring to bear the maximum critical scrutiny on the question of whether judges' powers of moral reasoning may serve as a justification for the moral discretion they often exercise. Further, the practical nature of this inquiry will not involve an attempt at rigorous empirical scrutiny but instead will track the appeals to common sense and common experience typically used by the proponents of the view that judges do possess special powers of moral insight.

To begin to answer this question, we have to ask ourselves what one might mean by phrases such as "better epistemic authority" or "special powers of moral insight" in the context of the judicial power.[10] How, indeed, should we go about defining an attribute such as "moral expertise"? One might begin by distinguishing between what one may call *substantive* or "thick" conceptions of moral expertise and *procedural* or "thin" conceptions of moral expertise.[11] A substantive conception of moral expertise defines a moral expert as someone who is simply reliable or accurate (i.e., "right") "substantively" on questions of morality and moral theory more broadly. Such a "thick" definition, however is not very helpful in the context of assessing judicial moral expertise for two reasons. First, it simply replicates our interminable substantive disputes over moral questions: Who has greater moral expertise—John Rawls, Michael Sandel, or John Finnis? And, second, a "thick" definition is also quite difficult to link to anything *intrinsic* to the nature of the judicial process as opposed to various social and political contingencies concerning what individuals and moral views tend to predominate in the judiciary at any given time. For instance, an argument for expansive judicial power premised on the moral truth of liberal individualism in conjunction with the federal judiciary's present tendency toward liberal individualist decisions fails on its own terms if *either* liberal individualism is false *or* the judiciary ceases to be more reliably liberal individualist than other institutions or actors. This line of argument thus has only a very narrow ideological appeal that comes very close to special pleading.[12]

We might then turn to a much less controversial definition of moral expertise, a "thin" or procedural definition. A procedural view defines moral expertise as some special skill in the basic requirements of the process of rational moral inquiry, involving at a minimum the Socratic dialectic and Rawlsian reflective equilibrium.[13] The purpose of such a process of moral inquiry is to develop a sophisticated, critical, reflective, reasoned, and coherent moral theory, and the "thin" conception of moral expertise defines this achievement as the true benchmark of heightened moral insight. As it might be stated in greater detail, procedural moral expertise is a product of

(1) a willingness to reason toward the truth and give reasons for one's conclusions; (2) the degree of critical reflection brought to bear on moral questions; (3) the seriousness of the attempt to formulate, principled, coherent answers; (4) vigorous confrontation of counter-arguments; (5) frequent and serious encounters with moral issues; (6) engagement of moral issues at varying levels of generality or particularity; (7) the ability to put aside bias, expediency, and self-interest in resolving them; (8) the habit of setting forth public justifications for one's moral conclusions.[14]

This "thinner" conception of moral expertise has two decided advantages in this context over a "thick" conception. First, it is much less controversial—virtually all moral realists and rationalists could subscribe to it in some basic form; and, on this view, theorists as diverse in their moral reasoning and conclusions as John Rawls, Michael Sandel, and John Finnis would clearly possess moral expertise. Second, this procedural conception of moral expertise would also be much easier to link to something intrinsic to the judicial process. The view that judges—when confronting questions of individual rights—are, say, especially fair-minded, reflective, and serious about crafting principled answers has a certain plausibility. Michael Moore, for instance, has made such an argument, noting:

First, judges are better positioned for . . . moral insight because every day they face moral thought experiments with the kind of detail and concrete personal involvement needed for moral insight. It is one thing to talk about a right to privacy in general; it is another to order a teenager to bear a child she does not want to bear. One might well think that moral insight is best generated at the level of particular cases, giving judicial beliefs greater epistemic authority than legislative beliefs on the same subject. Second, judicial reasoning is like moral reasoning in its focus on principled generality, so that judges might have an advantage even at the most abstract level. Moral rights, on such a view, are more safely left in the hands of those who can work out their content in a principled manner. Third, the institutional features of the judicial office—notably job security—make judges better able to focus their deliberations on the moral aspect of any problem, putting aside the questions of political expediency with which legislators must grapple. Thus, only judges can afford to take the long view that moral insight demands. Finally, the judicial temperament may be more suited to assessing moral questions than the legislative temperament. By temperament, I mean both the actual psychology of those who become judges rather than legislators and the culture of each institution that inculcates and reinforces that psychology. Evenhandedness, freedom from bias, prejudgment, and neutrality are the distinctly judicial virtues. They are also the virtues of the "ideal observer" in moral theory, that postulate of some moralists about who can best gain insight into moral trusts.[15]

We may conclude, then, that a plausible and defensible claim of special judicial moral expertise must rest on a procedural theory of moral reasoning rather than a substantive one.

Notably, even here we could question the link between highly sophisticated procedural moral reasoning and the actual discovery of "right" answers to the moral questions that actually divide us. For instance, it is obvious that sophisticated moral reasoners often disagree. John Rawls, Michael Sandel, and John Finnis certainly disagree in both their reasoning and their conclusions on a large number of moral questions. It is also quite obvious that many *un*sophisticated moral reasoners—drawing on their own traditions, religious beliefs, simplified ideologies, and various currents in the climate of opinion—often agree with the conclusions of more sophisticated moral reasoners. A large number of "ordinary" Americans, for instance, have moral outlooks that could be broadly defined as liberal individualist, communitarian, or traditionalist in nature. Therefore, if we are most concerned with the importance of reaching the *right* moral conclusions (and avoiding the injustice of a violation of rights) rather than merely crafting the most sophisticated moral rationales for what well might be the *wrong* moral conclusions, there is no reason to suppose that movement from less to more sophisticated "thin" moral reasoning is necessarily movement from error towards truth. The relationship of even highly sophisticated "thin" moral reasoning to the discovery of moral truth is simply much more complex than that.[16]

Even so, an inquiry into the relative capacity of judges to engage in sophisticated procedural moral reasoning is well warranted given the number of theorists who endorse this position linking the judicial process, moral sophistication, and moral accuracy. This chapter contends that the obvious and familiar arguments in favor of a special judicial power of moral insight in fact paint a skewed and idealized portrait of judges and courts; and it will contend that other aspects of the judicial process—such as the primacy of legal interpretation and the practical political constraints on judicial power—suggest that judges typically do not, and indeed cannot, openly engage in sophisticated moral reasoning or develop sophisticated, critical, reflective, reasoned, and coherent moral theories.

"COMMON SENSE" APPROACHES AND THE "COMMON SENSE" VIEW

Proponents of the view that judges possess some comparative advantage in moral reasoning can make of number of arguments grounded in common sense, intuition, and experience. As we have seen, Michael Moore, among others, has argued that there are aspects of the selection process for judges and features of the institutional dynamics of courts that might lead us to conclude that judges have special advantages in moral reasoning. Arguably, judges are specially selected for certain moral qualities and analytical abilities that are associated with sophisticated moral reasoning. And, arguably, the very structure of the judicial process with, say, its emphasis on argument and counterargument and its focus on the interaction of general rules and concrete cases tends to sharpen and clarify moral issues.

This chapter's response is that, in practice, judges are not selected for their ability to engage in sophisticated moral reasoning, and in fact they seldom engage in anything recognizable as such. On the contrary, common sense and experience strongly suggest that those who select judges and the judges themselves routinely do everything they can *to minimize the appearance of judicial moral discretion and thus overt judicial moral reasoning, largely precluding any form of serious judicial moral analysis.* As a starting point for our analysis, let us consider Kent Greenawalt's brilliant, imaginative dialogue between a candid Supreme Court justice and a disappointed litigant:

> *Justice Diepe*: . . . I have to confess to you that although my opinion tried hard to make your position look absurd, the case was pretty close. To be a bit more precise, the best judgment of myself and my colleagues was that the law was against you.
>
> *Faith*: . . . if you don't mind, I'd like to know just what it means to say "the law was against me." Do you mean the legal materials, that's what my lawyer referred to, were stronger on the other side?
>
> *Justice Diepe*: That is the judgment in many cases, but to be honest, not in your case. I thought the legal materials slightly favored you, but the position was much less appealing from the moral point of view.
>
> *Faith*: Are you saying that "the law was against me" even though the "legal materials," what my lawyer also called "fit arguments," were slightly in my favor?
>
> *Justice Diepe*: In a word, yes.
>
> *Faith*: Well, how do you know my arguments were so much worse morally? Do you mean that this was your best guess about existing community morality, or some objective moral realm that is rationally determinable by real people, or something like that?
>
> *Justice Diepe*: I'd be less than candid if I claimed that. I went by the moral ideas that seem right to me, but I am frankly perplexed by their status. Perhaps there is some sense in which there is a right moral answer to this question in terms of the arguments that would be more compelling to some ideal

person, sometime, but I'm not confident about that. I am not sure how far moral judgments can be measured by standards accessible to human understanding of a reasoned kind.

Faith: So, "the law" here comes down to the attempt of five justices to apply moral understandings that seem best to them.

Justice Diepe: Yes, that's right. Say, I'd love to talk to you about literary and biblical interpretation, about Gadamer and Habermas, and Fiss and Unger and Dworkin? Can you stay a little longer, say three more hours?[17]

This dialogue, with its candid appraisal of a "moralizing" judge, casts a great deal of commonsense light on the limited role that overt moral reasoning actually plays in the judicial process. First, what degree of "thin" realist-rationalist moral expertise can one actually expect from a typical judge? Greenawalt's dialogue suggests only a very limited degree. The character of Justice Diepe is by no means clearly within the realist-rationalist "philosophic mainstream": It is not even clear that Diepe is a moral realist, and he expresses definite doubts about moral rationalism. He is familiar with a number of academic theorists of various sorts but is still "perplexed" about the status and origin of his own moral views. Nor, one imagines, was he asked about his views on these issues at his confirmation hearing. Presidents and senators simply do not ask prospective judicial nominees: Are you a moral realist? Are you a moral rationalist? Are you capable of articulating your moral views in the sophisticated, rational manner of a professional philosopher or political theorist? Rather, common sense and experience suggest that the focus in judicial selection is on proven competence within the legal profession, on judicial philosophy, and political ideology. As to the last of these, to the extent that a judge's moral and political views do become an issue during the nomination and confirmation process, one can be sure that a "thick" "inferential" approach—an "expert" is someone one agrees with—is the method used to gauge moral "expertise" and not a neutral procedural method centered on the Socratic dialectic and Rawlsian reflective equilibrium.[18] Certainly, a selection process that in practice is not always able to give pride of place to merit from a traditional legal standpoint—as opposed to, say, "virtues" such as political connections or the lack of a controversial "paper trail"—is particularly ill suited to select sophisticated moral reasoners as judges.

Indeed, it is worth remembering that we typically do not know which judges are moral realists and which are moral rationalists. Nor do we typically know which judges *are* reflective about morality and able to articulate sophisticated moral justifications for the positions they favor—and which are happy unreflectively to allow their moral views to bubble up from the heady mix of social class, education, professional life, party affiliation, ideology, religion, regional background, life experience, personality, and even personal affections and attachments. For instance, John C. Jeffries, Justice Powell's law clerk and biographer, suggests that Justice Powell's position in *Roe* (in favor of a broad right to abortion) was essentially a visceral response and was "almost predictable" given his education, religious beliefs, and social class.[19] The realist-rationalist proponents of the concept of special judicial moral expertise might be surprised at the number of judges sitting on the federal bench who go with their "gut" feeling on questions of great moral importance. In short, then, judges are simply not selected for their ability to engage in sophisticated rational moral inquiry, and as a consequence many, perhaps most, of them have no particular inclination or capacity to do so.

Second, what about the degree of moral reasoning that actually makes it into a judge's opinion—his public justification of his decision—as evidence of his moral (in)expertise? Again, Greenawalt's dialogue suggests a common-sense answer in line with common experience. The form—as opposed to the substance—of Diepe's opinion is completely or largely "legal" or fit-oriented in nature. Faith, who has apparently read the opinion, is surprised to learn from Diepe in conversation that the meaning of "the law" actually pivoted on the judges' moral judgments rather than on the legal materials. Plainly, Justice Diepe's public justification of his decision did not make clear the pivotal role of the justices' moral concerns to the outcome of the case. Nor apparently did Diepe defend these moral concerns in any philosophic detail or explain his own inchoate thoughts on the nature of morality. In short, it would seem that one could read his opinion carefully without finding *any sort of overt reasoned moral argument.*

Indeed, it is clear that in virtually all controversial cases, judicial opinions consist almost *exclusively* of what purports to be the legal analysis of legal materials and that controversial moral arguments are glossed over even when one suspects that they are the real pivot of the case. Moreover, this state of affairs is widely recognized as such. Ronald Dworkin, for instance, observes, "It is patent that judges' own views about political morality influence their constitutional decisions, and though they might *easily* explain that influence by insisting that the Constitution demands a moral reading, they never do. Instead against all evidence, they deny the influence and try to explain their decisions in other—embarrassingly unsatisfactory—ways."[20] In short, whatever the substance, the *form* of judicial opinions routinely maximizes the appearance of legal "fit" and minimizes the appearance of moral "justification." This state of affairs, however, is *not*—contra Dworkin—the result of a judicial caprice and cannot be easily remedied simply by greater candor on the part of activist judges. On the contrary, it is a reasonable and almost inexorable judicial response to the severe prudential, felt-normative, and conventional constraints judges face, which limit their ability to resolve cases overtly on moral grounds.

REAL-WORLD CONSTRAINTS ON JUDGES: PRUDENTIAL, FELT-NORMATIVE, AND CONVENTIONAL

What are these constraints more precisely? First, there are powerful *prudential* concerns that limit a judge's ability to engage openly in sophisticated moral reasoning in judicial opinions. As Justice White has written: "The Court is most vulnerable and comes nearest to illegitimacy when it deals with judge-made constitutional law having little or no cognizable roots in the language or design of the Constitution."[21] As a prudential matter, the institutional integrity of the Supreme Court rests on the public's perception that the Court's decisions are grounded in something called "the Constitution," independent of the controversial moral and political views of the justices, a fact recognized in recent years by the *Casey* plurality.[22] That is to say that judicial legitimacy to a substantial degree depends upon maximizing the appearance of legal fit and minimizing the appearance of free-floating judicial moral judgment and the influence of other extrajudicial political concerns. There is good reason to suppose that if the American public ever becomes convinced that the Court routinely resolves controversial rights questions on controversial moral and political grounds, then the institutional integrity of the Court will suffer tremendously.

At this point, it is important that one keep two points clear. First, it is not a satisfactory answer to this problem simply to redefine the meaning of "the Constitution" so that it incorporates the judges' controversial moral and political views. What matters here is not the semantic or formal question of how we define "the Constitution," but the underlying reality of whether judges resolve controversial rights questions chiefly or largely on controversial moral grounds. They either do or they do not, to one degree or another, however one defines "the Constitution," and the authority of the Court would very likely erode substantially if the American people view the Court as routinely exercising a freewheeling moralistic or politicized approach to judicial review. Second, what matters for our practical inquiry is the public's *perception* of what the Court does, much more that what the Court actually does. As a retired federal judge is said to have remarked, "The only source of the authority of the Court is that the American people put up with it!"[23] As troubling as that may be from a normative standpoint, it is certainly true from a prudential one. It is in fact a truism: the courts have the power in practice to do that which they can get away with. Therefore, the maintenance of a plausible pretense of traditional legal interpretation—one sufficient to maintain a public perception of constitutional legitimacy—is of great importance to the Court's institutional integrity.

Second, there are important *felt-normative constraints* on judicial moral reasoning that many judges experience. There is good reason to suppose that judges recognize some outer limits on the scope of their authority and are troubled to at least some degree by the legal and moral-political structural implications of highly expansive exercises of the judicial power—such as the erosion of the separation of powers or representative democracy. Nor are we concerned here only with the most self-conscious and ideological of originalists or proponents of judicial restraint. In fact, even judges who disavow originalism or other philosophies of judicial restraint very likely do not think of themselves as moral free agents in constitutional interpretation entitled to roam wherever it is that their moral visions may take them in a particular decision. Instead, activist judges likely view their moral discretion as circumscribed to some not insignificant degree by legal materials and by structural constitutional and political norms such as representative democracy. Even Justice Brennan felt obliged to disclaim the mantle of Platonic guardianship and to make his obeisance to "conventional" morality."[24] Almost all judges, then, are unwilling to travel too far afield from where a fit with traditional legal materials takes them—though how far is "too far" is obviously the subject of substantial disagreement.

Third, it seems evident that there is a strong *judicial convention* in favor of maximizing the appearance of legal fit analysis and minimizing the appearance of moral analysis in the resolution of cases. Obviously, this convention of judicial decision-making is closely related to the prudential and felt-normative concerns discussed above. Even so, one suspects that this constraint is also rooted in an independent conventional understanding of the role of the judge. Indeed, the essence of the judicial function as traditionally understood is the fitting of legal claims to traditional legal materials; and the work of the judge is inevitably centered around the interpretation of law in this sense. A robust portrait of adjudication—such as Greenawalt's—will allow for the role that moral and political judgment inevitably plays; but the primacy of fit analysis, of technical legal interpretation, is clear. If moral justification analysis were to be reduced to a bare minimum, we would still recognize what remains as a form of legal adjudication. If, on the other hand, the legal fit analysis were to be reduced to a similar weightlessness, what remains would no longer be recognizable as adjudication, but simply ordinary moral and political judgment. It is not surprising, then, that the judicial conventions governing the scope of legal argument and the writing of opinions recognize the primacy of legal fit analysis—and maintain the form of such analysis even when the substance is substantially diminished in a particular case.

JUDICIAL MORAL REASONING: UNDERSTATEMENT, INCOMPLETE THEORIZATION, AND DISTORTION

The prudential, felt-normative, and conventional constraints on courts severely limiting judicial moral analysis affect the nature of the moral reasoning appearing in judicial opinions in at least three ways: First, the determinative force of the judicial moral reasoning tends to be *understated*; second, judicial moral conclusions tend to be *incompletely theorized*; and, third, judicial moral reasoning tends to be *distorted* by traditional legal materials.[25]

The first effect—understatement of the moral basis of judicial decisions—concerns the relative weights assigned to fit and justification analyses in judicial opinions. Given that the various constraints on judges lead them to maximize the appearance of legal fit and minimize the appearance of moral justification in their opinions, it is not surprising that the fit aspect of adjudication is always significantly overstated and the justification aspect *understated* whatever the actual pivot of a decision. Just as it is a judicial convention to overstate the force of one's argument generally,[26] it is also a judicial convention to overstate the determinative force of traditional legal analysis, and consequently to understate the determinative force of controversial moral and political analysis or opinion. As the dialogue between Faith and Justice Diepe suggests, judges may not always identify or fully adduce the actual moral ground of a decision even if it is the deciding factor in the case. In some instances, a decision may actually pivot on a moral judgment that is nowhere openly discussed or defended in the opinion.

Roe v. Wade provides a notable example of the significant understatement of the decisional force of moral analysis or opinion. Justice Blackmun in his opinion cites text, precedent, and tradition in support of his contention that there is a general constitutional right to abortion, but one can scarcely suppose that a disinterested examination of the legal materials compels his reading or his legal conclusion as a matter of legal fit. In fact, an equal protection argument in favor of a fetal right to life has at least as much support in legal materials. Further, from a traditional legal fit perspective, by far the most compelling answer to *Roe's* legal question is that abortion is a question for legislative resolution: As a general matter, neither the right to abortion nor the fetal right to life has sufficient support in the constitutional text, original historical context, or longstanding American legal traditions to justify elevation to the status of a constitutional right. One can thus conclude that the decision in *Roe* pivoted on an implicit (pro-choice) moral judgment about abortion, but a moral judgment that was left largely unstated by the Court. Blackmun resolved the question of fetal personhood under the Fourteenth Amendment on narrow textual and historical legal grounds; he left open as putatively unresolvable the question of fetal personhood as a "state interest," given perennial disagreement on the question; he cited mere judicial precedent in favor of an unenumerated right to privacy; and he found a right to abortion within the scope of the "right to privacy" in a highly conclusory fashion, simply stating that the "right of privacy" is "broad enough to encompass a woman's decision whether or not to terminate her pregnancy."[27] Notably, Blackmun's deployment (without explanation) of inconsistent interpretive methodologies in *Roe*—using a legalistic or "tight" fit approach to determine the meaning of "person" in the Fourteenth Amendment and a "loose" fit approach to determine the meaning of "liberty" in the same amendment—is particularly suggestive of an underlying political motive.

Blackmun thus did not attempt to articulate an openly *moral* defense of abortion, identify it as the pivot of the decision in *Roe*, or even discuss his proabortion moral concerns as a primary moral consideration in resolving the legal issue before the Court. Nor could he have done so, one imagines, without very likely (further) severely damaging the Court's institutional authority. In short, given the politically controversial nature of the legal conclusion in *Roe*, it was of crucial importance that the reasoning be as legally uncontroversial and thus as legalistic or fit-oriented in form as possible, however political and discretionary its actual substance. Blackmun, therefore, grounded the form and expression of his analysis—to the extent possible—in text, history, and precedent; and he carefully minimized any appearance of overt moral analysis of the abortion question.

Second, the prudential, felt-normative, and conventional constraints on judicial moral reasoning lead judges to *undertheorize* their moral conclusions. As Cass Sunstein has argued, sweeping judicial opinions with fully theorized philosophical bases tend to create political controversy, including potentially intense scrutiny of the decision and the broader judicial process.[28] Thus there are strong prudential incentives for judges to issue narrower rather than broader rulings in order to minimize disagreement and criticism. For the same reasons, there are also strong prudential incentives for judges to issue morally conclusory or undertheorized opinions: By arguing a legal or moral conclusion as "shallowly" as possible, the Court will alienate the minimum number of those persons who agree with the conclusion—but who might ultimately disagree with a particular line of reasoning. In particular, this "shallow" approach can take full advantage of the numerous instances where there is broader agreement about conclusions than about the reasons for the conclusions—what Sunstein calls incompletely theorized agreements. Moreover, moral "undertheorizing" is closely related to moral "understatement": Not only does a "shallow" moral argument maximize support and minimize conflict, it is also typically much easier to link plausibly to traditional legal materials. Therefore, judicial moral reasoning tends not only to be understated as the basis of decision but incompletely theorized, conclusory, or shallow in nature as well.

Here again we can turn to *Roe* for an example of incomplete theorizing of the moral basis of a decision. As noted, it was of crucial importance to the institutional integrity of the Court that the reasoning in *Roe* be as legalistic or fit-oriented in form as possible—whatever its actual substance. The achievement of this goal could not have been maximized if Blackmun's opinion had openly constitutionalized a controversial moral argument in favor of abortion. If Justice Blackmun had, say, openly grounded *Roe* in some form of Millian utilitarianism or Rawlsian neo-Kantianism, then the institutional integrity of the Court would very likely have suffered significant additional harm. Or if Justice Blackmun had expressly endorsed a highly controversial moral argument about the nature of personhood—say, grounding personhood in the possession of significant level of rationality, moral agency, or self-awareness (a view favored by Peter Singer among others) rather than in a being's individual membership in the human species (a view favored by John Finnis among others), then, again, the Court's institutional integrity would have suffered substantial additional harm. Plainly, such openly morality-based opinions would have been highly controversial politically, and they would be very difficult to link to a traditional fit analysis of legal materials, raising questions of the constitutional legitimacy of the decision in a stark and highly confrontational form. In short, a decision in *Roe* openly rooted in a highly sophisticated but also highly controversial fully theorized moral argument about abortion would have been likely to damage the Court as an institution even more severely than *Roe* did as it was actually decided.

Third, the constraints on judicial reasoning discussed above lead to legal *distortion* of moral reasoning and conclusions. There should be no doubt that legal materials exercise a significant "gravitational pull" on the moral reasoning of even activist judges and thus that judicial moral reasoning is refracted through and distorted by legal materials. The reasons for this are clear enough. They are essentially the same as the general reasons why judges emphasize legal fit arguments over moral justification arguments in their opinions, though our focus here is on both the effect of legal materials on the substance of the judge's own (often private) moral analysis, and the public (quasi-)moral analysis that the judge actually presents in his opinion. Distortion effects occur in at least three related ways. First, there is the effect of the prudential incentives judges have to adduce moral arguments that they can link most plausibly to existing legal materials. Second, there is the effect of the felt normative constraints judges experience requiring that their moral analysis fit to some degree with the existing legal materials. And, third, there is the effect of legal conventions on the judicial moral analysis, including both judicial training in legal analysis and the fact that a judge qua judge confronts legal materials in a fit-oriented adjudicatory setting. Thus the moral reasoning of judges is shaped, guided, and constrained to a substantial degree by legal materials such as text, history, and precedent. As a result, a typical judge—even when exercising a significant degree of moral discretion—is likely to make very different moral arguments and reach different moral conclusions than he would if he were sitting in a political philosophy seminar, policy roundtable, or a legislative chamber debating the moral issues without reference to adjudication.

We can call these effects *distortion* effects simply because it is clear that the dynamics of the judicial process influence judicial moral reasoning in ways that typically both alter and impoverish that moral reasoning. For instance, in many cases, it is clear that a much weaker moral and political argument may be related to a stronger legal argument because of the latter's fit with existing legal materials. Often the moral-cum-legal analyses that actually make it into a legal opinion may not contain the strongest moral argument for the decision or in fact its real moral basis; instead, it may contain a morally weaker, but legally stronger (albeit perhaps still very weak) line of argument. Again, *Roe* provides a notable example. Justice Blackmun grounded the right to abortion in the "right to privacy," but abortion, a medical procedure typically performed by a physician in a hospital or clinic, as a putative right, is surely much more about individual "liberty" or "autonomy" than it is about "privacy."[29] In fact, *Roe*'s characterization of abortion as a "privacy" issue was clearly driven by a need to minimize the controversy surrounding the decision by grounding *Roe* as firmly in legal precedent as possible. Thus the Court built its decision in large part on the recent *Griswold* precedent. *Griswold*, in turn, had grounded a right to use contraceptives in the marital bedroom in a "right to privacy" derived from "emanations" and "penumbras" from the Bill of Rights rather than in the "liberty" language of the due process clause of the Fourteenth Amendment in part because of a felt need to avoid a highly controversial and historically freighted substantive due process argument associated with decisions of the *Lochner* era.[30] Thus the analytic framework, "the right to privacy," the Court used in *Roe* was selected for its perceived *legal* advantages despite its obvious shortcomings as a matter of moral analysis.[31] Notable also in this context is the fact that judicial discussion of the abortion question also continues to discuss issues related to fetal personhood using Justice Blackmun's ill-chosen language of when "life begins" and "potential life," despite the fact that no one doubts that a fetus is "alive" from the moment of conception and that the real debate centers abound the definition of personhood and the attributes necessary for the possession of a personhood-order right to life.[32] This is another example of the distortion and impoverishment of judicial moral argument by the gravitational pull of legal materials such as precedent.

In sum, when a judicial decision does in fact pivot on a controversial moral basis, that moral basis is likely (1) to be under- or unidentified as the pivot of the decision, (2) to be stated in a "shallow," undertheorized, or conclusory form, and (3) to have been distorted by the argumentative pull of traditional legal materials. And this is so largely as a result of political, felt-normative, and conventional constraints on courts that are unlikely to change without a major shift in American political and legal culture.

CASEY: A STUDY IN MORAL INCOMPETENCY

Let us turn to a final example to illustrate these points further. In *Planned Parenthood v. Casey*, the plurality of the Court enunciated in the famous "mystery" passage what has been called the "megaright": "At the heart of liberty is the right to define's one's own concept of existence, of meaning, of the universe and the mystery of human life."[33] In a work of serious philosophy, one would expect such a sweeping statement of individual autonomy—were it ventured—to be carefully defended. What did the justices cite in defense of the "megaright?" John Stuart Mill? John Rawls? Ronald Dworkin? Or an original, detailed, sophisticated line of moral analysis? No, to the contrary, the plurality cited principally judicial precedent and the doctrine of stare decisis, leaving any moral basis for the decision un- or dramatically understated.[34] In short, however much the "megaright" pivoted on moral and political considerations—which it certainly may have substantially—it was defended almost entirely on the traditional legal ground of precedent. Nor did the justices make any attempt to define the scope of this right more specifically or to qualify it. The "mystery passage" as a moral judgment is, in other words, naked, indiscriminate, unsupported, and conclusory—the sort of statement that one would circle in red and decorate with question marks if one were to read it on a freshman philosophy exam.

Even so, if the justices were in fact determined to plant such a broad statement of individual autonomy in the case law, one wonders how they could have done it any differently—given the various constraints on judicial power discussed above. If the justices had simply decreed that the Fourteenth Amendment guarantees our "liberty" in the abstract and that the Court must determine what "liberty" means in the concrete through purely moral and political analysis, it would have raised quite serious questions of constitutional legitimacy in an overt and confrontational manner likely very damaging to the Court's institutional integrity. Plainly, citing precedent in favor of an (otherwise) unargued-for moral conclusion was by far the least controversial way to do it. Even a dubious reading of a dubious line of precedents is far less likely to provoke a major controversy on judicial power grounds than an openly moral and political approach.[35]

Moreover, even had the plurality conceded that it was exercising a fair degree of moral discretion, it would have been unlikely to have articulated a fully theorized moral defense of the mystery passage, rather than simply stating a "shallow," conclusory, or undertheorized moral conclusion. Had the justices simply endorsed the political liberalism of, say, John Rawls, they would have been subjected to a great deal of criticism from a number of quarters, not the least of which would have come from non-Rawlsian liberal individualists. There is little agreement even among prominent academic liberal individualists about the precise moral grounding of autonomy rights. In brief, the Court would have been endorsing not simply a controversial moral conclusion, but an even more controversial moral argument—inviting additional scrutiny and criticism. Further, the plurality would have had even more difficulty explaining why the theories of John Rawls are the particular mandate of the Constitution rather than, say, Robert Nozick's, John Finnis's, or even James Madison's. Finally, in putting together a majority, the justices might have had to paper over a number of their own moral differences about the basis and likely limitations of the "megaright" or written separate opinions—assuming, of course, that they had actually thought the matter through. A series of opinions citing different "deep" or completely theorized moral arguments in support of the "mystery passage" and perhaps disagreeing on its precise scope would have gone even further to undermine the Court's authority. John Hart Ely once deflated the pretensions of theorists who advocate judicial grounding of decisions in moral philosophy by imagining an opinion reading: "We like Rawls, you like Nozick. We win, 6–3."[36] One wonders what the public response would be to a highly philosophical but also highly fragmented liberal individualist decision concluding: "Two of us like Rawls, one of us likes Nozick, one of us likes Dworkin, and one of us likes Judith Jarvis Thomson. Our moral conclusion wins, 5–4."

Finally, the plurality's "moral" reasoning in *Casey* may have been significantly distorted by legal materials. For instance, the plurality's (in)famous mystery passage, as noted, is not supported by overt moral analysis but rather by citation to judicial precedents, suggesting that these precedents may have in fact influenced and thus potentially distorted judicial moral reasoning on the question of the scope of individual autonomy. Further, if we do take the plurality at their word, their specific holding on abortion was also significantly determined by precedent, by the doctrine of stare decisis, and by related concerns about the Court's institutional reputation and standing. Or, in other words, the justices of the plurality may have reaffirmed the right to abortion, not solely or even principally because they concluded after careful moral analysis that it is indeed a requirement of objective morality, but rather because of a two-decade-old judicial precedent and because they were concerned that the Court would look "unprincipled" and its reputation and authority would suffer if it changed its mind on the issue in the face of significant political criticism. Therefore, if we can actually call what the plurality did *moral* reasoning, it was moral reasoning radically *distorted* by extramoral legal and political concerns. In sum, to someone really doing his best to "take abortion seriously," to grapple with the difficult cluster of moral arguments surrounding that vexing question, there can be few things more dispiriting than reading *Roe* and *Casey*.

THE PRACTICAL LIMITS OF JUDICIAL MORAL REASONING

The severe prudential, felt-normative, and conventional constraints on judicial moral reasoning typically cause judicial moral reasoning to be understated, incompletely theorized, and distorted. What, then, are the consequences for *the level of sophistication* that judicial moral reasoning is actually able to achieve? As a practical matter, it is clear that judges cannot achieve any special degree of procedural, or "thin," moral expertise, in light of the minimum requirements of rational moral inquiry as defined above.

Judges typically do not publicly reason toward moral truth or give moral reasons for their conclusions, bring much that we can see in the way of critical moral reflection to bear on moral questions, formulate coherent moral answers, or vigorously confront moral counterarguments. Judges, of course, do encounter moral issues frequently and at varying levels of particularity, but, again, as we have seen, they tend to encounter them through the prism of law and also to treat them publicly as legal rather than moral issues. Judges also tend to put aside bias, expediency, and self-interest when resolving cases, but again the focus here is on the parties before the court and on legal analysis rather than moral analysis, where, as we have seen, there is good reason to think judges often go with "gut" impulses reflecting class and other demographic biases and evince real concern about the "political standing" of the courts. Finally, judges simply do not publicly set forth clearly moral justifications for their moral conclusions, but rather often subsume those concerns, or disguise them, in traditional forms of legal fit analysis. Judges, then, cannot engage in dialectic about difficult moral questions, develop "deep" moral theories, vigorously meet moral counterarguments, achieve a substantial degree of moral "reflective equilibrium,"or publicly justify and defend their moral conclusions. To the contrary, judicial reasoning *in practice* is, or purports to be, fundamentally "technical" legal reasoning—ordered toward traditional forms of legal interpretation—rather than freewheeling moral reasoning. The substance of some judges' reasoning in some, perhaps many, cases may approach freewheeling moral reasoning, but significantly the form continues to be that of a much more narrow legal fit analysis. Inevitably such constraints on the form of judicial reasoning limit its substantive sophistication in significant ways as well.

There is no reason, then, to suppose that judges engage in anything even approaching sophisticated moral reasoning and certainly no obvious reason to suppose that they are better moral reasoners than voters or legislators. In fact, voters and legislators, because they are free to engage in moral reasoning without the pretense of legal interpretation, have certain obvious advantages relative to judges in meeting the basic requirements of sophisticated moral reasoning. If nothing else, the moral reasoning of voters and legislators is not driven by the institutional dynamics of the judicial process into recurrent patterns of moral understatement, incomplete theorization, or distortion by legal materials. Further, even if one has one's doubts about the moral competency of the typical legislator or voter, one could always advocate the creation of elite panels or "task forces" stocked with real "moral experts"—professional philosophers, ethicists, theologians—such as Governor Mario Cuomo's New York State Task Force on physician-assisted suicide. Such a task force could bring real moral expertise to bear on hard moral questions and, as Governor Cuomo's did, "represent[ ] a broad spectrum of ethical and religious views and ethical, health, legal, and medical competencies."[37] Indeed, if one thinks that rights questions should be subjected to the maximum of serious moral scrutiny, one very likely should not support an expansion of the judicial process, but rather a contraction.

Conclusion

Taking judicial power seriously requires testing rival conceptions of the proper scope of the judicial power for structural "fit" and "justification" with the structure of the governmental design established by the Constitution. As noted, the sweeping degree of judicial power that flows from a judicial "moral" reading of the Bill of Rights is very likely precluded by its lack of structural legal fit with the traditional legal materials establishing the broad contours of the American constitutional design. Still, even if this highly expansive conception of the proper judicial role under the Constitution were thought to meet some threshold requirement of structural fit, it would still require additional structural moral-political justification in order qualify as the best interpretation of the constitutional scope of the judicial power in the structure of the Constitution. This last point is particularly important given the counterweight of other moral-political concerns, such as the value of representative democracy. As we have seen at length, one possible defense for expansive judicial power, the case for a special judicial power of moral insight, cannot be sustained in the face of serious critical scrutiny. Judges simply do not and, practically speaking, cannot engage in anything approaching sophisticated moral reasoning or develop the kind of "thin," or procedural, moral expertise discussed here. On the contrary, judges face severe prudential, felt-normative, and conventional constraints that lead them to radically understate, incompletely theorize, and distort their moral analysis. Judges, therefore, cannot meet even the most basic requirements of fair-minded rational moral argument, and in fact, this moral "incompetency" is quite evident in their typically shallow and impoverished treatment in judicial decisions of difficult moral questions such as abortion. This point in turn suggests that the familiar arguments in favor of the comparative advantage of courts in moral reasoning are in fact seriously flawed and radically overstate the moral expertise of the judiciary. In the final analysis, then, expansive judicial power must be justified in the face of competing moral values such as representative democracy without any reliance on a "special" judicial power of moral expertise.

NOTES

1. The formulation of this project in part as one of "taking judicial power seriously" invites a comparison to the work of Ronald Dworkin and the project of "taking rights seriously." See Ronald Dworkin, *Taking Rights Seriously* (Cambridge: Harvard University Press, 1978).

2. Ronald Dworkin originated this formulation of the nature of legal interpretation, breaking down its essence into aspects of legal "fit" and moral-political "justification." See Ronald Dworkin, *Law's Empire* (Cambridge: Harvard University Press, 1986).

3. See *Federalist*, No. 78 (Alexander Hamilton); *Marbury v. Madison* 5 U.S. (1 Cranch) 137 (1803).

4. For a discussion of implicit structure-based constitutional limits on the use of judicial review, see Jack Wade Nowlin, "The Constitutional Limits of Judicial Review: A Structural Interpretive Approach," 52 *Oklahoma Law Review* 521 (1999); "The Constitutional Illegitimacy of Expansive Judicial Power: A Populist Structural Interpretive Analysis," 89 *Kentucky Law Journal* 387 (2001); "The Judicial Restraint Amendment: Populist Constitutional Reform in the Spirit of the Bill of Rights," 78 *Notre Dame Law Review* 171 (2002).

5. Thus a legal "fit" and "moral justification" structural interpretation of the scope of judicial power under the constitutional design could either preclude or endorse a judicial "moral" reading of the Bill of Rights.

6. See, e.g., See Ronald Dworkin, *Freedom's Law: The Moral Reading of the American Constitution* (Cambridge: Harvard University Press, 1996); Michael Moore, "Moral Reality Revisited," 90 *Michigan Law Review* 2424, 2479 (1992); Sotirios Barber, *The Constitution of Judicial Power* (Baltimore: Johns Hopkins University Press, 1993); Stephen Macedo, *The New Right v. the Constitution*, 2d ed. (Washington, D.C.: Cato Institute, 1987).

7. For instance, Dworkin, while emphasizing the constraints of "history and [legal] integrity," also observes that "[v]ery different, even contrary, conceptions of constitutional principle—of what treating men and women as equals really means, for example—will often fit language, precedent, and practice well enough to pass these tests, and thoughtful judges must then decide on their own which conception does most credit to the nation." See Dworkin, *Freedom's Law*, 11.

8. Ibid., 3–4 (arguing that the "moral" reading "is almost never openly endorsed even by judges whose arguments are incomprehensible on any other understanding").

9. For an argument that expansive judicial power is precluded by a structural "fit" analysis of the American constitutional design, see Nowlin, "Constitutional Illegitimacy," 472–74.

10. For a detailed discussion of issues related to moral realism, epistemic theory, and the judicial process, see Jack Wade Nowlin, "Natural Law, the Constitution, and Judicial Moral Expertise: An Epistemic Analysis," n.s., 2, nos. 1–2, *Vera Lex* 71–113 (2001); Jeremy Waldron, "The Irrelevance of Moral Objectivity," in *Natural Law Theory: Contemporary Essays*, ed. Robert P. George (Oxford: Oxford University Press, 1992); Michael Moore, "Law as a Functional Kind," in George, *Natural Law Theory*; Moore, "Moral Reality Revisited," 2477; Barber, *Constitution of Judicial Power*, 184; John Hart Ely, *Democracy and Distrust: A Theory of Judicial Review* (Cambridge: Harvard University Press, 1989), 56–60.

11. For a fuller discussion of this distinction "thick" and "thin" theories of moral expertise, see Nowlin, "Natural Law," 80–92.

12. For a detailed discussion of the substantive, or "thick," conception of judicial moral expertise, see ibid., 77–88.

13. Sotirios Barber, for instance, maintains that the Socratic dialectic and Rawlsian reflective equilibrium constitute a widely-agreed upon method for reaching moral truth. See Barber, *Constitution of Judicial Power*, 184.

14. This formulation is borrowed from an earlier work. See Nowlin, "Natural Law," 89. It was inspired in part by Sotirios Barber and by Michael Moore. See

Barber, *Constitution of Judicial Power*, 184; Moore, "Moral Reality Revisited," 2477.

15. Moore, "Moral Reality Revisited," 2477.

16. For an elaboration of this point concerning the uncertain link between "thin" moral reasoning and moral truth, see Nowlin, "Natural Law," 92–108.

17. Kent Greenawalt, *Law and Objectivity* (Oxford: Oxford University Press, 1992), 226–27.

18. See Dworkin, *Freedom's Law*, 5–6 (observing that Senate hearings on Supreme Court nominations implicitly reject overtly "moral" readings of the Constitution as illegitimate and therefore consider it "inappropriate to ask the nominee any questions about his or her own political morality").

19. John C. Jeffries Jr., *Justice Lewis F. Powell, Jr.* (New York: C. Scribners Sons, 1994), 346–47. Powell was, Jeffries writes, a "well-educated, non-Catholic, upper-class male—a group then, as now, overwhelmingly supportive of freedom of choice" on abortion. Ibid., 347.

20. See Dworkin, *Freedom's Law*, 3–4 (emphasis added). Dworkin overstates the reach of "moral" readings of the Constitution to include even those interpretive theories that strain to limit the moral discretion of judges. Even so, his broader point about the unwillingness of judges to acknowledge the influence of moral judgment in adjudication is certainly valid. Hadley Arkes has also observed that Supreme Court justices often "act[ ] in the style of men who have rediscovered natural law, and yet they themselves can speak only the language of legal positivism." The "result," Arkes concludes, "is that our jurists have reached decisions untethered by the traditional formulas in the Constitution, but without having the least comprehension, themselves, of the moral philosophy that would render this whole enterprise intelligible." Hadley Arkes, *Beyond the Constitution* (Princeton: Princeton University Press, 1990), 110–11.

21. *Bowers v. Hardwick*, 478 U.S. 186, 194 (1986). Justice White here may be seen as making both a prudential claim ("most vulnerable") and a normative claim ("nearest to illegitimacy").

22. *Planned Parenthood v. Casey*, 505 U.S. 833, 865–66 (1992).

23. Francis Canavan, *The Pluralist Game* (Lanham, Md.: Rowman and Littlefield, 1995), 55.

24. William J. Brennan, "The Constitution of the United States: Contemporary Ratification," in *Interpreting the Constitution*, ed. Jack N. Rakove (Boston: Northeastern University Press, 1990): "The act of interpretation must be undertaken with full consequences that it is, in a very real sense, the community's interpretation that is sought. Justices are not platonic guardians appointed to wield authority according to their personal moral predilections" (25). Ronald Dworkin also attempts to minimize democratic objections to the "moral" reading of the Constitution by (over)emphasizing the "constraints of history and integrity" that his theory places on the moral reasoning of judges. See, e.g., *Freedom's Law*, 11–12.

25. The concept of incomplete theorization is borrowed from Cass Sunstein. See *Legal Reasoning and Political Conflict* (Oxford: Oxford University Press, 1996), 35–61.

26. Kent Greenawalt maintains that judges seldom admit just how close a close case really is. See *Law and Objectivity*, 226.

27. See *Roe v. Wade*, 410 U.S. 113 (1973).

28. See Sunstein, *Legal Reasoning*, 35–61.

29. *Roe v. Wade*, 152–53.

30. *Griswold v. Connecticut*, 381 U.S. 479, 484 (1965).

31. Notably, the Court in *Roe* "split the difference" by retaining the "right to privacy" language of *Griswold* but grounding the "right to privacy" in the "liberty" language of the Fourteenth Amendment due process clause. *Roe v. Wade*, 153.

32. *Roe v. Wade*, 159–63; *Planned Parenthood v. Casey*, 870–72.

33. *Planned Parenthood v. Casey*, 851.

34. Ibid.

35. Of course, the precedents themselves, we are told, are the product of the Court's exercise of "reasoned judgment," but we are not told of what that consists with any precision—other than it has something to do with "tradition" and that "it does not mean [the Court is] free to invalidate state policy choices with which [it] disagree[s]." *Planned Parenthood v. Casey*, 849–50. Even so, "reasoned judgment" in practice seems to involve an ill-defined and uneasy mix of judicial reasoning about *both* objective morality and conventional morality—with the judges own moral judgments often playing the pivotal role, as they clearly do in *Roe*. Certainly, there is no reason to think that either *Roe*'s right to abortion or the plurality's own unqualified statement of a "megaright" in *Casey* was (or is) a direct reflection of traditional or conventional American moral norms.

36. Ely, *Democracy and Distrust*, 58.

37. *Compassion in Dying v. Washington*, 49 F. 3d 586, 592 (1995).

CHAPTER 8

Toward a More Balanced History of the Supreme Court

Michael W. McConnell

WHILE MANY specialists in the study of the American constitutional system recognize that each of the branches of government—and even the individual citizen—has a legitimate role in the interpretation of our foundational document, it is all too common to hear some version of the idea that "the Constitution is what the Supreme Court says it is." In recent years, this inflated view of the authority of the High Court has crept into the Court's own discussion of its position in American life. In *Planned Parenthood v. Casey*, for example, the controlling joint opinion asserted that the belief of the American people "in themselves" as "a Nation of people who aspire to live according to the rule of law . . . is not readily separable from their understanding of the Court invested with the authority to decide their constitutional cases and speak before all others for their constitutional ideals." When the nation faces an "intensely divisive conflict," the justices went on, "the Court's interpretation of the Constitution calls the contending sides of a national controversy to end their national division by accepting a common mandate rooted in the Constitution."[1] This comes perilously close to the suggestion that the People should acquiesce in the Court's decisions, right or wrong.

The same high judicial self-regard can be seen behind the Court's more recent decision, in *City of Boerne v. Flores*, to strike down the Religious Freedom Restoration Act.[2] In this decision, the Court held that Congress could not enforce its own understanding of the meaning of free exercise of religion in the course of discharging its constitutional function of passing laws to enforce the Bill of Rights. The most troubling aspect of this opinion was that the Court did not think it necessary to set forth the substance of Congress's theory of the free exercise clause, or to explain why that theory was an untenable interpretation of the Constitution. When Congress legislates "against the background of a judicial interpretation of the Constitution already issued," the Court declared, "it must be understood that in later cases and controversies the Court will treat its precedents with the respect due them."[3] There was not so much as a footnote addressing the possibility that Congress, and not the Court, might have had the better understanding of the Constitution, even for the purpose of refuting that possibility. It was sufficient that Congress had disagreed with the Court.

It is not difficult to understand why justices of the Supreme Court take a generous view of their own powers. When does a power holder not do so? It is not much more difficult to see why lawyers and law professors would tend to share this view. Who does not see advantages to rule by one's own social class? The difficulty is in understanding why the rest of society—the People, whose democratic authority is thereby diminished—put up with it.

My thesis here is that an important part of the explanation lies in the nature of education about the history of the Supreme Court. In high school civics class, in undergraduate courses in government, and even—I am embarrassed to say—in most introductory courses in constitutional law in law school, students are imparted a celebratory history of the Supreme Court that goes something like this.

THE STANDARD, CELEBRATORY HISTORY OF THE SUPREME COURT

In the beginning is *Marbury v. Madison*.[4] Almost all courses in American constitutional government begin with *Marbury*. It is literally true that in many constitutional law classes the students read and analyze *Marbury* before they ever read the Constitution. One of the two best selling casebooks in constitutional law—Gerald Gunther's magisterial *Constitutional Law*, now in its thirteenth edition—begins with *Marbury* and relegates the Constitution to appendix A.[5] The subtle point conveyed by this organization is that the fountainhead of constitutional law is not the act of the People in 1787, but the decisions of the justices of the Supreme Court.

And the picture of *Marbury* presented in most constitutional law classes is one in which the heroic chief justice, John Marshall, refutes one bad argument after another against judicial review, thus casting the Court in its majestic role as the expositor of the Constitution.[6] Put aside the fact (to be addressed below) that this story bears little resemblance to what *Marbury v. Madison* was actually about in its own historical context. The key point is that constitutional law is defined, from the beginning, as the study not of the Constitution but of judicial review under the Constitution. In a sense, the rest of constitutional law is a series of footnotes to *Marbury*. Once the key question—who decides?—is behind us, the rest of the course can be devoted to such interesting questions as

"What does the Supreme Court think about freedom of speech?" "What does the Court think are proper procedures for welfare administration?" "What is the Court's opinion of term limits?" and the like. Students learn to parse cryptic opinions for clues about what the justices are thinking, to use doctrinal language out of Supreme Court opinions rather than the language of the Constitution, to manipulate multipart tests, and to speculate about the authority of plurality opinions and concurrences—all this in place of serious reflection on the words of the Constitution, its historical context, or the philosophy of government that it reflects. Much constitutional doctrine has no actual content, but simply tells us how much or little regard the Court will have for the decisions of the representatives of the people: strict scrutiny, rational basis, and the like.

After *Marbury*, the next important development touched upon in the typical course of study is the Fourteenth Amendment. This amendment, of course, vastly expands the power of the United States Supreme Court. Indeed, most of modern constitutional law consists of interpretations of "due process" and "equal protection." Do these clauses sound vague and open-ended (especially if yanked from any historical context)? This is taken as proof that the framers of the Fourteenth Amendment must have intended the justices to have broad and unconfined powers to promote the cause of liberty and equality (as they see it).

The result? Protections for the downtrodden, protection for civil liberties, defending the unity of the nation.

This cheery account of the Supreme Court's role as protector and defender of the Constitution has some hard going for a brief period—say, 120 years, between 1835 and 1954. How, for example, can it deal with *Dred Scott v. Sandford*,[7] the second time in American history that the Supreme Court actually struck down an act of Congress, and in so doing conjured up rights for slaveholders not to be found in the constitutional text, took away congressional power over slavery in the territories, which had been exercised since the first days of the Republic, and brought on the Civil War? One answer: ignore it. *Dred Scott* is nowhere to be found in the Gunther casebook.[8] In another casebook, the editors leave out the section of *Dred Scott* in which the doctrine of substantive due process makes its first appearance—thus depriving students of the irony that the most potent tool of modern progressive judicial activism had its birth in protecting slaveowners.[9]

But most heroic sagas sometimes show the hero's weaker moments. Accordingly, the standard history does not attempt to cover up the dark period after Reconstruction and before the New Deal. This period is characterized by *Plessy v. Ferguson*[10] and *Lochner v. New York*.[11] The message that most students take from this period, however, is not that legislative and judicial institutions departed from their proper roles, but that the judicial personnel appointed at this particular juncture of history were lacking in proper liberal sensibilities.

But, in any event, most courses skip relatively quickly through this period and get to the good stuff, starting with *Brown v. Board of Education*,[12] in which a creative and innovative Supreme Court rescues the nation from segregation by overriding precedent and disregarding the intentions of the Framers.[13] Now the students get to *Cooper v. Aaron*,[14] in which the notion comes forth that the opinions of the Supreme Court are actually on a level with the Constitution itself. The Court's opinions, the Court opines, are not just *interpretations* of the law, but are *themselves* the supreme law of the land.[15] So officials around the country who swear an oath to support and defend the Constitution of the United States are in fact swearing to uphold and defend the Supreme Court's decisions, and not just the Constitution.

Then we come to the glorious civil rights revolution: *Reynolds v. Sims*, *Miranda*, *Gideon*, *Mapp v. Ohio*, leading up to the *really* good stuff: *Griswold* and *Roe*. These are the glory days of the Court: judicial review in the service of fair representation, the rights of criminal defendants, sexual liberation, autonomy, and the transformation of gender roles. The Court is the agent of social change, accomplishing revolutionary deeds that the slow-moving representative system would never be able to accomplish.[16]

To be sure, there has recently been a fall from grace. The Rehnquist Court does not live up to its predecessors. It mostly leaves legislative decisions intact, and when it does intervene, it tends to be in service of benighted ideas: color-blind laws, limited federal power, property. But even though it has been some fifteen years since the beginning of the Rehnquist Court, most law professors seem to treat it as a kind of interregnum, an unfortunate period that will come to an end pretty soon, so that the nation can again experience the blessings of social transformation through the decisions of the Supreme Court.

The Need for a More Balanced History

It is no wonder that Supreme Court decisions declaring for themselves the extraordinary power to dictate to the rest of us with respect to such important subjects are treated as legitimate. That seems to be the way it always has been—if history is studied this way. I think we need to look back and see American constitutional history in a different light. We need a more balanced history of the role of the Court in American democracy. This would require an adjustment in two respects. First is that through most of our history the Supreme Court has *not* viewed itself as the body with exclusive authority to tell us what the Constitution dictates. Instead, the Court has understood its role as limited by a principle of self-restraint, sometimes called the presumption of constitutionality. There are dozens of decisions from the early days of the Republic in which the Court made clear that it would not invalidate the acts of the legislature unless conflict between the legislative act and the Constitution was clear. Judicial review was not a matter of balancing this against that and coming up with the right answer. The function of the courts was to police the outer boundaries and make sure the Constitution was not flouted.

The second principle is that the Court is not the exclusive, and maybe not even the most important, expositor of the Constitution. The Constitution is a frame of government that governs the activities of every actor in the constitutional system, right down to the individual citizens. And all actors in the system, within the scope of their own authority, have not just the right but the responsibility to read and understand the Constitution and interpret it for themselves. This has been called the principle of "coordinate review," to distinguish it from the idea of "judicial review."

In light of these two ideas, let us take a look at the same history that we just explored, but with a different eye.

One of the striking facts about the early history of the Republic is that after the Constitution was ratified, we managed to get along without any significant constitutional judicial action at all. There were almost no constitutional decisions of any real significance—other than one, *Chisolm v. Georgia*,[17] which was promptly overturned by constitutional amendment. Did this mean that there was no constitutional law? By no means. A great deal of constitutional law was being made. It just happened not to be made in the courts. The principal forum for constitutional deliberation and decision was the Congress of the United States. In Congress, there were extensive discussions about the meaning of the Constitution, and a broad range of important constitutional questions were resolved.[18] Other constitutional issues were debated and resolved within the executive branch, as in the case of Hamilton's opinion on the Declaration of Neutrality. Even state legislatures got into the act of constitutional interpretation, most notably in the case of the Kentucky and Virginia Resolutions challenging the legitimacy of the Alien and Sedition Acts. The Supreme Court, by contrast, played almost no role in shaping constitutional interpretation during the Federalist period.

This relatively modest role for the Supreme Court was *not* attributable to the supposed fact that judicial review had not yet been invented by Marshall in *Marbury*. The historical record is clear that judicial review was expected from the beginning (by which I mean that if a case of a judicial nature were properly presented in which the meaning of the Constitution is implicated, the court would read the Constitution for itself, come to its own independent judgment about what the Constitution means, and in the unlikely event that a statute passed by Congress was inconsistent with that meaning, the court would disregard the statute). It was just that judicial review and invalidation of statutes was expected to be a rather unusual event. The principal institution for enforcement of the Constitution, it was widely agreed, was not the courts but the People. The Constitution was deliberately written in understandable language, and the People had the power and the incentive to hold their representatives to the terms of the document.

It may be helpful to consider an example. During the First Congress, representatives and senators debated at length where the Constitution had vested the power to discharge the head of an executive department. This was an extremely important issue, since the character of executive administration would be vastly different if the President were not able to control his cabinet officers through removal or threat of removal. Indeed, this issue is with us still: one of the several constitutionally problematic features of the Independent Counsel statute was that it vested executive authority in an officer not subject to removal by the President. The First Congress ultimately concluded that the Constitution, although not explicit on the subject, should be interpreted as vesting the President with the power of removal. Interestingly, participants in this debate contemplated that it was possible that the issue might later be raised in court. But far from thinking that the courts were the primary interpreter, it was said that the judges "would feel great relief in having had the question decided by representatives of the people"[19] and that the courts would probably not overrule the legislative judgment on a point that the constitutional language did not explicitly resolve.[20] This was typical of the way Congress envisioned the relationship between congressional and judicial constitutional interpretation in those key years in the late 1780s and 1790s, when our system was being established.

Marbury v. Madison comes later. In the standard view, *Marbury* is taught as the great triumph of the principle of judicial review. I cannot do justice to the argument in the space of this short essay,[21] but that was not the issue in *Marbury* at all. No one in the case challenged the proposition that a court has power within a case properly brought before it to disregard an act of Congress it concludes to be unconstitutional. Nor was that a controversial proposition in the legal and political culture of the day. Indeed, to the best of my knowledge, the first time a public figure disputed this proposition in public debate was 1802, the very year before *Marbury*. John Breckinridge of Kentucky, the most radical of the Jeffersonians, argued in connection with the judiciary reform act that if Congress passed the act within the scope of its authority, no other institution could question its constitutionality. Since the Constitution gives each department "exclusive authority on the subjects committed to it," Breckinridge argued, "therefore the Legislature have the exclusive right to interpret the Constitution, in what regards the law-making power, and the judges are bound to execute the laws they make."[22] That, however, went beyond the orthodox doctrine of the Jeffersonian party. First Madison and then Jefferson himself staked out a position to the effect that the courts' power is to decide the case or controversy before them, but that any constitutional conclusion they might reach is binding only on the particular parties to the case. The other branches of government are not required to accept the courts' interpretation, and are free to act in ways contrary to that interpretation in all other matters.[23] For example, after *Marbury v. Madison* itself, Jefferson felt no compunction to deliver commissions (which the Court had held were wrongfully withheld) to the thirteen other appointees who were in the same position as William Marbury. Under Jefferson's theory of coordinate review, those appointees might have been able to go to court in a proper action and get their commissions, but he, having concluded that the Court was wrong, was under no obligation to deliver their commissions without court order. More famously, Jefferson did not feel bound by lower-court decisions upholding the Alien and Sedition Acts, but used his pardon power to free those jailed under those acts.

The Jeffersonian-Madisonian theory of coordinate review still leaves the judiciary in the position of having the final word in all cases of a judicial nature where litigants care enough to pursue their remedies in court. Insofar as the other branches of government need the judicial machinery to accomplish their ends (for example, in prosecuting criminals, collecting taxes, or seizing property), a judicial conclusion that it would be unconstitutional to cooperate will be the end of the matter. That is why the requirement of trials in advance of takings of life, liberty, and property has a separation-of-powers dimension, and is so important: In these cases, government power cannot be successfully asserted unless all three branches concur in its constitutionality—Congress by passing the law authorizing the taking, the executive by prosecuting the action, and the judiciary by entering the legal judgment. More controversially, insofar as the courts have authority to issue writs of mandamus, prohibition, or injunction directing executive officials in their conduct of their offices, or to entertain suits for money damages and other relief against governmental officials or agencies, courts are able to impose their constitutional interpretations on the other branches. Moreover, both for reasons of prudence (fear of suit) and comity (respect for the judgments of a coordinate branch within its field of expertise), the other branches of government are likely to give great weight to judicial interpretations of the Constitution even outside the particular case or controversy. Thus, the judiciary is the most potent interpreter of the Constitution even under the theory of coordinate review.

But this leaves cases in which parties have no standing to sue, the case is not ripe or is moot, the case presents a nonjusticiable political question, the government has sovereign immunity, or there is no statutory basis for suit. In those cases, the constitutional judgments of the other branches will be final. Moreover, since the burden is on litigants dissatisfied with the actions of the political branches to litigate, judicial power is limited by the judicial capacity to hear and decide cases, and by the energies and resources of the litigants. It is *not* unconstitutional for government officials to defy Court precedent outside the strict limits of decided cases. Thus, the Jeffersonian-Madisonian view of coordinate judicial review recognizes that the judiciary will have the final word in many, though not all, constitutional controversies; but it reserves both theoretical equality and substantial practical interpretive authority to Congress, the President, and the states.

A close reading of the *Marbury* opinion suggests that Marshall was in substantial agreement with this view. The real controversy in *Marbury* was not over judicial review, but over the idea that the courts could order executive officers how to conduct their office. The real conflict was executive-judicial, not legislative-judicial. Jefferson and Madison took the position that the "Take care Clause," which says that "the President shall Take care that the laws be faithfully executed," means that it is the *President*—not the Court—who has the obligation to ensure that executive officers are faithfully executing the laws. This is why Madison made the gesture of failing to show up in court in the *Marbury* case. It was the most dramatic way in which he (and Jefferson) could express their view that the court had no authority over the Secretary of State. That is why Marshall's discussion of mandamus, which many constitutional law professors treat as a boring way-station to the really interesting and important question of judicial review, is actually the heart of the case. The law of mandamus would determine the forms of law under which the court might have authority to issue orders to the executive. The proposition that the court would be able to engage in judicial review was not questioned.

In fact, the Court's decision in *Marbury* did not reflect a radical or strongly judicial approach to constitutional adjudication. The arguments in support of judicial review in *Marbury* are based, not on the proposition that the Supreme Court has any special or exclusive role in constitutional interpretation, but on the proposition that the Constitution is supreme over the actions of every officer in government. This was entirely consistent with Jefferson's doctrine of coordinate review—the idea that all branches of government have authority to interpret the Constitution for themselves within the scope of their own duties. To be sure, many members of the Federalist Party took a stronger line, and came close to the judicial supremacy position later found in *Cooper v. Aaron*, *Planned Parenthood v. Casey*, and *City of Boerne v. Flores*. During the Alien and Sedition Act controversy, for example, the Rhode Island legislature passed a declaration that the Constitution "vests in the Federal Courts, exclusively, and in the Supreme Court of the United States, ultimately, the authority of deciding on the constitutionality of any act or law of the Congress of the United States."[24] But nothing in John Marshall's opinion in *Marbury*, or in his other statements on the subject, suggests that he adopted that High Federalist view.

Nor was *Marbury* a harbinger of judicial activism. Not until 1838, in *Kendall v. United States ex rel. Stokes*,[25] did the Court again issue a directive to an executive branch official, and review of executive agency action did not become routine until the end of the century, or—arguably—until passage of the Administrative Procedure Act in 1947. Not until 1857, in *Dred Scott v. Sandford*,[26] did the Court again hold an act of Congress unconstitutional. Almost all judicial review in the antebellum period was directed at the actions of the states.

The role of the courts continued to be a contested question in the antebellum years. Andrew Jackson and his Democratic Party continued to adhere to the Jeffersonian position of coordinate review, and this was probably the dominant position. There was, however, some dissent, especially among the Daniel Webster wing of the Whig Party, who tended to be supporters of a more powerful judicial role. But after the 1830s they were a fairly weak force in American politics.

Alignments on the issue changed, however, as the slavery question came to dominate American politics. It is important to recognize that during this period the Supreme Court was a reliable bastion of Southern power. The reason for this was not that there "happened" to be a Southern majority on the Supreme Court, but that the judiciary act of 1837 gerrymandered judicial circuits so that five of the nine circuits were made up entirely up of slave states, even though they constituted far less than a majority of the population.[27] Since the Supreme Court had one justice chosen from each of these circuits, there was a guaranteed Southern majority on the Supreme Court. Meanwhile, population was shifting to the north, improving the electoral prospects of the new Republican Party. The Democrats accordingly began to take refuge in the courts, much as the Federalists had done a half century before. Accordingly, the political parties abandoned their traditional positions on judicial authority. Democrats began to espouse a strong view of judicial authority inconsistent with their Jeffersonian and Jacksonian heritage, in the hope that the Supreme Court would be the institution to resolve the slavery question.

This produces *Dred Scott*. Whatever our leading casebook editors may think, *Dred Scott* was no inconsequential event in American history. It was the Court's earliest attempt to "call the contending sides of a national controversy to end their national division by accepting a common mandate rooted in the Constitution."[28] It declared that Congress had no authority to deal with the great question of slavery by regulating its entry into the territories, and held that any exclusion of slavery was a denial of due process of law. It was the first decision in American history to hold a significant act of Congress—the Missouri Compromise—unconstitutional, and the first to assert a power to strike down legislation under the rubric of what would later be called substantive due process.

The *Dred Scott* decision was the focal point of the debates between Abraham Lincoln and Stephen Douglas, which in turn framed the central political debate of the late 1850s. Lincoln was elected President on a platform of restoring the Jeffersonian-Jacksonian (and Marshallian) doctrine, that the Supreme Court is *not* the final and exclusive arbiter of the Constitution. In his inaugural address, Lincoln explained that a judicial decision bound only the parties to the lawsuit, and declared that if the "policy of the government, upon vital questions affecting the whole people, is to be irrevocably fixed by the decisions of the Supreme Court of the United States, . . . the people will have ceased to be their own rulers, having to that extent practically resigned their government into the hands of that eminent tribunal."[29]

The next few years after Lincoln's election form the immediate background and context for the Fourteenth Amendment. That amendment is central to modern constitutional law and stands as the principal justification for modern judicial activism. The actual background and context may therefore come as something of a surprise to most readers. Let us consider the attitude toward the judiciary that was shared by the authors of the Fourteenth Amendment.

In 1862, by mere statute, Congress passed a law abolishing slavery in the territories.[30] This was in defiance of a Supreme Court decision that was directly on point. Congress again explicitly violated a Supreme Court decision in 1866; the first section of the Civil Rights Act of 1866 declared freemen to be citizens,[31] which *Dred Scott* had held was unconstitutional. Members of Congress during this period also engaged in rather remarkable court packing. First they increased the number of justices to ten, so that Lincoln would be able to make an additional appointment, improving their chances of having reconstruction and wartime legislation upheld. Then, when Lincoln was assassinated and they were faced with a hostile Andrew Johnson as President, Congress reduced the size of the Court to seven to ensure that he could not make any appointments. None of this suggests that the party of Lincoln treated judicial independence as any kind of sacrosanct principle.

Congress also engaged in judicial jurisdictional stripping. When the Supreme Court announced that it was going to decide the case of *Ex Parte McCardle*,[32] the Republicans feared that the Court would strike down key aspects of reconstruction legislation. To prevent that from happening, Congress voted to strip the Supreme Court of its appellate authority.

Of more general significance, in 1868 John Bingham, the author of the Fourteenth Amendment, proposed a bill similar to a recent proposal by Robert Bork, to prohibit the Supreme Court from striking down any acts of Congress as unconstitutional without a two-thirds majority vote. (Another Republican congressman proposed a unanimity requirement.) This measure was defended as an institutional means of guaranteeing adherence to the traditional position that acts of Congress should only be held unconstitutional in clear cases. Bingham's two-thirds reform passed the House of Representatives by an overwhelming majority,[33] though it was ultimately buried in the Senate.

As these incidents illustrate, the framers of the Reconstruction amendments did not have a high view of judicial authority. The notion that by using vague language they intended to empower the courts to second-guess legislatures on an almost infinite range of issues is lacking in historical context. In *City of Boerne*, Justice Kennedy wrote of the Supreme Court's "primary authority to interpret [the Bill of Rights],"[34] and suggested that the framers of the Fourteenth Amendment deliberately acted to preserve that authority. The real history of this period shows anything but. Indeed, in the first principal draft of the amendment, introduced by Bingham in February and again in April 1866, the Court was given no authority with respect to the new rights created; enforcement was entirely left to the Congress.[35] Had that version passed, we would have a Fourteenth Amendment that is a grant of power to Congress, without any independent basis for judicial review whatsoever. For a variety of reasons, however, the amendment was altered to include Section 1, which forbids states from abridging the privileges or immunities of citizens or denying due process of law or equal protection of the law, and Section 5, which empowers Congress to enforce those limitations. This version undoubtedly was designed to authorize judicial review under the new amendment, but it was also designed to ensure that Congress had the primary role. Oliver Morton, Republican of Indiana, explained that "the remedy for the violation of the fourteenth and fifteenth amendments was expressly not left to the courts. The remedy was legislative, because in each the amendment itself provided that it shall be enforced by legislation on the part of Congress."[36]

For the next seventy years after passage of the Fourteenth Amendment, the Supreme Court's performance was substantially less than heroic. It abandoned the core purpose of the Fourteenth Amendment—protection of the civil rights of black Americans—and embarked on a role of second-guessing economic legislation. The general outlines of this period are well known, and I shall not describe them in detail. The extremity of the Court's dereliction of its duty to civil rights enforcement, however, may not be widely appreciated.

The segregation issue serves as an example. Between 1870 and 1875, Congress debated and enacted legislation that would have outlawed racial segregation in inns, railroads, and other common carriers and places of public accommodation. This became the Civil Rights Act of 1875. (A provision extending the law to public schools was accepted by majorities in both the House and the Senate but, because of procedural maneuvering, could not be adopted without a two-thirds vote, which it did not attain; consequently, schools were left out of the bill.)[37] In congressional debate, it was widely assumed, even by Democratic opponents, that Congress had authority to pass such legislation if the states themselves were responsible for the segregation. The controversial issue was whether Congress had authority to pass such legislation when state law was silent or even (as many opponents of the law insisted) provided a legal remedy.[38] When the constitutionality of the legislation reached the Supreme Court in 1883, the Court sided with the Democratic opponents, holding that Congress lacked the power to enact civil rights legislation unless the states themselves had violated the Constitution. "If the [state] laws themselves make any unjust discrimination," the Court observed, however, "Congress has full power to afford a remedy."[39] This was, in my opinion, a needlessly narrow interpretation of congressional authority,[40] but it was not beyond the pale of reasonable construction.

Later in the decade of the 1880s, southern states began to enact Jim Crow legislation requiring strict racial segregation of railroads and other facilities. This was precisely the sort of legislation that even Democratic opponents of the Civil Rights Act of 1875 had conceded was within the prohibitory scope of the Fourteenth Amendment.[41] Yet in *Plessy v. Ferguson*, in 1896, the Supreme Court upheld state segregation laws, on the preposterous proposition that if segregation is perceived as inferior treatment, this is "solely because the colored race chooses to put that construction upon it."[42]

But, egregious as this was, the Court was to do worse. In *Cumming v. Board of Education*,[43] the Court effectively abandoned even the requirement that separate schools be equal. In that case, the school board of Augusta, Georgia closed the only black high school "for economic reasons," while supporting several high schools for white children. Despite this blatant inequality, the Supreme Court, in an opinion by Justice John Marshall Harlan, author of the famed dissent in *Plessy*, held that the court could supply no remedy. The court could not order the expenditure of funds on a black high school, and to order closure of the white high schools "would only . . . take from white children educational privileges enjoyed by them, without giving to colored children additional opportunities."[44] That made any enforcement of the "equal" half of "separate but equal" impossible. Then, in perhaps the most extreme of this series of decisions, the Court upheld the power of the Commonwealth of Kentucky to forbid even a private religious college to educate black and white children together, on pain of criminal prosecution.[45]

Thus, in a few short decades, the nation proceeded from a legal regime in which the federal government barred racial segregation, to one in which only formal state-mandated segregation was unconstitutional, to one in which segregation was permitted when facilities are materially equal, to one in which facilities could be not only separate but unequal and indeed nonexistent, to one in which even private, noncommercial, religious associations with conscientious beliefs to the contrary could be required to conform to the state's segregationist ideology.

The Court's record in enforcing voting rights under the Fifteenth Amendment was, if anything, even more dismal. The Fifteenth Amendment, ratified in 1870, had been an immediate success. Black citizens voted and were elected to office in large numbers during the 1870s and into the 1880s. After the end of Reconstruction, however, black voters were progressively disenfranchised.

The Supreme Court's failure to defend black voting rights is best illustrated by its 1903 decision in *Giles v. Harris,* written by no less eminent a jurist than Oliver Wendell Holmes.[46] The case involved an intricate scheme, embodied in the Alabama Constitution, to limit the vote to white citizens. The Supreme Court upheld jurisdiction in the case, but denied relief on two grounds. First, noting that the "plaintiff alleges that the whole registration scheme of the Alabama constitution is a fraud upon the Constitution of the United States," the Court held that it would "make the court a party to the unlawful scheme" if the court "accept[ed] it and add[ed] another voter to its fraudulent lists."[47] In other words, since the disenfranchisement of black voters made the entire system a fraud and a sham, the Court could not order the registration of black voters without becoming a party to the sham. This is surely one of the greatest examples of double talk in the annals of the U.S. Reports. Second, the Court held that it lacked "practical power" to enforce relief. "[S]omething more than ordering the plaintiff's name to be inscribed upon the lists of 1902 will be needed," because "[i]f the conspiracy and the intent exist, a name on a piece of paper will not defeat them." In other words, because the state might not honor the voting registration, the Court would not require the registration, even if the plaintiff had established a right to be registered. If that is not an invitation to lawlessness, what is?

This failure to enforce the Fifteenth Amendment was arguably more serious than any dereliction under the Fourteenth. The principal reason the black citizens of the South required protection from unequal laws is that they had been deprived of any political clout in the southern legislatures. The vote is the most effective protection of all. Without the vote, the black population of the South was at the mercy of hostile legislators.

Some may point out that, even if it was belated, the courts eventually were the instrument of reform of segregation and voting rights, citing *Brown v. Board of Education*. It is important to give the courts their due, and there were heroic moments in the great civil rights struggle of the 1950s and 1960s. But the courts should not be allowed to take all the credit. As Gerald Rosenberg has shown, serious desegregation of southern school systems did not occur until more than a decade after *Brown*, and the institution that forced the eventual change was not the Court, but Congress.[48] And the courts did not begin to address the disenfranchisement of black citizens until Congress enacted the Voting Rights Act of 1965. That was one of the most successful pieces of reform legislation in American history, resulting in the enfranchisement of substantial numbers of black voters within a very few years.

But we are now getting ahead of the story. Between the end of Reconstruction and the middle of the twentieth century, the Supreme Court succeeded in inverting the Fourteenth Amendment. Although the principal purpose of the Amendment was to guarantee civil equality of the races, the Court essentially abandoned that purpose and ushered in Jim Crow with decisions like *Plessy*, *Cumming*, and *Giles*. At the same time, the Court embarked on a period of judicial activism in the service of laissez-faire economics, in the name of the due process clause. The most famous of these decisions was *Lochner v. New York*, in which the Court held that the State of New York could not constitutionally enact a maximum-hour law for bakers. *Lochner* has been so thoroughly condemned by so many commentators, and the Court itself, that I will not pause to heap on more criticism. But it is important to stress that *Lochner* was misguided not because it protected rights of an economic nature; the Constitution contains many economic liberties, which are and should be enforced as vigorously as any others. *Lochner* was misguided because the right it purported to protect is nowhere to be found in the Constitution, and the doctrine of "substantive due process" on which the decision rested is nothing more than a roving commission for courts to second-guess legislative judgments.

Unfortunately, in the decades following the New Deal, and especially after *Brown v. Board of Education*, the courts became ever more aggressive in their review of political judgments, and took ever more imaginative liberties with the constitutional text. Part of the activism of the Warren Court was salutary and legitimate; part was politically desirable (from my point of view) but illegitimate; and part was neither wise nor legitimate. The Burger Court, far from being an improvement, exacerbated the worst tendencies of the Warren Court, and rendered some of the most far-fetched and misguided decisions, on subjects such as abortion, aid to religious schools, family law, and federalism. Under the Burger Court, the multipart "test," which means anything or nothing, became the centerpiece of constitutional interpretation, thus maximizing judicial power and discretion and rendering Congress, the President, and the states secondary authorities, free to decide only those matters not important enough to be captured by courts and lawyers. The Rehnquist Court has retreated substantially from this high-water point of judicial activism, but the major precedents have not been reexamined, and the vision of the justices as the high priests of our constitutional religion continues to capture their vanity and their imagination. Indeed, in some respects (state sovereign immunity and its relation to Congress's power to enforce the Fourteenth Amendment being the most prominent), the Rehnquist Court carries on the tradition of judicial activism, though in service of a different set of constitutional principles.

There is no particular reason to suppose that judges will make better decisions than elected legislators. Moreover, it is clear that judicial error can have more severe and long-lasting consequence than legislative error. When legislators are wrong, the people can turn them out of office and adopt new policies. Judicial errors, by contrast, are embedded in the law and extraordinarily difficult to correct. It is one thing to say that the time-honored principles reflected in the text of the Constitution should prevail over the products of representative government, quite another to say that the political judgments of judges should take precedence.

As of 1940, Attorney General Robert Jackson, later to become one of the more distinguished members of the Court, offered this assessment of the Supreme Court's historic role in the constitutional order. Jackson wrote that "time has proved that [the Supreme Court's judgment] was wrong on the most outstanding issues upon which it has chosen to challenge the popular branches." He continued:

[The Court's] judgment in the *Dred Scott* case was overruled by war. Its judgment that the currency that preserved the Union could not be made legal tender was overruled by Grant's selection of an additional Justice. Its judgment invalidating the income tax was overruled by the Sixteenth Amendment. Its judgments repressing labor and social legislation are now abandoned. Many of the judgments against New Deal legislation are rectified by confession of error. *In no major conflict with the representative branches on any question of social or economic policy has time vindicated the Court.*[49]

And the Court's mistakes have not been confined to peripheral questions. Some have concerned the most important moral, political, constitutional question that any society has to face: whether a category of human persons is unworthy of the protection that is accorded their fellow human beings. The Court has too frequently stumbled on that question, beginning with *Dred Scott*, and moving through *Plessy*, *Giles*, and *Korematsu*; many would add *Roe* and *Casey* to that list. Jackson's conclusion that "in no major conflict with the representative branches on any question of social or economic policy has time vindicated the court" is too harsh. But the usual celebratory account of the Supreme Court's role in our history is too generous. A more balanced understanding, I believe, should lead to greater humility in the exercise of the power of judicial review.

Notes

1. 505 U.S. 868, 866–67 (1992).
2. 117 S.Ct. 2157 (1997). See Michael W. McConnell, "Comment: Institutions and Interpretation: A Critique of City of Boerne v. Flores," 111 *Harvard Law Review* 153 (1997).
3. *City of Boerne v. Flores*, 2172.
4. 5 U.S. (1 Cranch) 137 (1803).
5. Gerald Gunther and Kathleen M. Sullivan, *Constitutional Law*, 13th ed. (Foundation Press, 1997).
6. In more recent times, it has become common for daring professors to present the revisionist view: that Marshall's arguments were not very good. This may be worse. It suggests to the students that the legitimacy of constitutional decisionmaking does not depend on sound reasoning from proper authority, but from raw judicial power.
7. 60 U.S. (19 How.) 393 (1857).
8. See Gunther and Sullivan, *Constitutional Law*.
9. Paul Brest and Sandford Levinson, *Process of Constitutional Decisionmaking: Cases and Materials*, 3d ed. (Boston: Little, Brown, 1992), 193.
10. 163 U.S. 537 (1896).
11. 198 U.S. 45 (1905).
12. 347 U.S. 483 (1954).
13. But see Michael W. McConnell, "Originalism and the Desegregation Decisions," 81 *Virginia Law Review* 947 (1995).
14. 358 U.S. 1 (1958).
15. "[*Marbury*] declared the basic principle that the federal judiciary is supreme in the exposition of the law of the Constitution, and that principle has

ever since been respected by this Court and the Country as a permanent and indispensable feature of our constitutional system. It follows that the interpretation of the Fourteenth Amendment enunciated by this Court in the Brown case is the supreme law of the land, and Art. VI of the Constitution makes it of binding effect on the States." Ibid., 18.

16. I am not suggesting that any, or all, of these cases were wrongly decided by conventional legal interpretive standards, but that whether they were correctly decided as a matter of law is seen as beside the point. Good results are what matter.

17. 2 U.S. (2 Dall.) 419 (1793).

18. See David P. Currie, *The Constitution in Congress: The Federalist Period, 1789–1801* (Chicago: University of Chicago Press, 1997); Kent Greenfield, "Original Penumbras: Constitutional Interpretation in the First Year of Congress," 26 *Connecticut Law Review* 799 (1993).

19. 1 *Annals of Congress* 560 (Joseph Gales, ed., 1789) (Abraham Baldwin).

20. Ibid., 486 (John Lawrence).

21. For excellent discussions of these issues, see David E. Engdahl, "John Marshall's 'Jeffersonian' Concept of Judicial Review," 42 *Duke Law Journal* 279 (1992); James M. O'Fallon, "Marbury," 44 *Stanford Law Review* 219 (1992).

22. 11 *Annals of Congress* 179; see Engdahl, "John Marshall's 'Jeffersonian' Concept," 320–21.

23. See Engdahl, "John Marshall's 'Jeffersonian' Concept," 297–304.

24. Reprinted in Richard Hofstadter, ed., *Great Issues in American History* (New York: Vintage, 1958), 2:184, 185.

25. 37 U.S. (12 Pet.) 254 (1938).

26. 60 U.S. (19 How.) 353 (1857).

27. See Stanley Kutler, *Judicial Power and Reconstruction Politics* (Chicago: University of Chicago Press, 1968), 14.

28. *Planned Parenthood v. Casey*, 867.

29. Abraham Lincoln's First Inaugural Address, in *A Documentary History of the United States*, ed. Richard Heffner, 5th ed. (New York: New American Library, 1991), 144, 149. On Lincoln's views of judicial authority, see, e.g., John Agresto, *The Supreme Court and Constitutional Democracy* (Ithaca: Cornell University Press, 1984), 86–95; Sanford Levinson, *Constitutional Faith* (Princeton: Princeton University Press, 1988), 39; Michael Stokes Paulsen, "The Most Dangerous Branch: Executive Power to Say What the Law Is," 83 *Georgia Law Journal* 217, 272–84 (1994).

30. 12 Stat. 432 (June 19, 1862).

31. 14 Stat. 27 (1866).

32. 74 U.S. (7 Wall.) 506 (1869).

33. *Congressional Globe*, 40th Cong., 2d Sess. 488.

34. *City of Boerne v. Flores*, 2166.

35. "The Congress shall have power to make all laws which shall be necessary and proper to secure to the citizens of each state the privileges and immunities of citizens in the several states and to all persons in the several states, equal protection in the rights of life liberty and property." *Congressional Globe*, 39th Cong., 1st Sess. 1034 (1866).

36. *Congressional Globe*, 42d Cong., 2d Sess. 525 (1872).
37. See McConnell, "Originalism and the Desegregation Decisions," 947.
38. Ibid., 1029–36.
39. *The Civil Rights Cases*, 109 U.S. 3, 25 (1883).
40. See McConnell, "Originalism and the Desegregation Decisions," 1091.
41. Ibid., 1029–36, 1122–23.
42. *Plessy v. Ferguson*, 551.
43. 175 U.S. 528 (1899).
44. Ibid., 544.
45. *Berea College v. Kentucky*, 211 U.S. 45 (1908).
46. 189 U.S. 475 (1903).
47. Ibid., 486.
48. Gerald Rosenberg, *The Hollow Hope* (Chicago: University of Chicago Press, 1991).
49. Robert H. Jackson, *The Struggle for Judicial Supremacy* (New York: Alfred Knopf, 1949), ix–x.

CHAPTER 9

Judicial Review and Republican Government

Jeremy Waldron

I

IN THIS COUNTRY we pride ourselves on having a republican form of government. By that I do not mean government by the likes of Herbert Hoover, Richard Nixon, or Ronald Reagan, of course; I mean "republican" in the sense used in Article 4 of the U.S. Constitution: "The United States shall guarantee to every State in this Union a Republican form of Government."[1]

The word *republican* refers to a form of government in which public affairs are governed *as* public affairs by the members of the public—the citizens—acting together as statesmen. A good definition of "republican government" should include two aspects that command our attention.[2] First and more important, it should emphasize the responsibility of the whole citizenry for the public affairs of the society, not just a particular elite. And second, it should draw an important connection between the subject matter of government—public affairs—and the spirit in which the citizenry are supposed to participate. They are to participate in politics not merely as acquisitive egoists devoted to their private interests, but as statesmen, that is, as people who feel a strong responsibility for public affairs qua public affairs. This does not mean that individual interests have nothing to do with public affairs. It is surely the case that the public interest is some function of individual interests (though perhaps not a simple function); and it is certainly not the case that the public-spirited citizen makes no mention or takes no cognizance at all of his own interests in his public deliberations. There are many views about the proper relation between private interests and public interest in republican politics, but the important point is that the relation between them is an open question: in other words, "my views about the public interest" and "my pursuit of my own interest" denote distinct ideas for each citizen, and in republican politics the former, not the latter, is taken as the leading idea.

In modern discussions of "civic republicanism,"[3] the second of these aspects is emphasized in a way that sometimes eclipses the first. Civic republicans stress that *whoever* participates in politics should do so in a public-spirited way: so the claim that judges, legislators, and other officials (as well as scholars, commentators, and lobbyists) should take the public good rather than private interest as their point of orientation is sometimes regarded as a republican claim irrespective of its connection or lack of connection with any proposition about the suffrage or about citizen participation generally. This truncated view of republican government is perhaps understandable in the light of two important points. First, civic republicans have been at pains to emphasize their differences with traditional liberalism, and the issue about political motivation or point of orientation is crucial for that. Liberals (especially those of the "pluralist" persuasion)[4] are reputed to model politics in terms of individual participants' pursuit of their own interests, with the public interest emerging (if at all) by some sort of invisible hand.[5] Civic republicans are opposed to that, so they tend to seize on *any* opportunity to highlight political roles devoted explicitly to the pursuit of the public good.

Second, republican government is rightly regarded as not exactly identical with democratic government; and it is sometimes thought that this can be brought out only by downplaying the role of full citizen-suffrage in republican models. There are important differences between the concept of a republic and the concept of a democracy. Democracy implies that in principle citizenship and suffrage should be extended to every adult member of the society, whereas republicanism is compatible with the idea of the citizenry comprising only those with a substantial stake in the society (like a property franchise, for example). Also, the idea of democracy is indifferent as to the issue of participants' motivation or orientation or virtue, in a way that republicanism is not. Nevertheless, there are important affinities between the two ideals. Many modern democratic theorists phrase their ideal in terms of "*deliberative* democracy."[6] The idea of deliberative democracy is quite close to that of republican government, inasmuch as it stresses citizens' orientation to the public good. Moreover, although the term *republican* does leave open the issue of criteria for citizenship, still we can say something like this: the more restrictive the criteria for citizenship, the more the citizen body begins to look like a special elite of nobles, oligarchs, or plutocrats, and the less republican the system of government appears. Thus the *tendency* of republicanism is to attribute citizenship to everyone who has anything approaching a permanent stake in the commonwealth. Certainly in our own time, republican politics without something like familiar institutions of democratic suffrage is unthinkable; and it could not be offered today as a plausible interpretation of the American system of government (let alone as a plausible interpretation of the provision in Article 4).

Let me add one or two more comments about the importance of citizen participation in a republic, for it is a delicate issue, and easily misunderstood. We need to understand the republican approach to the suffrage in two steps. First, the republican sets up the idea of "the citizen." The idea of the citizen is not the idea of a political specialist, and it does not simply expand or contract its meaning according to a user's views about how political authority should be distributed. The idea of the citizen is in the first instance the idea of an ordinary full member of the society—a member of the public whose affairs are properly comprised in the res publica, or a member of the community whose interests are properly comprised in the idea of the "commonwealth." The second step—a distinct and crucial step—is to say that, in a republic, politics should be conducted among those who are full ordinary members in this sense. Politics should not be seen as the special preserve of some extraordinary subset of the members: politics is about the public and common affairs of the citizens and it is to be conducted among the citizens on that basis.

It does not follow that republican politics is necessarily participatory politics, along the lines (say) of direct democracy. Republican politics may operate through a settled system of representation and offices, and there may even be in a republic (as there certainly are in ours) people who make officeholding their vocation. The acceptance of such structures is not incompatible with republican opposition to the idea of an exclusive political caste. If there *are* representatives or professional politicians, their role is to be understood (in republican theory) as one of responsibility to the ordinary citizens who make up the public. That responsibility is not just a matter of ethos—a sort of noblesse oblige, like the sense in which a king might feel responsible for his subjects. It is characteristically a matter of institutionalized accountability, so that the system of representation and the professional pursuit of politics are understood by everyone as a means—a complicated but still a realistic means—by which the members of the public ultimately govern their own public affairs. In modern republics, presidents, governors, senators, and legislators are chosen by elections in which all citizens are eligible to participate; and they have terms at the end of which they must either abandon their office, or offer themselves to the members of the public for reelection (in circumstances where the members of the public may choose someone else instead). These electoral structures, and the apparatus of parties, primaries, and campaigns that go with them, enable us to see high executive and legislative office as a representative form of republican government. Thus in a system of this sort, important decisions about public affairs—lawmaking, policymaking, or the great issues of state—are still made by officials and institutions in the name of the public and in a way that is responsive, directly or indirectly, to all the members of the public whose affairs these decisions ultimately are. Moreover, if an ordinary individual offers herself for public office, or puts forward some criticism of the conduct of those in public office, in a republic she is not to be told that this is none of her business, or that that is an inappropriate posture for the likes of her.[7] Unless there is some special reason for disqualifying her (such as felony, lunacy, infancy, or association with royalty), an ordinary citizen in a republic has as much standing to participate in politics, even professional politics, as anyone in the society. In this sense, republican government involves a deep commitment to political equality. As citizens we are one another's equals so far as our stake and standing in political affairs are concerned. Structures of office and representation and political career may establish forms of political inequality; but the republican conviction is that these are both superficial (by comparison with the deeper political egalitarianism) and answerable to that fundamental republican equality.

This may all sound quite weak. It may appear that we can always concoct "a justification" for a given surface inequality (between representative and constituent, say, or between ruler and subject). In fact, however, it involves insistence on something quite robust. Effectively, republicanism limits the kind of justification one can offer for political inequalities. One may not say: "This limit on the franchise or this system of plural voting is a way of getting the best rulers, and that is why the inequality is acceptable." Nor may one say: "This political hierarchy furnishes the best means by which the polity can serve the equally considered interests of the citizens." To appeal to the idea of "the best ruler" as a fundamental evaluative criterion is to introduce nonrepublican aristocratic ideas. And to appeal only to what serves citizens' interests is, at most, to fall back on a liberal conception of why citizenship matters, ignoring the active side of it—government *by* the people, not just *for* the people—that is equally, if not more, important for republicanism. A republican theorist can defend specialization and even functional inequality; but the defense must be that such structures represent the best way of articulating and applying the background ideal of active self-government by citizens who are to treat one another as equals, in the circumstances of a modern crowded state. For even if those circumstances are such as to make the active equality of citizens difficult to discern, it becomes all the more important that it be seen as a point of reference and the basis of justification in republican political argument.

I have gone on at length about this, because there is one other approach to the revival of republican theorizing (besides "truncated" republicanism) that I would like to caution against. Classic thinkers whom we categorize as "republican" or "civic republican"—Aristotle, Cicero, Machiavelli (in some moods), Harrington, Sidney, Rousseau (in some moods), Montesquieu, James Wilson, Publius (in some moods), even Hannah Arendt—all held a variety of political, constitutional, and jurisprudential positions. Some of these positions are explained by their republican commitments, others are rationalized on republican grounds, while still others have only the most tenuous connection, or no connection at all, with anything recognizable as republicanism.[8] Once we recognize this, it is clearly dangerous to attempt to define republicanism either as the union or the intersection of all the political positions held by the thinkers we call "republican."[9] The union-set would obviously be way too capacious. But even the apparent rigor of looking only in the intersection-set might be misleading: for there may be a position that every republican theorist happened to be committed to, and for which every one of them was eager to concoct a "republican justification," even though the best explanation of their holding such a position had nothing to do with their republican commitments. I suspect that the commitment of many republican thinkers to values like "the rule of law" and (throughout much of the history of republican thinking) "male suffrage" and "virtual representation" is of this kind. Accordingly I would like to warn against the sort of "hunt and peck" approach that many self-styled republican theorists take today. They have a favorite political position of their own that they want to defend (judicial supremacy, for example); they think they can defend it on the basis of a value like the rule of law; they notice that many classic republican theorists were committed to the rule of law; so they call that a "republican" justification. In my view, that sort of hunt-and-peck approach is sophomoric. It not only fails to distinguish between fundamental, derivative, and merely rationalized positions, but even on the occasions that it comes up with a genuinely republican commitment—civic virtue, for example—it usually applies that to modern political problems in a literal-minded way without any consideration of how the deeper republican values that the position embodies might play out in the complex circumstances of modern life.[10] Accordingly, in what follows I will take time out to excoriate what I see as instances of this approach, whenever they appear, together with the "truncated" republicanism I talked about earlier in this section.

II

The question for this chapter concerns judicial review of legislation, and it can be formulated as follows. If we begin with the underlying idea of republican government, what view should we take of a political system in which important issues of public principle are decided finally by majority-voting in panels of professional judges, appointed for life, whose decisions are made after, and whose decisions prevail over, decisions made in legislative assemblies by the accountable representatives of the people?

That is a rather abstract (not to mention long-winded) description of a political system: but I mean it to capture the gist of political decision-making in the United States of America, so far as the protection of individual rights is concerned. The same question can be posed more specifically. When a court strikes down a statute restricting abortion,[11] or reforming campaign finance laws,[12] or regulating the marketplace[13]—a statute passed after careful deliberation by Congress or a state assembly, by legislators responsible directly to the people the ordering of whose affairs is at stake—how does that square with the constitutional guarantee that in this country politics will be republican in character? How does it square with the idea that in this country and in these states, the public will be its own governor on matters of high principle as well as on matters of low policy, and that ordinary men and women, ordinary citizens, should be the ones who decide, ultimately on equal terms, about the conditions and ordering of their common life together?

I must confess that these questions are intended to sound rhetorical, indeed to prejudice readers in favor of the view that something sits ill in the juxtaposition of judicial review of legislation and the guarantee of republican government. But answers have been offered, and we should take the time to evaluate them. I want to consider three main classes of answer. First, in section III, I shall consider the view that judicial review is compatible with republicanism inasmuch as it represents the view of the people as to how their self-government should be conducted. Second, in section IV, I shall consider the opinion (defended by Ronald Dworkin in a recent book) that judicial review of legislation promotes republican values by improving the quality of public debate on matters of principle. Third, in section V, I shall look at the argument that judicial review is necessary as a means of safeguarding a republican framework—the view put forward by John Hart Ely and others. Each of these arguments is important in its own right, but each of them also in various ways offers to betray the idea of republican government in the light of something that seems to the proponent more important—popular sovereignty, scholarly culture, and procedural respectability.

Finally—in section VI—I will insist again, as I insisted in the opening section, that republican government is a demanding ideal and that many of the current, rather sloppy attempts to reconcile it with the institution of judicial review seriously underestimate what is involved in self-government by the citizen body.

III

If we did not want an interesting discussion, we could simply say that the very same Constitution that guarantees republican government also re-

quires judicial review of legislation, and so there cannot be any contra-
diction or tension between the two. But, first, that assumes the U.S. Constitution is consistent, which may be one of the points at issue. Second, it
begs the question of whether the Constitution actually *does* require judicial review. It is possible to read the text in a way that generates such a
requirement: Articles 3 (1) and 6 (2) are certainly open to that interpretation.[14] It is less clear, however, that this is a *republican* interpretation.
Would a true republican theorist move as readily as Chief Justice Marshall did from the texts just mentioned to the proposition that it is emphatically the province and duty of the judicial department to say what
the law is?[15] Would a republican be happy with the way in which this has
developed into a general doctrine that when Congress and the Court differ as to the general meanings they attribute to the constitutional text, the
meaning held by the least representative branch is the one that should
prevail?[16] More generally, one might emphasize how strongly classic republicans were committed to the value of *the rule of law*.[17] But if that
were not to lapse into the "hunt and peck" approach I warned against
earlier, it would have to involve a showing that the rule of law *in a republican sense* (as opposed to any of the other senses in which that extraordinarily complex and popular ideal could be cashed out) requires judicial supremacy over representative lawmaking institutions even when
the law is quite uncertain and controversial.[18]

I do not mean to deny the constitutional legitimacy of judicial review.
It is evidently a well-established practice in the United States, and has established itself as part of the real (even if not the textual) constitution.
But it has never been without its critics, at least as regards judicial supremacy. Indeed, one of the best-known misgivings by one of the best-
known Americans—

> [T]he candid citizen must confess that if the policy of the government upon
> vital questions, affecting the whole people, is to be irrevocably fixed by deci-
> sions of the Supreme Court, the instant they are made, in ordinary litigation
> between parties, in personal actions, the people will have ceased to be their
> own rulers, having, to that extent, practically resigned their government, into
> the hands of that eminent tribunal[19]

—sure sounds like a *republican* misgiving to me. So the questions I have
posed about an apparent tension between republican ideas and judicial
review remain open.

One of the reasons judicial review of legislation flourishes as a constitutional practice in the United States despite its ambiguous textual pedigree is that it has always enjoyed a great deal of public support. Might its
republican credentials be restored therefore by arguing—not implausibly—that this is one of the means by which the citizens of the United
States have elected to govern themselves? An argument along these

lines—though in the context of proposals to introduce judicial review in the United Kingdom—was once attempted by Ronald Dworkin. On his view, any objection to judicial review based on the republican ideal of self-government by the citizens would be self-defeating because polls reveal that more than 71 percent of the citizens of the United Kingdom believed that the British system of government would be improved by the incorporation of a Bill of Rights.[20] Indeed if judicial review is introduced in the United Kingdom (as it has been, very recently, though in a rather attenuated form),[21] it will not be as something that the British have inherited because it seemed like a good idea to a bunch of slave-owning white supremacists living on the edge of an undeveloped continent more than two hundred years ago, but because the British people have decided to take control of their politic institutions and, for the first time, govern themselves in the way that *they* want and not their ancestors.

Unfortunately, however, the republican difficulty cannot be disposed of so easily. The fact that there is support among the citizens, even overwhelming support, for a constitutional practice does not make the practice republican. I guess that if the people want a regime of judicial review, then that is what they should have: that is what the idea of republican self-government requires, so far as constitutional practice and constitutional change are concerned. But we must not confuse the reason for carrying out a proposal with the character of the proposal itself. If the citizens voted to experiment with dictatorship, republican principles might give us a reason to allow them to do so. But it would not follow that dictatorship is a republican form of government.

Let me put the matter more theoretically. There is a distinction between republican self-government and popular sovereignty. The principle of popular sovereignty requires that the people should have whatever constitution, whatever form of government they want. But popular sovereignty does not remove or blur the differences that exist among the various forms of government on the menu from which the people are supposed to choose.[22] It is possible for republican self-government to self-destruct by republican means, and one of the questions we have to confront is whether popular enthusiasm for judicial review (where it does not presently exist) should count as an example of that.

IV

A different line of argument, also pursued by Ronald Dworkin,[23] concerns the effect of judicial review on the character of public debate.[24] Dworkin acknowledges that modern civic republicans (among others) are concerned that citizens should engage actively in political deliberation, and that some of them have misgivings about judicial review because they think it tends to undermine this engagement by removing important decisions of principle from the democratic forum. Dworkin believes, however, that from a republican point of view the quality of public debate may actually be better on this account:

> When an issue is seen as constitutional . . . and as one that will ultimately be resolved by courts applying general constitutional principles, the quality of public argument is often improved, because the argument concentrates from the start on questions of political morality. . . . When a constitutional issue has been decided by the Supreme Court, and is important enough so that it can be expected to be elaborated, expanded, contracted, or even reversed by future decisions, a sustained national debate begins, in newspapers and other media, in law schools and classrooms, in public meetings and around dinner tables. That debate better matches [the] conception of republican government, in its emphasis on matters of principle, than almost anything the legislative process on its own is likely to produce.[25]

He cites as an example the great debate about abortion surrounding the Supreme Court's decision in *Roe v. Wade*, saying it has involved many more people and has led to a more subtle appreciation of the complexities involved than in other countries where the final decision about abortion was assigned to elected legislatures. As a result of entrusting it to the courts,

> Americans better understand, for instance, the distinction between the question whether abortion is morally and ethically permissible, on the one hand, and the question whether government has the right to prohibit it, on the other; they also better understand the more general and constitutionally crucial idea on which that distinction rests: that individuals have rights that may work against the general will or the collective interest or good.[26]

In this way, Dworkin thinks, a system of final decision by judges on certain great issues of principle may actually enhance the republican character of our politics.

I am afraid I do not agree with any of this. Consider first what is said about political discussion. Dworkin acknowledges that he is making tentative empirical claims about the quality of public debate. My experience is that national debates about abortion are as robust, as statesmanlike, and as well informed in countries like the United Kingdom and New Zealand, where they are not constitutionalized, as they are in the United States—the more so perhaps because they are uncontaminated by quibbling about how to interpret the text of an eighteenth-century document. It is sometimes liberating to be able to discuss issues like abortion directly, on the principles that ought to be engaged, rather than having to scramble around constructing those principles out of the scraps of some sacred text, in a tendentious exercise of constitutional calligraphy. Think of how much more wisely capital punishment has been discussed (and disposed of) in countries where the debate has not had to center around the moral reading of the phrase "cruel and unusual punishment," but could focus instead on broader aims of penal policy and on dangers more morally pressing than "unusualness," such as the execution of the innocent. It is simply a myth that the public requires a moral debate to be, first, an interpretive debate before it can be conducted with any dignity or sophistication.

Or consider the debate about homosexual law reform initiated by the 1957 Wolfenden Report in Great Britain, and sustained in the famous exchange between Lord Devlin and H. L. A. Hart in the 1960s.[27] Despite their focus on the decisions of a legislature (the British Parliament), these authors seemed to evince a perfectly adequate grasp of the distinction between whether something is morally permissible and whether government has the right to prohibit it. They did not need to be taught that by a court. Indeed, if the U.S. Supreme Court's intervention on a similar issue is anything to go by, the American debate is actually impoverished by its constitutionalization. As Mary Ann Glendon has remarked, the decision in *Bowers v. Hardwick*[28] is remarkable for the "lack of depth and seriousness of the analysis contained in its majority and dissenting opinions," compared with the discussion that has taken place in other countries.[29] If the debate that actually takes place in American society and American legislatures is anywhere near as good as that in other countries, it is so *despite* the Supreme Court's framing of the issues, not because of it.

Still, suppose Dworkin is right that the quality of public discussion may be improved by citizens' awareness that the final disposition of some issue of principle is to be taken out of the hands of their elected representatives and assigned instead to a court. The idea that civic republicans should count this as a gain is a travesty: it is the "truncated" version of republicanism we noted in section I. True republicans are interested in *practical political deliberation among the citizenry*, which is not just any old debating exercise, but a form of discussion among those who are about to participate in a binding collective decision. A starstruck people may speculate about what the Supreme Court will do next on abortion or some similar issue; they may even amuse each other, as we law professors do, with stories of how *we* would decide, in the (unlikely) event that we were elevated to that eminent tribunal. The exercise of power by a few black-robed celebrities can certainly be expected to *fascinate* an articulate population. But that is hardly the essence of active citizenship. Perhaps such impotent debating is nevertheless morally improving: Dworkin may be right that "there is no necessary connection between a citizen's political impact or influence and the ethical benefit he secures through participating in public discussion."[30] But independent ethical benefits of this kind are at best desirable side-effects, hardly the primary point of civic participation in republican political theory.

And this is to say nothing of the negative effects of judicial review on a political culture. The low quality of legislative debate and electoral politics in the United States—unique among modern advanced democracies—makes it hard to resist the impression that political deliberation suffers when final decisions on issues of principle are assigned to a nonparticipatory and nonaccountable body. If legislators are encouraged to think that they need not address great issues of right and principle—because those issues will be taken care of by the courts—or if they know that the courts exist as backup to remedy whatever impulsive or irresponsible decisions they make, they may pay less attention to the quality of their contributions, and make them less seriously and more irresponsibly. Certainly, to the extent that there is an institutional division of labor in the United States—with final political decisions on matters of high principle being assigned to nonelective institutions and final political decisions on matters of policy being assigned to elective institutions—it is easy for those who participate in the latter to come to think of their deliberation as appropriately different in form and orientation from serious moral statesmanship. If this is true then the danger that ordinary politics will be taken over once again by the interplay of private interests is heightened, not lessened, by the practice of judicial review.

There is another danger also, and that is of a political culture increasingly dominated by the idea of *litigation* as the dominant form of social and political initiative. I see this in American law schools where the best and brightest of our young people who might be expected to engage with politics are encouraged to think of the courts and constitutional litigation, rather than republican politics, as the main agents of legal change. The encouragement comes from their teachers—law professors—many of whom remain utterly preoccupied with a sort of fetishism of the higher judiciary and oriented almost exclusively to the courts as agents of the kind of changes in the law that they as legal scholars think themselves entitled to propose.[31] The result is a sort of marginalization in legal thought of what one would expect to be the major source of law in a democratic society: the elected state and federal legislatures. U.S. jurisprudence has almost nothing to say about legislatures, certainly nothing positive or helpful. Even theorists of the "legal process" school, who pride themselves on treating adjudication as just one process among others in an interlocking array, relegate legislation by a democratic assembly "to a residual status, a last ditch instrument to be used when the powers of rational deliberation fail."[32] Legislatures exist, of course, and no one in the law schools denies that the elective legitimacy of these institutions plays an important role in the ordinary citizen's understanding of the law. But the consensus among legal scholars is that this is an ill-informed layman's conception: legislation, they suggest, is much less important, jurisprudentially, than most people think. Certainly they give the impression that legislative decision is not a source of law that in itself requires much philosophical attention.[33] The main contribution of legal theorists, so far as legislative assemblies are concerned, is to downplay the importance of what they do, impugn the legitimacy (and sometimes the rationality) of their procedures, and reclaim as much of their work as humanly possible for the courts to perform in the elaboration (or truncation) of legislative schemes. There is virtually no developed discussion in the legal theory literature of the moral or political basis of legislative authority and very little on the relation between their authority, the procedures they use, and the interpretation of the statutes they enact. Most theorists content themselves with saying that legislative assemblies claim democratic credentials and that the claim is largely unfounded. They accept that once a piece of legislation has been enacted, we all have a duty to make the best of it. But making the best of it means handing it over to the courts for revision and reconstruction; it rarely has anything to do with orienting its interpretation systematically to the ideal of popular self-government.

In a recent book, Roberto Unger relates all this to what he calls "discomfort with democracy," which, he says, is one of the "dirty little secrets of contemporary jurisprudence."[34] I think he is right,[35] and that the scandal he refers to must also be understood as a discomfort with self-government, and thus as an implicit repudiation of fundamental principles of republicanism. The discomfort with self-government shows up, Unger says, in every area of our legal culture:

> in the ceaseless identification of restraints upon majority rule, rather than of restraints upon the power of dominant minorities, as the overriding responsibility of judges and jurists; in the consequent hypertrophy of countermajoritarian practices and arrangements; in the opposition to all institutional reforms, particularly those designed to heighten the level of popular political engagement, as threats to a regime of rights; in the equation of the rights of property with rights of dissent; in the effort to obtain from judges, under cover of improving interpretations, the advances popular politics fail to deliver; in the abandonment of institutional reconstruction to rare and magical moments of national refoundation; in the single-minded focus upon the higher judges and their selection as the most important part of democratic politics; in an ideal of deliberative democracy as most acceptable when closest in style to a polite conversation among gentlemen in an eighteenth century drawing room; and, oc-

casionally, in the explicit treatment of party government as a subsidiary, last-ditch source of legal evolution, to be tolerated when none of the more refined modes of legal analysis applies.[36]

The explanation for all this is bitter and dishonorable. As much as anyone, the legal academic wants to be taken seriously. He wants to be thought of as doing important work, work that makes a difference to the world, a difference which is traceable *to him*. From this point of view, ordinary republican politics, conducted among the mass of citizens on roughly equal terms, is somewhat unappetising. The differences made by individuals are much harder to trace in the democratic process. There one acts collectively with millions of others, and an individual citizen can seldom bolster his vanity by pointing to the vote he cast or the dollars or energy he contributed to a campaign and saying, "There's the difference *I* made."[37] If one focuses, however, on courts as agents of change, then things are different. There the legal scholars can "stand in the imaginative position of judges, or whisper, figuratively or literally, into their ears." They can preen or fancy themselves as effective individual participants among only a few dozen "Madisonian notables" in a powerful political process—Unger calls it "black-robed providence"—which bypasses the unflatteringly cluttered realities of democratic life.[38] Never mind the patient and laborious business of assembling a legislative majority or getting someone elected: we are *legal* scholars; we know how to argue for change in a way that dispenses with all that.

I think this is terribly corrupting from a republican point of view. So my suggestion is almost exactly the opposite of the one by Dworkin with which this section began. Far from improving civic discourse, judicial review has had the effect in the United States of undermining our faith in any form of self-government that would take place genuinely among our hundreds of million of citizens. By furnishing the political culture with an alternative and flattering image of principled governance by a high-minded few, our legal scholars have turned their backs on the task of constructing a philosophy of law that is predicated seriously on the idea of self-government and the settling of principled disputes among the citizens in a republican manner.

V

A third, and somewhat more plausible attempt to reconcile republican government and judicial review goes as follows. Republican government is a great achievement (where it exists), but it is not self-sustaining. It depends on the integrity of certain structures and processes, and on the existence and effective maintenance of certain conditions and guarantees. If these are not attended to, then republican government may wither away or self-destruct. One of the ways in which this might happen is through legislation: a legislative enactment may attack or undercut republican structures. That, then, is why we have the institution of judicial review of legislation. The special task of the courts, on this suggestion, is to underwrite and uphold the conditions that are necessary for self-government, not to preempt it or its outcomes.

This form of argument is best known from the work of John Hart Ely, where it is presented as a way of reconciling judicial review with democracy.[39] Democratic self-government means that everyone has to have the right to vote; it means that genuine and open deliberation must be guaranteed; and it means that equal representation (particularly of minorities) must somehow be defined and secured. The idea is that legislation (or other forms of political action) that undermines these structures cannot be tolerated if the form of government is to remain republican (or democratic). So far, there is nothing that republican theorists need disagree with. Republican government certainly does require vigilance and constraint.

Whether it requires constraint of elective institutions by nonelective institutions is another matter. Ely, referring to a couple of situations where representative government seems to be undermining itself (such as when "the ins are choking off the channels of political change to ensure that they will stay in and the outs will stay out"), observes that "[o]bviously our elected representatives are the last persons we should trust with identification of . . . these situations."[40] He may be right; but if he is, that is, if the identification and remedy of these situations requires the intervention of a class of persons who are "comparative outsiders"[41] vis-à-vis self-government, then what has been shown is that republican self-government is *impossible* in an unalloyed form, not that the ideal of republican self-government involves or comprises the practice of judicial review.

For consider this. The issue of what count (in detail) as the appropriate forms and procedures for republican government is a matter of political and theoretical controversy. As citizens in a republic, we disagree among ourselves on a whole host of issues that may be presented as issues about what universal suffrage, unclogged channels of political change, and fair representation amount to. We disagree about proportional representation, the use of referendums or citizen initiatives, the frequency of elections, the imposition of term limits, the basis of electoral districting, state-funded access to television airtime for candidates, the publication of opinion polls in the final stages of election campaigns, and of course campaign finance restrictions. The existence of disagreements like these is characteristic of all modern democracies and all modern societies in which there is anything approaching a republican form of government. The situation that faces us is *not* one in which there is a well-known set of requirements for republican government, upon which legislatures will be tempted to trespass if not restrained by impartial judges. Instead, in the United States, for example, the situation is one in which citizens disagree and disagree reasonably about all these things, and when they attempt to resolve these disagreements (for the time being) by legislation or initiative, the judges (who also disagree among themselves about these matters) insist on the right to intervene, to review and invalidate legislation, and to impose their own view of these matters, arrived at, of course, by majority voting on the bench. That may or may not be a wise way of proceeding, but it is certainly not a republican way of proceeding. For the republican ideal, concerning any reasonable disagreement among the citizens on a matter of principle, is that the citizens should settle this by deliberation and decision among themselves, not by submitting to the tendentious decision-making of those whom Ely calls "comparative outsiders."

The decision on campaign finance legislation in *Buckley v. Valeo* is a fine example of this. Reasonable citizens disagreed on the matter; they still do. Throughout the 1970s there was a long debate on the issue both inside and outside our political institutions; eventually legislation was drafted and despite opposition and after considerable amendment to secure majority support, it was enacted. Then a lawsuit was brought by people who took—perhaps quite reasonably—a view different from that of the proponents of the legislation about what counts as fair campaigning in a democratic republic. When the matter reached the Supreme Court, this persuaded most, though not all of the nine justices, and so much of the legislation was struck down. Maybe this was the best outcome, but it is impossible to say that it was arrived at by a process that either embodied or respected the ideal of republican self-government. On the contrary, the settlement that the citizens had arrived at—carefully and deliberatively—among themselves, through representative politics, was set aside by the majority decision of a body that prides itself on its *distance* from the ordinary body of citizens. I do not see how this can be regarded as an instance of republican self-government, even on the assumption that the Supreme Court's decision was the right one.[42]

Ely suggested that, to secure genuine democratic self-government, the citizenry has no choice but to entrust these matters to the courts. If this is true in the United States, it may well be as a matter of self-fulfilling prophecy, along the lines of the points made earlier, in the second half of section IV, about the way in which judicial review has corrupted and undermined legislative politics. In other countries, not similarly corrupted, it is patently false that existing majorities or incumbent representatives are incapable of deciding these matters fairly or in ways that respect republican values. Voters in New Zealand recently adopted and made use of a system of proportional representation; voters in the United Kingdom have decided on issues of devolution and the setting up of assemblies in Wales and Scotland to ensure a greater voice for regional minorities; the same voters will soon have the opportunity to decide among various proposals for reform of the second chamber of their legislature; electoral campaign finance is on the legislative agenda almost everywhere, and has in many countries been settled by legislatures in ways that many American citizens (with their "constitutional guarantees") look on with envy. Each country studies the constitutional experience of the others; in every one of these debates, citizens weigh complex arrays of pros and cons; and though people and their professors may plead passionately for one option or another, debates about constitutional structure are by and large conducted in a spirit of mutual respect and in common acknowledgment that this is not an area of life where the truth is well known and self-evident.

Much the same can be said about more substantive versions of Ely's suggestion, put forward (among others) by Stephen Holmes and Ronald Dworkin. I cannot go into this in detail here,[43] but let me just outline the general shape of the positions and the response.

Stephen Holmes makes the point that in setting up institutions of self-government, the members of a society intend to commit themselves not just to any old form of majoritarianism but to a particular form of politics, namely to decision by popular "will formed in vigorous and wide-open debate."[44] This, they cannot do without at the same time doing their best to create an open and tolerant climate for the effective expression of political opposition and dissent. And that in turn requires them to establish certain guarantees that minority opposition and dissent will not evoke any backlash from either temporary or permanent majorities. Such guarantees—the argument goes—are not credible unless the people have put in place constitutional mechanisms to restrain their own natural repressive response to the irritation of minority criticism. A precommitment of this kind may look negative, and members of the majority may feel that its immediate effect is to prevent them from doing things that they want to do. But in the medium and long term, constitutional guarantees of free speech and loyal opposition are indispensable for meaningful political debate. Thus they are conditions for the very thing that republican citizens want from their constitution: the emergence of an informed and effective basis for popular civic decision.

In *Freedom's Law*, Ronald Dworkin takes a similar line, though he orients it not so much towards what the people want from their politics, as to the conditions under which they may plausibly be regarded as bound to their society. He argues that a person is not bound by democratic decisions unless he is in some satisfactorily substantive sense a member of the community whose democracy it is. Membership in a self-governing republic is not just a matter of geography, nor is it simply a matter of formal participation: it is also a matter of a person's interests being treated with appropriate concern. Even if she has a vote, a citizen can hardly be expected to accept majority decisions as legitimate if she knows that other members of the community do not take her interests seriously or if the established institutions of the community evince contempt or indifference towards her or her kind.[45]

I have no doubt that *some* arguments along these lines must be respected. There are surely some conditions under which what called itself a self-governing republic would cease to be attractive under that description. And there are surely some rights such that, if they were not respected in a community, no political legitimacy could possibly be accorded to any republican decision-procedure. Is it not appropriate, then, for political decision-making to be constrained by rights that satisfy this formula? One could hardly complain about such constraints on democratic or republican grounds, for a democratic republic unconstrained by such rights would be scarcely worthy of the name.

But does that provide a basis for reconciling republican self-government, on the one hand, with constitutional constraint and judicial review, on the other? It might—*just*—amount to a plausible republican case for constitutional constraints immune to subsequent legislative revision if everyone agreed about the conditions or the substantive rights necessary for good republican self-government. It might amount to a plausible case if there were no good-faith disagreement about these conditions or rights in any society that was to be governed by constitutional constraints of the sort we are imagining. Or—even if there were disagreements—it might amount to a plausible case for constitutional constraints if minorities had reason to fear that any legislative rethinking of the rules about these matters in their society, any allegedly "republican" deliberation about them, would inevitably turn out to be a way of crushing minorities and silencing dissent.

In fact, neither condition is satisfied. As we saw earlier with procedural issues, so with these more substantive ones: even citizens who accept the general form of Holmes's or Dworkin's approach disagree about what the conditions of republican self-government are. Some think American-style free speech is necessary; others favor a more limited British-style regime, with restrictions on hate speech, pornography, and so on. Some think welfare guarantees are necessary; others maintain exactly the opposite. Some—like Dworkin—think that a country cannot really call its system of government democratic or republican, unless its members have free choice in matters like abortion; needless to say, many oppose this. And the list goes on and on. Under these conditions of reasonable disagreement, it simply cannot be the case that the republican approach is to impose a particular set of solutions simply on the ground that they are favored by a scholarly or judicial elite.

The second condition is not satisfied either. It is true that dissidents in a republic need an assurance that their opposition will not elicit a repressive or murderous response, and that the reopening of fundamental questions in the legislature will not undermine their equal standing as citizens. In some countries (even in some that call themselves republics) that assurance is tenuous or nonexistent. This is a matter of great concern, but it is not what interests us here; in those countries, constitutional structures have failed altogether. There may, however, be one or two countries where the assurance dissidents need actually does exist by virtue of constitutional structure, but where it is so fragile that any attempt by the people or their representatives to revisit and vote upon issues of political structure would reasonably be seen by minorities as a way of attacking and undermining their guarantee of freedom and loyal opposition. Perhaps some of the new democracies of eastern Europe and the former Soviet Union fall into this category. Arguably, however, these are the countries that can *least* afford constitutional rigidity; their people need to be able to experiment with a variety of detailed procedural forms as, slowly, over the *decades*, they attempt to elaborate their own republican traditions. At any rate, the conditions I have set out certainly do not apply to the countries that have been the main focus of discussion in this chapter—the United States, the United Kingdom, and other countries like Australia, New Zealand, and Canada, that are influenced by their example. In those countries there are robust and established traditions of republican liberty (which have flourished often *despite* the best efforts of the judiciary); and there are vigorous debates about political structure that seem able to proceed in good faith without threatening minority freedoms.

VI

Republican self-government is a demanding ideal. Many of those who would combine it with constitutional constraint and judicial review accept that. They emphasize the restraint and discipline, the acceptance of limits, that good republican government requires, if it is to survive under modern political conditions. Indeed, they are not sure the citizenry are up to these demands. They think that some of the demands that republican government places upon us are so exacting that they must be enforced by nonrepublican institutions such as courts oriented to the imposition of final decisions about matters of great controversy in the community.

The message that I have tried to convey is that civic republicanism is demanding in another way. Faith in a people's ability to govern themselves demands that we accept certain risks—including the risk that the very system of self-government might self-destruct. As much as the faith of a parent in a young adult's autonomy or the faith of a colonial power in the new political system of its erstwhile dependency, the theorist of republicanism advocates that we take a chance on a people's ability to govern themselves. Sure it means that things are up for grabs,[46] and it is not unimaginable that the newly enfranchised entity will grab at something dangerous or ill conceived. To be exercised by this possibility is only human, but to be obsessed by it, in one's thinking about institutional design, is to turn one's back on the republican aspiration, and to commit oneself instead to some form of paternalistic or aristocratic tutelage.

Beyond this, the worst form of republican apostasy is to worry that social issues that one regards (perhaps rightly) as of great importance may be settled in ways that do not depend purely on *one's own* thinking, or *one's own* conscience, or *one's own* convictions about justice, and to portray *that* as the sort of danger that we need judicial review to guard against. For each of us, to engage in politics is to accept that we share the world with others—millions of others—who are constituted not just as objects of our moral concern but as individual thinkers with their own views on the matters that we take so seriously. There is a danger that when one moves from a politics dominated by interest to a politics dominated by principle, people will find it harder (*morally* harder) to accept compromise or to submit to social decisions with which they do not agree. Republicanism requires this move of us—it requires us to take matters of principle seriously; but because it is a political philosophy, it requires each of us as a citizen to loosen a little the connection between our own convictions and what we can expect from our polity. Though each of us reasonably regards his own moral views as tremendously important, we must also (each of us) respect the elementary condition of *being with others*, which is both the essence of republican politics and the principle of mutual recognition that lies at the heart of the idea of citizenship. When one confronts a fellow citizen, one is not just dealing with a person entitled (on one's own favorite moral theory) to liberty, justice, sustenance, rights, and protection. One is confronting above all a particular *intelligence*—a mind and consciousness that is not one's own, that is not under one's intellectual control, that has its own view of the world and its own account of the proper basis of relations with those whom it too sees as other. The worst thing, then, about judicial review from a republican standpoint, is that it tempts us away from that recognition, and entices us into a politics that offers a more direct vindication of the power and importance of our own moral convictions.

Notes

1. U.S. Constitution, Article 4, Section 4.

2. There is a fine definition of "republican" in David Miller et al., eds., *The Blackwell Encyclopaedia of Political Thought* (Oxford: Basil Blackwell, 1987), 433–34: "The term is defined by contrast with monarchy. Whereas a traditional king enjoys personal authority over his subjects and rules his realm as his personal possession, government in a republic is in principle the common business (*res publica*) of the citizens, conducted by them for the common good."

3. Civic republicanism is a body of legal and political theory oriented specifically to the affirmative evaluation of republican government. For useful summaries, see Philip Pettit, *Republicanism* (Oxford: Oxford University Press, 1997); also M. N. S. Sellers, *American Republicanism* (New York: New York University Press, 1994).

4. For "pluralism," see Anthony Downs, *An Economic Theory of Democracy* (New York: Harper and Row, 1957); and R. A. Dahl, *Dilemmas of Pluralist Democracy: Autonomy vs. Control* (New Haven: Yale University Press, 1982). See also Frank Michelman, "Law's Republic," 97 *Yale Law Journal*, 1493, 1507–8 (1988).

5. Whether this is an *accurate* portrayal of liberalism—particularly liberal political philosophy—is something I will not pursue here.

6. See Amy Gutmann and Dennis Thompson, *Democracy and Disagreement* (Cambridge: Harvard University Press, 1996); and Jon Elster, ed., *Deliberative Democracy* (Cambridge: Cambridge University Press, 1998).

7. So one can define the republican approach by contrasting it with the well-known saying of Charles I on the scaffold at Westminster in 1649: "For the People: And truly I desire their Liberty and Freedom as much as anybody whomsoever, but I must tell you that their Liberty and their Freedom, consists in having of Government; those Laws, by which their Life and their Goods may be most their own. It is not for having a share in Government (Sir) that is nothing pertaining to them; a subject and a Sovereign are clean different things" "King Charles his Speech," an anonymous narrative of Charles I's execution, January 30, 1649, in *Politics, Religion, and Literature in the Seventeenth Century,* ed. William Lamont and Sybil Oldfield (London: Dent, 1975), 132.

8. I suspect there is a similar taxonomy for conservatives, liberals, socialists, and so on: sometimes we argue from our deep philosophical ideas to surface-level commitments, while other times we scramble around to find a congenial "justification" for a surface position that, independently, we are unwilling to give up.

9. I am using "union" and "intersection" in their set-theoretic sense.

10. See also Jeremy Waldron, "Virtue *en Masse,*" in *Debating Democracy's Discontent: Essays on American Politics, Law, and Public Philosophy*, ed. Anita L. Allen and Milton C. Regan (Oxford: Oxford University Press, 1998), esp. 35–39.

11. *Roe v. Wade*, 410 U.S. 113 (1973); *Planned Parenthood v. Casey*, 505 U.S. 833 (1992).

12. *Buckley v. Valeo*, 424 U.S. 1 (1976).

13. *Lochner v. New York*, 198 U.S. 45 (1905).

14. See Henry P. Monaghan, "*Marbury* and the Administrative State," 83 *Columbia Law Review*, 1 (1983), for about the most persuasive case that can be made.

15. *Marbury v. Madison*, 5 U.S. (1 Cranch) 137, 177 (1803).

16. See *City of Boerne v. Flores*, 117 S.Ct. 2157. See also Michael W. McConnell, "Institutions and Interpretation: A Critique of *City of Boerne v. Flores*," 111 *Harvard Law Review* 153, 169–83 (1997).

17. See Harrington's "Preliminaries" to *Oceana* in James Harrington, *The Commonwealth of Oceana* and *A System of Politics*, ed. by J. G. A. Pocock (Cambridge: Cambridge University Press, 1992), 8ff.

18. See Michelman, "Law's Republic," 1501ff. for a very helpful discussion.

19. Abraham Lincoln, 'First Inaugural Address,' in his *Speeches and Writings, 1859–1865* (New York: Library of America, n.d.), 221.

20. Ronald Dworkin, *A Bill of Rights for Britain* (London: Chatto and Windus, 1990), 36–37.

21. Human Rights Act 1998.

22. See also the discussion in Jeremy Waldron, *Law and Disagreement* (Oxford: Clarendon Press, 1999), 255–57.

23. This time in Ronald Dworkin, *Freedom's Law: The Moral Reading of the American Constitution* (Cambridge: Harvard University Press, 1996).

24. The argument in the next few pages is adapted from Waldron, *Law and Disagreement*, 289–91.

25. Dworkin, *Freedom's Law,* 345.

26. Dworkin, *Freedom's Law*, 345.

27. See H. L. A. Hart, *Law, Liberty, and Morality* (Oxford: Oxford University Press, 1963) and Patrick Devlin, *The Enforcement of Morals* (Oxford: Oxford University Press, 1965), debating the *Report of the Committee on Homosexual Offences and Prostitution*, Cmd. no. 247 (1957).

28. *Bowers v. Hardwick*, 478 U.S. 186 (1986).

29. Mary Ann Glendon, *Rights Talk: The Impoverishment of Political Discourse* (New York: Free Press, 1991), 151.

30. Dworkin, *Freedom's Law*, 30.

31. For a complex and persuasive argument about the effect of this on the type of change that legal scholars tend to advocate, see Roberto Mangabeira Unger, *What Should Legal Analysis Become?* (London: Verso, 1996), 83–104. Some of what follows is adapted from my review of this book in Jeremy Waldron, "Dirty Little Secret," 98 *Columbia Law Review* 510 (1998).

32. The quotation is from Unger, Legal Analysis, 107. Unger seems to have in mind passages like the following from Henry M. Hart and Albert M Sacks, *The Legal Process: Basic Problems in the Making and Application of Law*, ed. William N. Eskridge and Philip P. Frickey (New York: Foundation Press, 1994), 164: "A legislature has a primary, first-line responsibility to establish the institutions necessary or appropriate in the everyday operation of government. For example, it must create courts. . . . But in relation to the body of general directive arrangements which govern private activity in the society its responsibility is more accurately described as secondary in the sense of second-line. The legisla-

ture characteristically functions in this relation as an intermittently intervening, trouble-shooting, back-stopping agency. . . . The private lawmakers, the courts, and administrative agencies are . . . the regularly available continuously functioning agencies of growth in the legal system."

33. For elaboration of this point, see Jeremy Waldron, "The Dignity of Legislation," 54 *Maryland Law Review* 633, 641–48 (1995).

34. Unger, *Legal Analysis*, 72. Unger is not alone in this. Another jurist who warns explicitly of the law's "discomfort with democracy" is Antonin Scalia, *A Matter of Interpretation: Federal Courts and the Law* (Princeton: Princeton University Press, 1997), 10.

35. See also Waldron, *Law and Disagreement*, 8–9.

36. Unger, *Legal Analysis*, 72–73.

37. Cf. Benjamin Constant, "The Liberty of the Ancients Compared to That of the Moderns" (1819) in *Political Writings*, ed. Biancamaria Fontana (Cambridge: Cambridge University Press, 1988), 316: "Lost in the multitude, the individual can almost never perceive the influence he exercises. Never does his will impress itself upon the whole; nothing confirms in his own eyes his own cooperation."

38. The quoted phrases are Unger's, *Legal Analysis*, 134 and 117, respectively.

39. John Hart Ely, *Democracy and Distrust: A Theory of Judicial Review* (Cambridge: Harvard University Press, 1980).

40. Ibid., 103.

41. Ibid.

42. These lines were written before the decision of the U.S. Supreme Court in *McConnell v. Federal Election Commission* 124 S.Ct. 619 (2003), which revised some of the issues in *Buckley v. Valeo*.

43. For more complete accounts, see Waldron, *Law and Disagreement*, 275–81 (Holmes) and 291ff. (Dworkin).

44. Stephen Holmes, *Passions and Constraint: On the Theory of Liberal Democracy* (Chicago: University of Chicago Press, 1995), 171.

45. Dworkin, *Freedom's Law*, 25.

46. For the various connotations of "up for grabs," see Waldron, *Law and Disagreement*, 302–12.

CHAPTER 10

The *Casey* Five versus the Federalism Five: Supreme Legislator or Prudent Umpire?

Keith E. Whittington

CONSTITUTIONAL LAW professors have been very upset lately with the U.S. Supreme Court. Actually, this has been true for a few years now. One encounters anguished and bitter words in the places where such faculty gather. The words are only somewhat less heated in print. "Arrogant" and "imperious" are common adjectives, and the nature and meaning of judicial supremacy and judicial activism are again on the academic agenda.

Planned Parenthood v. Casey is not at the center of that discussion.[1] The 1992 *Casey* decision has certainly generated a critical response, as several contributions to this volume evidence, but these have been more likely to appear in nonacademic intellectual journals such as *First Things* than in the law reviews published by the major law schools.[2] Legal academia more generally met the *Casey* plurality opinion with a sigh of relief than with a shout of outrage. In the mainstream of academic legal commentary, *Casey* has been recognized as an important case with complicated implications for the regulation of abortion and future litigation on abortion rights, but it has rarely been regarded as especially imperious.[3] Even now, when scholarly criticisms of the Rehnquist Court as antidemocratic are rampant, *Casey* is rarely mentioned as supporting evidence.[4]

It is the Rehnquist Court's decisions regarding the structural features of the Constitution—in particular, federalism—that have generated controversy in the legal academy. *Bush v. Gore* certainly ratcheted up the level of emotions swirling about the Court, but that decision only reinforced the set of beliefs about the recent Supreme Court that were already well settled in the academy.[5] The Rehnquist Court had startled observers by showing relatively little deference to Congress and by substantially altering the judiciary's constitutional agenda.

Among the most notable features of the late Rehnquist Court has been its willingness to strike down acts of Congress as unconstitutional. Throughout its history, even in such relatively dormant periods as the early nineteenth century or the years immediately following the judicial capitulation to the New Deal, the Supreme Court has been active in monitoring the constitutionality of the actions of state and local governments and has been willing to nullify such actions on a regular basis. By contrast, the Court has been much more tentative in addressing itself to the actions of the other branches of the national government. The Supreme Court struck down more acts of the state and local governments in the single decade of the 1960s than it had of the federal government over the entire course of its first two centuries.[6] By contrast, the Rehnquist Court, especially since 1995, has struck down federal statutes at a historically unprecedented rate. Although no subsequent Court has bested the mark of seven congressional laws struck down in 1935 at the height of the judicial war against the New Deal, the Rehnquist Court has come the closest and far exceeds the record of the Hughes Court over the course of a few years. No prior Court has embarked on such a sustained assault on congressional power. At the same time, the recent Supreme Court has found relatively little cause to strike down the actions of state and local governments. Far from being "activist" across the board, the Supreme Court in the 1990s has returned to the languid pace of the famously restrained Court of the 1940s in its record of invalidating state and local actions.

In turning its sights on Congress, the Supreme Court has also altered its constitutional agenda. Under Chief Justices Earl Warren and Warren Burger, the Court drew attention for its rulings regarding individual rights. Across a wide range of substantive areas of public policy, the federal judiciary hemmed in government power and limited democratic decision making in the name of individual liberty and equality. Most of those decisions were aimed at state and local governments, which have primary responsibility for preserving the peace, running the schools, and regulating society. In its first substantial foray with *Brown v. Board of Education*, the Court found heated controversy and only limited practical success but eventually won widespread public approval and a moral victory. Nearly two decades later in *Roe v. Wade*, the Court was able to make a more immediate impact on policy, but it did not find anything like the same moral consensus. In a host of only slightly less well known decisions, the Court was willing to discover numerous newfound rights in such areas as criminal justice, legislative apportionment, speech and the press, and religious liberty. Those "discoveries" and their implications dominated the Court's attention until only very recently.

While still dealing with the aftereffects of some of those earlier decisions and occasionally tackling relatively new controversies such as euthanasia and homosexual rights, the Rehnquist Court has been most innovative in addressing matters of constitutional structure.[7] The Court has been active in evaluating the constitutionality of government action in relation to separation of powers such as the line-item veto and the independent counsel, in relation to state involvement in federal elections such as congressional term limits and the 2000 presidential election controversy, in relation to the scope of federal power under the commerce clause and the Fourteenth Amendment, and in relation to the federal authority to regulate the states themselves.

This shift in focus is no accident. It reflects a different conception of the judicial role within the constitutional system and what the benefits, and dangers, of judicial review might be. For many scholars and judges, the so-called *Lochner* Court of the early twentieth century had a decisive influence on their understanding of the appropriate use of the judicial power to review the constitutionality of legislation. For most, the trajectory of the *Lochner* Court, ending in political retaliation and popular and scholarly rejection, is a cautionary tale about the exercise of judicial power. For many proponents of the judicial activism of the 1960s and 1970s, the primary difficulty with the *Lochner* Court was that it used the power of judicial review to protect the wrong set of rights from democratic decision-making. From this perspective, there is little wrong with judges trumping the popular will. The only question is what set of values judges will enforce. If not a generalized "right to contract," then perhaps a generalized "right to privacy." For others, by contrast, the lesson of the *Lochner* Court, and indeed the Warren and Burger Courts, is that judicial review should not be used to protect controversial rights claims at all but rather should focus on other sorts of constitutional issues, such as the protection of constitutional rights that are widely recognized in the abstract but perhaps not always respected in practice (following, for example, Justice Felix Frankfurter's lead of invalidating police conduct that "shocks the conscience") or the maintenance of constitutional structures within which democratic decisions are made.[8]

The Rehnquist Court is regarded by many as a very activist Court. The activism that has drawn the most attention, however, has been the Supreme Court's assertions of authority against Congress over the meaning of the Constitution and the scope of federal powers. This has drawn scholars to consider the possibility of "conservative judicial activism" and what such a term might mean. Scholars have pondered both the substance and form of the Rehnquist Court's constitutional jurisprudence. The recent activity of the Court has also tended to disrupt traditional scholarly alignments. Many (mostly liberals) who had no difficulty with the active use of the power of judicial review by the Warren and Burger Courts and who view decisions such as *Casey* with restrained approval, have reacted to the recent invalidation of federal statutes with alarm and dismay. Others (mostly conservatives) who could be counted on to voice strenuous disapproval of those earlier decisions have been relatively quiet in the face of the Rehnquist Court's actions, or have even responded with mild approval. The strongest voices for judicial restraint can now be found on the ideological Left, with some reaching so far as to call for the end of judicial review itself. Although the conservative critique of judicial activism is now well entrenched and has not yet disappeared, voices from the ideological Right are increasingly being raised to urge the Court onward to further feats of judicial muscle-flexing. This is not simply a matter of ideological antagonists switching roles, however.

There is a distinction to be made between the kind of judicial activism at work in a decision such as *Casey* and in decisions such as *Lopez* and *Boerne*. In brief, *Casey* is about stopping political debate and legislative action. *Lopez* and its brethren are about redirecting political activism into different channels. Ultimately, *Casey* is intended to have substantial political and policy consequences. By contrast, *Lopez* has only modest policy consequences. For those concerned about judicial supremacy, *Casey* should be far more disconcerting than *Lopez*.

A Caveat

Before considering that argument in more detail, however, an important qualification should be offered. I do not consider here the question of which, if any, of these decisions can be adequately justified as a correct substantive interpretation of the Constitution and application of constitutional principles. In the first instance, whether a judicial decision should be praised or condemned depends upon its fidelity to the Constitution. When the Court claims to be enforcing the strictures of the Constitution against the usurpations of elected officials, we would immediately want to know whether that claim is warranted and whether the Court has gotten the Constitution right. This is, of course, a difficult matter, and much can be said regarding the interpretive fidelity of decisions such as *Casey* on the one hand and those such as *Lopez* on the other.

I do not wish to examine that question here. The very basis for determining whether or not a particular judicial decision is faithful to the meaning of the Constitution is controversial, as scholars and jurists disagree as to how, even in the abstract, the Constitution should be interpreted by courts. I have elsewhere defended a mode of constitutional interpretation that emphasizes original understandings of the text, and my final judgment on the decisions of the Court would turn on whether they could be justified in originalist terms.[9] Others would insist on a different metric, and there would remain the complicated enterprise of evaluating the quality of the interpretations of particular features of the Constitution being offered by the Court even if a single standard of constitutional interpretation could be agreed upon. Widespread disagreements persist as to the substantive merit of constitutional claims on behalf of a right to abortion or a robust congressional power of social regulation. Even so, critics of the recent Rehnquist decisions are often quite willing to embrace creative approaches to constitutional understanding in other circumstances. Much of the criticism of the Court's recent activities has been less focused on the claim that the Court has gotten the Constitution wrong than on the claim that the Court is overreaching and seriously obstructing the political process. This claim of judicial imperialism is worthy of separate consideration.

Although we might well hesitate before embracing the Court's recent doctrinal statements as valid interpretations of the constitutional text, we might still want to know the extent to which they raise problems for our understanding of the judicial role within the political system. If the Court is correct in its constitutional understandings in *Roe* or *Lopez*, then we might not be disturbed if it intervenes aggressively to block unconstitutional policies. Our sense of the implications of these decisions for democratic politics, however, may well affect how tentative or risk-averse we believe the Court should be when pondering contestable claims about constitutional meaning.

THE COURT AS ARBITER

Early in his career William Rehnquist signaled his views on the proper role of the Court within the constitutional system. After graduating from Stanford Law School in 1951, Rehnquist went to Washington, D.C., to serve as a clerk for Justice Robert Jackson. Jackson had served in the Department of Justice when President Franklin Roosevelt waged his war with the Supreme Court over the constitutionality of the New Deal, and Roosevelt later placed him on the Court, where he helped solidify the New Deal revolution in constitutional law. Rehnquist served as Jackson's law clerk for sixteen months, and was working in the justice's chambers when *Brown v. Board of Education* first reached the Supreme Court. In preparation for that case in 1952, Rehnquist wrote Jackson a brief memo that became public during the Senate deliberations on Rehnquist's own appointment in 1971 to serve as an associate justice on the Supreme Court.

Brown having reached the Court just fifteen years after Franklin Roosevelt had proposed his Court-packing plan, the reactions of judges and scholars to it reflected the lessons that they had drawn from the New Deal. Rehnquist's memo to Jackson evidenced one common response.

Though the Constitution clearly "deals with individual rights," Rehnquist wrote, "as I read the history of the Court, it has seldom been out of hot water when attempting to interpret these individual rights."[10] When looking into the constitutional clauses relating to individual rights, the justices often found their own political and social preferences reflected back to them. Just as John Marshall sought to protect "infant business" and Roger Taney sought "to protect slaveholders from legislative interference," so the early-twentieth-century justices "ventured into the deep water of protecting certain types of individuals against legislative interference."[11] Eventually "the Court called a halt to this reading of its own economic views into the Constitution," apparently recognizing "that where the legislature was dealing with its own citizens, it was not part of the judicial function to thwart public opinion except in extreme cases" that might "command intervention from one of any conviction."[12] Though the "sentiments of a transient majority of nine men" may attempt to "read its own sociological views into the Constitution," "in the long run it is the [political] majority who will determine what the constitutional rights of the minority are." Where the rights at issue are controversial and not firmly grounded in "precedent" and "legislative history," the Court should defer.[13] The power of judicial review was premised on the belief that "there are standards to be applied other than the personal predilections of the Justices," but that condition was rarely met when controversial rights claims were at issue.[14]

Despite this rather pessimistic conclusion, the young William Rehnquist still saw a clear role for the courts exercising the power of judicial review. In the century and a half since *Marbury* held that the Supreme Court "was the ultimate judge of the restrictions which the Constitution imposed on the various branches of the national and state governments," experience had suggested another path for the Court to take.[15]

> As applied to questions of inter-state or state-federal relations, as well as to interdepartmental disputes within the federal government, this doctrine of judicial review has worked well. Where theoretically co-ordinate bodies of government are disputing, the Court is well suited to its role as arbiter. This is because the problems involve much less emotionally charged subject matter than do those discussed below [individual rights]. In effect, they determine the skeletal relations of the governments to each other without influencing the substantive business of those goverments [sic].[16]

This was, without question, a controversial conclusion to draw from the Court's history, and a controversial application of it in the case of *Brown*. The moral instincts of the justices on the segregation question proved to be durable rather than transient, and perhaps by 1952 it had even become possible that the myriad injustices of Jim Crow were among those "extreme cases . . . [that command] intervention from one of any conviction" even if the obstacles to success were great.[17] Moreover, Jackson himself had been instrumental, first as attorney general and then as justice, in the judicial abandonment of "its role as arbiter" in disputes over the scope of federal powers vis-à-vis the states and likely took a different view from that of his clerk as to whether judicial review had "worked well" in the context of federalism.[18]

Nonetheless, this view of judicial review clearly continues to shape Chief Justice Rehnquist's, and to a great extent the Rehnquist Court's, approach to the task. Especially in the context of individual rights, the fear of the "political seduction of the law," as Robert Bork phrased it, and belief that a line can be readily drawn from *Dred Scott* to *Lochner* to *Roe* led many conservatives to turn to a jurisprudence of original intent and a commitment to judicial restraint as ways of trying to tie the hands of judges.[19] The calculation has been somewhat different in the context of the structural features of the Constitution, however. Justice Sandra Day O'Connor has recently echoed Rehnquist, asserting that "*Marbury v. Madison* confirmed not only the power of judicial review generally, but specifically the competence of courts to enforce the constitutionally enshrined balance of power among the different organs of government."[20] In guarding against "transgression of constitutional borders, . . . the courts should strive to emulate a prudent umpire, who allows the contestants to play hard between the lines but takes swift and sure action when those lines are crossed."[21] Away from the essentially political decisions about the "substantive business" of politics, in this view, the Court has a more active role to play and can play it with less fear of unduly restricting the political sphere.[22]

CASEY

The imperialistic ambitions and effects of decisions such as *Casey* are fairly evident, regardless of whether one thinks those ambitions are warranted in such cases or not. I note two ways in particular in which this is true in *Casey*. The first, and lesser, way is how the *Casey* plurality opinion, authored by Justices Sandra Day O'Connor, Anthony Kennedy, and David Souter, treats constitutional disagreement. *Casey* is remarkably frank about certain aspects of its decision, and its treatment of its concerns for judicial legitimacy is among them. "The Court's power lies . . . in its legitimacy, a product of substance and perception that shows itself in the people's acceptance of the Judiciary as fit to determine what the Nation's law means, and to declare what it demands."[23] The opinion notes that "the underlying substance of this legitimacy is of course the

warrant for the Court's decisions in the Constitution," but those substantive warrants are often challenged. Not everyone will be persuaded
that the Court's decision really is warranted by the Constitution. There
will be those who will claim that the Court has gotten the Constitution
wrong. Perhaps for this reason, the *Casey* plurality quickly falls back to
a weaker claim for judicial legitimacy. Echoing the cry familiar to every
teacher who has listened to students disappointed with their grades, what
truly matters is not whether the justices got the constitutional answer
right or wrong but that they really tried. The claim that the Court's arguments are "conscientious" and "principled" must be "sufficiently plausible to be accepted by the Nation" as such. The people must be willing "to
accept its decisions on the terms the Court claims for them" and sustain
a "belief in the Court's good faith."[24]

This "belief in the Court's good faith," the plurality justices avow,
would be undermined to the extent that the judicial decisions are overturned often or in the context of substantial external criticism. Interestingly, although both circumstances would on their face tend to suggest
that "a prior decision was wrong," the justices are far more concerned
that the suspicions of bad faith would fall on the overturning Court
rather than on the Court that was overturned. Apparently, "there is a
limit to the amount of error that can plausibly be imputed to prior
Courts."[25] Especially "when the Court's interpretation of the Constitution calls the contending sides of a national controversy to end their national division by accepting a common mandate rooted in the Constitution," the justices must close their eyes to the questions that might be
raised about the accuracy of the Court's constitutional interpretation. To
subsequently admit that the original constitutional declaration was mistaken would be to "surrender to political pressure" and "subvert the
Court's legitimacy beyond any serious question."[26] The Court must not
admit to fallibility lest it lose its claim to finality.

The *Casey* plurality contends that the Court cannot recognize the possibility of good-faith disagreement over constitutional meaning. Judges
who disagree with prior decisions would only be viewed as political
pawns rather than good-faith constitutional interpreters in their own
right. *Casey* seeks to close the door on any opening by which the people
might attempt to influence the course of "the policy of the government,
upon vital questions, affecting the whole people," as Abraham Lincoln
once feared.[27] The Court, according to *Casey*, must "speak before all others for their [the American people's] constitutional ideals." It is precisely
where judicial error is widely perceived that the Court must steadfastly
refuse to "address error."[28] To live under a constitution, *Casey* asserts,
means to live not only under judicial supremacy but also under a judiciary unresponsive to criticism.

The second way in which *Casey* is imperialistic is in its operation. Like all cases involving rights claims, *Casey* seeks to remove a subject of political disagreement from the realm of democratic decision-making and place it under judicial supervision. This is, of course, the "awful responsibility" of judicial review, to borrow John Marshall's phrase.[29] *Casey* does not flinch from it. The burden of the second section of the *Casey* plurality opinion is to demonstrate that the right to abortion is part of the "promise of the Constitution that there is a realm of personal liberty which the government may not enter."[30] *Casey* turns forthrightly, if somewhat self-consciously, to "substantive due process," the much vilified heart of *Lochner* jurisprudence.[31]

If the second section of the *Casey* plurality opinion is persuasive, then the imperialism of the decision may well be taken as justified. But accepting that the Court may be justified in taking such a step should not obscure the nature of the step that it is taking. The Court hopes to put an end to "the national division" and remove a subject of ongoing political controversy from democratic politics. In practice, of course, the Court cannot end the controversy by fiat. Moreover, by claiming to open a window for the regulation, but not the prohibition, of abortion, the Court invites some continuing legislative activity on the subject. But like the *Lochner* Court before it, the *Casey* Court insists that such substantive policy decisions will always be answerable to the particular "reasoned judgment" of the judges.[32]

Casey does not involve some technical flaw in legislative drafting or some excess of passing popular passion. It involves a regular subject of twentieth-century public policy and a central issue of late-twentieth-century electoral politics. To proponents of the policies at stake in *Casey*, the Court offers no other place of redress. A substantial element of the polity is simply told to abandon its policy objectives, that they have been "irrevocably fixed by decisions of the Supreme Court."[33] Judicial supremacy in such a context has real teeth.

THE FEDERALISM REVIVAL

Although often accompanied by aggressive judicial rhetoric, the Rehnquist Court's federalism decisions are far different. Since 1991, the Supreme Court has sought to revive federalism as a judicially enforced constraint on congressional power after nearly half a century of disuse.[34] In 1976, then–Associate Justice Rehnquist was able to enlist a slim majority of the Court to come to the defense of "state sovereignty" and limit the enforcement of federal economic regulations against the state governments and their subsidiaries in *National League of Cities v. Usery*.[35]

That majority proved short-lived, however, and the Court officially abandoned *National League of Cities* less than a decade later, pointing to the political process rather than the judiciary as the appropriate mechanism for preventing Congress from encroaching on the constitutional authority of the states. In a brief dissent, Rehnquist expressed confidence that the core principles of judicially enforced federalism would "in time again command the support of a majority of this Court."[36] His confidence proved to be justified.

Briefly, the Court's recent federalism decisions come in four broad, and somewhat overlapping, categories. First, the Court has revitalized the constitutional clause giving Congress the power "to regulate Commerce . . . among the several States" as a limited grant of authority to Congress, and has been willing to pare back federal statutes that the justices believe regulate activities only tangentially related to interstate commerce.[37] Second, the Court has limited congressional authority under Section 5 of the Fourteenth Amendment. Section 5 grants Congress the "power to enforce, by appropriate legislation, the provisions" of the Fourteenth Amendment, most notably a variety of individual rights protections against the state governments. The Court has held that congressional authority to "enforce" the Fourteenth Amendment cannot significantly outrun the Court's interpretive understanding of the obligations that the amendment places on the states. Congress cannot place substantial new burdens on the states in the name of remedying constitutional violations that the Court does not recognize as occurring.[38] Third, the Court has held that the federal government may not "commandeer" state and local governmental bodies, such as the state legislature or executive branch officials, to carry out federal policy.[39] Fourth, the Court has held that in a variety of circumstances the federal government cannot waive the sovereign immunity of the state governments from lawsuits, as recognized by the Eleventh Amendment, and empower private litigants to force the state governments into court.[40]

In these cases, the Court has sometimes voiced fairly sweeping claims for its own interpretive authority. Perhaps most notably, Justice Kennedy took Congress to task for challenging the judiciary's authority to give meaning to the Constitution in his majority opinion in *City of Boerne v. Flores*. At issue in *Boerne* was the federal Religious Freedom Restoration Act (RFRA), which was passed in response to the Supreme Court's 1990 decision to alter doctrines that had guided the Court's understanding of the free exercise clause of the First Amendment since the 1960s. With RFRA, Congress sought to reimpose the older doctrine on not only the federal government but also the states and localities. Justice Kennedy reminded Congress that "the Constitution is preserved best when each part of government respects both the Constitution and the proper actions and determinations of the other branches." Once the Court has declared "what the law is," then Congress may not "define its own powers by altering the Fourteenth Amendment's meaning."[41] Chief Justice Rehnquist added in a later case that it is a "central principle of our constitutional system" that "the limitation on congressional authority is not solely a matter of legislative grace." "[E]ver since *Marbury* this Court has remained the ultimate expositor of the constitutional text" and has been obliged to invalidate policies adopted under contrary constitutional understandings.[42]

As claims about judicial authority, such statements would be fairly unremarkable if made in other contexts. If the judiciary has the right, and perhaps the duty, to evaluate federal statutes for their consistency with the constitutional grant of authority to Congress, then it is surely true that the Court cannot take congressional assertions of its authority at face value. If the judiciary has recognized a constitutional right, for example, then it is unlikely to allow Congress to legislate as if such a right did not exist. If, contrary to prior judicial determinations, legislators expressed constitutional understandings that had the effect of increasing legislative power, then judges might be expected to look on such claims with some skepticism. If two political bodies claim constitutional authority over the same subject matter, then courts might reasonably play the role of independent arbiter of those competing claims, and the availability of such a constitutional umpire might well be preferable to assuming that the claim of one of the interested parties simply trumps that of the other.

An important thing to note about these recent federalism decisions is their modest effect on public policy. Although these cases have provoked a scholarly uproar, they have generated relatively little political heat. This is perhaps unsurprising. The doctrinal innovations were sure to draw the attention of students of the Court and the Constitution. Political actors, however, are most concerned with results, and these cases have not imposed a very high political or policy cost. Of course there was a constituency for these policies or they would not have been adopted in the first place, but the political support for the invalidated legislative provisions was not especially deep.

Moreover, the federalism decisions do not significantly impair the possibility of a political response to the policy concern at issue. Unlike *Casey*, which sought to remove the disputed policy from the political arena, the federalism decisions allow for the underlying policy dispute to be resolved politically. Rather than judicially imposing a policy outcome, the federalism decisions simply reorganize the political process by which policy outcomes might be reached.

The policy effects of these decisions have been uniformly small. In some cases, the statutory provisions at issue were either largely symbolic or already out-of-date. In the commerce clause cases, the Court struck down federal statutes that essentially duplicated state and local policies. Justice Kennedy noted in his concurring opinion in *Lopez*, which struck down the federal Gun-Free School Zones Act, that "over 40 States already have criminal laws outlawing the possession of firearms on or near school grounds."[43] In any case, Congress soon passed a very similar statute that essentially covered the same ground but limited to cases involving guns that had been transported in interstate commerce, which is the vast majority of them. Similarly, states already provide criminal and civil remedies for violence against women. The provision of the Violence Against Women Act at issue in *Morrison* simply provided a federal venue for local crimes. Such statutes provide political benefits to congressmen who can demonstrate their concern for crime, but they do little about the targeted social problem. The provisions of the Brady Act that required local law enforcement officials to carry out federal background checks on gun purchasers and that were invalidated in *Printz* was itself only a transitional feature of the statutory scheme until the national computerized system came online. By the time the provision was struck down by the Court, it was of little practical significance.

The policy consequences of the Court's actions in other federalism cases were likewise small, but for somewhat different reasons. In the state sovereign immunity cases, the Court has generally limited the application of otherwise valid statutes. In the 1976 *National League of Cities* case, the Court objected to the 1974 extension of the terms of the New Deal–era Fair Labor Standards Act to public employees. State and local governments are economic actors in the national marketplace, but they remain only a small part of the overall economy and their economic activities have not generally been of primary concern to national policymakers considering economic and social regulations. Relatively speaking, the application of federal minimum wage laws to state and local employees is of little policy consequence. Many of the recent state sovereign immunity cases take the same form, involving, for example, provisions of the American with Disabilities Act (ADA)[44] or the Age Discrimination in Employment Act (ADEA).[45] If state and local governments, as employers, sometimes escape the net of federal economic regulation, the social and policy effects, though real, are of limited consequence.

In such cases, the Court has prevented the application of federal laws to state and local governments, but they have not blocked the policies themselves or defined the policy goals as illegitimate. Though state and local governments are exempted, such policies can still be applied against private actors and arms of the federal government itself. In many cases, the Court has only blocked one means by which the federal government might apply these policies against the states (namely, civil damage lawsuits by private individuals) while leaving various other means still available (e.g., injunctions, direct federal enforcement, federal incentives for state waivers of sovereign immunity). Moreover, the Court has left the door completely open to the adoption of such policies by the states themselves. For this particular purpose, the Court has simply instructed advocates of such policies to direct their political efforts at state, as well as national, policymakers. Though the individual rights recognized in the federal Religious Freedom Restoration Act (RFRA) could not be applied against the states, they could be applied by statute to the federal government and a variety of circumstances with a federal jurisdictional nexus.[46] More importantly, states are free to adopt "mini-RFRA's" on their own and make the same individual rights claims available in state courts. By the same token, states and local governments are free to bind themselves to legal requirements similar to those contained in federal statutes such as the ADA.

If the primary effect of the recent judicial activity on federalism is to redirect political activism toward the states, is this a cause for concern? There are circumstances under which this might be, but the Court has to date refrained from venturing into such relatively hazardous territory. A central concern of the New Deal era was that the Supreme Court's stringent federalism doctrines had contributed to a constitutional " 'no-man's land' where no Government—State or Federal—can function."[47] By leaving the channels of state policymaking open and only slightly constraining the lawmaking authority of the federal government, the Rehnquist Court's federalism decisions create no such impasse. It might be possible, however, that these decisions create an effective no-man's-land, even though they formally leave the authority to act in the hands of the state governments. The risks here are relatively small, however. The Court has taken pains to signal that, although it is revitalizing judicially enforced federalism, it is not seeking to disrupt the essential elements of the New Deal settlement of the 1930s and 1940s. Most directly, in his majority opinion in *Lopez* Rehnquist claimed to be making no significant doctrinal innovation but simply to be elaborating and applying the New Deal precedents. Though there is language in those cases that might make Rehnquist's approach textually plausible, on the whole it seems disingenuous, since those cases clearly had the intent and effect of abandoning judicially enforced federalism. At another level, however, Rehnquist is sending an important signal by embracing those precedents even as he takes them in a somewhat different direction.[48] The Court has been explicit that the federal authority to regulate virtually any aspect of the economy remains unquestioned.[49]

The Court's decision to focus federalism on noneconomic issues has important implications for how we might evaluate its effects. Most immediately, of course, the federalism revival does not threaten the national economic regulatory state built up since the early-twentieth-century. Relatedly, the Court's federalism decisions do not directly challenge central political issues, as the early twentieth century Court did in striking down the primary elements of the reform agenda first during the Progressive Era and then during the early New Deal. The Court's recent federalism decisions have case-by-case effects, but they do not strike at a larger political and policy agenda.[50]

More generally, the economic issues faced by the Court in the early twentieth century had a systematic relation to federalism that further increased the significance of those cases.[51] Reformers of the early twentieth century needed to be able to call upon the power of the national government in order to effectuate their policy goals. The mobility of economic actors across state jurisdictions, and the increasing size and reach of large corporations, rendered state-level economic reforms relatively ineffective. Reformers were often stymied by fears of a political "race to the bottom" when regulations that imposed costs on businesses threatened local economic growth and placed reformist states at a competitive disadvantage. The prohibition of child labor is a classic example, as the anti–child labor movement was driven into national politics in order to prevent "unfair" competition from child-labor states. A decentralized federal system tends to hamper activist regulatory policies. The reform agenda of the early twentieth century also tended to tax the administrative and budgetary resources available to the states, which were completely swamped by the Great Depression. Once unleashed from its constitutional and ideological shackles, the national government proved capable of providing the bureaucratic and fiscal muscle needed to meet the political demands of the twentieth century. In the realm of economics, states are not practically capable of responding to policy demands as the national government does.

Earlier frustrations with judicially enforced federalism also reflected the fact that states often were not as politically responsive to reform demands as the federal government. The case of racial civil rights is the classic example here. Leaving the security of black civil rights in the hands of southern state and local officials proved disastrous through much of the nation's history. More generally, in an era in which state governments were often anemic and unprofessional, and state legislatures were often grossly malapportioned, channeling political demands into states was often equivalent to stifling them. State politics was not just a different venue than federal politics, but often a much less promising one.

In the early and middle-twentieth century, the judicial enforcement of federalism could be expected to have dramatic policy consequences, given the issues at stake and the structure of the state governments. In that context, judicially enforced federalism did have the fairly direct effects of "influencing the substantive business of those governments" and "thwart[ing] public opinion" that Rehnquist sought to avoid in individual rights cases.[52] In the current context, the judicial enforcement of federalism cannot be expected to have the same effect. There was ample reason to believe that many state governments, especially in those places where it mattered most, would not have been open to adopting the equivalent of the Civil Rights Act of 1964. There is little reason to believe that state governments would be systematically unresponsive to political mobilization in support of local equivalents of the Religious Freedom Restoration Act, the Americans with Disability Act, the Age Discrimination in Employment Act, or the Gun-Free School Zones Act. Advocates of such policies are not guaranteed success at the state level, of course, but there is little reason to expect that such advocates face undue burdens in state politics as opposed to national politics. The political means for responding to, and nullifying the policy consequences of, the Court's federalism decisions are readily available.

It is certainly true that the Rehnquist Court has shown less deference to Congress than has been the historical norm. Several of the justices seem to share the belief, widely held in the general public, that the federal judiciary is a more trustworthy institution than the federal legislature. Cries of "judicial imperialism," however, seem best reserved for those decisions that remove subjects of political controversy from the political arena. Decisions such as *Casey* have this ambition and effect to a far greater degree than the Court's federalism decisions. The Court's federalism might well be open to criticism, but such criticisms should be made on other grounds. The federalism decisions may be mistaken as a matter of substantive interpretation of the Constitution. If so, then we might wish that the Court would correct its errors in constitutional judgment. It is judicial imperialism, however, to make government policy from the bench and then to recognize judicial error but fail to correct it.

NOTES

1. *Planned Parenthood of Southeastern Pennsylvania v. Casey*, 505 U.S. 833 (1992).

2. On the 1996 *First Things* symposium and the responses to it, see Mitchell S. Muncy, ed., *The End of Democracy?* (Dallas: Spence Publications, 1997); Muncy, ed., *The End of Democracy? II* (Dallas: Spence Publications, 1999).

3. Significantly, one journalistic account of the Rehnquist Court took *Casey* as primary evidence that "the center holds and moderate continuity had prevailed at

the Supreme Court." James F. Simon, *The Center Holds* (New York: Simon and Schuster, 1995).

4. Jeffrey Rosen did, however, turn to *Casey* in his critical profile of Justice Sandra Day O'Connor, observing that her "performance in *Casey* was characteristically self-assured and judicially aggressive" and employed some of the "same reasoning that she would turn to in *Bush v. Gore*" to "short-circuit the political debate" and "save the country from legislative battles that could only polarize and divide Americans." Rosen, "A Majority of One," *New York Times*, June 3, 2001, sec. 6 (Magazine), 64. Rosen has expressed similar misgivings about Justice Anthony Kennedy's "particularly expansive" opinion in *Lawrence v. Texas*, which built primarily on the plurality opinion in *Casey*. Jeffrey Rosen, "How to Reignite the Culture Wars," *New York Times*, September 7, 2003, sec. 6 (Magazine), 48; *Lawrence v. Texas*, 123 S.Ct. 2472 (2003).

5. Though I recognize the importance of *Bush v. Gore* in this context, I do not address that rather sui generis case here.

6. Although the Court was quite active in the 1960s, that decade did not prove to be exceptional. The Court exceeded those numbers in each of the next two decades.

7. This builds on a trend begun during the Burger Court with such decisions as *INS v. Chadha*, 462 U.S. 919 (1983).

8. *Rochin v. California*, 342 U.S. 165, 172 (1952).

9. Keith E. Whittington, *Constitutional Interpretation* (Lawrence: University Press of Kansas, 1999); Whittington, "Dworkin's Originalism: The Role of Intentions in Constitutional Interpretation," 62 *Review of Politics* 197 (2000).

10. William H. Rehnquist, "A Random Thought on the Segregation Cases," reprinted in Senate Judiciary Committee, *Nomination of Justice William Hubbs Rehnquist: Hearings before the Committee on the Judiciary*, 99th Cong., 2d Sess., 1986, 324.

11. Ibid., 324.

12. Ibid., 324–25.

13. Ibid., 325.

14. Ibid., 324.

15. Ibid.

16. Ibid.

17. Ibid., 325.

18. See *U.S. v. Darby*, 312 U.S. 100 (1941); *Wickard v. Filburn*, 317 U.S. 111 (1942). For an account of Jackson's role in *Wickard*, see Barry Cushman, *Rethinking the New Deal Court* (Oxford: Oxford University Press, 1998), 212–25.

19. See Howard Gillman, "The Collapse of Constitutional Originalism and the Rise of the Notion of the 'Living Constitution' in the Course of American State-Building," 11 *Studies in American Political Development* 191 (1997). On Rehnquist specifically, see Keith E. Whittington, "William H. Rehnquist: Nixon's Strict Constructionist, Reagan's Chief Justice," in *Rehnquist Justice*, ed. Earl M. Maltz (Lawrence: University Press of Kansas, 2003). The "political seduction of the law" is the subtitle of Robert Bork, *The Tempting of America* (New York: Free Press, 1990).

20. Sandra Day O'Connor, "Altered States: Federalism and Devolution at the 'Real' Turn of the Millennium," 60 *Cambridge Law Journal* 501 (2001).

21. Ibid.

22. Rehnquist, "Random Thought," 324. See also, Keith E. Whittington, "The Death of the Legalized Constitution and the Specter of Judicial Review," in *Courts and the Culture Wars*, ed. Bradley C. S. Watson (Lanham, Md.: Lexington Books, 2002).

23. *Planned Parenthood v. Casey*, 865.

24. Ibid., 865–66.

25. Ibid., 866.

26. Ibid., 867.

27. Abraham Lincoln, 'First Inaugural Address,' in *Abraham Lincoln: His Speeches and Writings*, ed. Roy P. Basler (New York: Da Capo Press, 1990), 585.

28. *Planned Parenthood v. Casey*, 868, 869.

29. *McCulloch v. Maryland*, 17 U.S. 316, 400 (1819). It should be emphasized that *Casey* and the *Casey* majority are, of course, not unique in identifying a rights claim that is sheltered from democratic decision making. The *Casey* majority shares this ambition with, for example, the *Lawrence* majority and the *Grutter* dissenters. *Grutter v. Bollinger*, 123 S.Ct. 2325 (2003).

30. *Planned Parenthood of v. Casey*, 847.

31. *Lochner* is discreetly omitted from this section of the opinion, though interestingly the opinion goes on to indicate that *Lochner* was abandoned not because it incorrectly "read Mr. Herbert Spencer's *Social Statics*" into the Constitution, as Oliver Wendell Holmes and William Rehnquist would have it, but because the factual preconditions of *Lochner* ceased to hold. Ibid., 861–62. *Lochner v. New York*, 198 U.S. 45, 75 (1905) (Holmes, J., dissenting). Justice Kennedy has since employed the substantive due process analysis of *Casey* to find constitutional protection for the choice to giving sexuality "overt expression in intimate conduct with another person," in contravention, in this case, to laws prohibiting sodomy. *Lawrence v. Texas*, 2478. He again avoids *Lochner* when citing early-twentieth-century cases providing "broad statements of the substantive reach of liberty under the Due Process Clause," and turns quickly to *Griswold* as interpreted by *Casey* as the touchstone of modern substantive due process. *Lawrence v. Texas*, 2476; *Griswold v. Connecticut*, 381 U.S. 479 (1965).

32. *Planned Parenthood v. Casey*, 849.

33. Lincoln, First Inaugural Address, 585.

34. In 1991, the Court created a presumption against interpreting statutes to alter federal relations. *Gregory v. Ashcroft*, 501 U.S. 452 (1991). The following year, it held that Congress could not force state legislatures to enact specified laws. *New York v. United States*, 505 U.S. 144 (1992). The federalism revival truly took off, however, in 1995. *United States v. Lopez*, 514 U.S. 549 (1995).

35. *National League of Cities v. Usery*, 426 U.S. 833 (1976).

36. *Garcia v. San Antonio Metropolitan Transit Authority*, 469 U.S. 528, 580 (1985) (Rehnquist, J., dissenting).

37. E.g., *United States v. Lopez*; *United States v. Morrison*, 529 U.S. 598 (2000).

38. E.g., *City of Boerne v. Flores*, 521 U.S. 507 (1997); *United States v. Morrison*; *Board of Trustees of the University of Alabama v. Garrett*, 531 U.S. 356 (2001).

39. E.g., *New York v. United States*; *Printz v. United States*, 521 U.S. 898 (1997).

40. E.g., *Seminole Tribe v. Florida*, 517 U.S. 44 (1996); *College Savings Bank v. Florida Prepaid Postsecondary Education Expense Board*, 527 U.S. 666 (1999); *Alden v. Maine*, 527 U.S. 706 (1999); *Kimel v. Florida Board of Regents*, 528 U.S. 62 (2000); *Federal Maritime Commission v. South Carolina* 535 U.S. 743 (2002).

41. *City of Boerne v. Flores*, 521 U.S. 507, 535–536, 529 (1997).

42. *United States v. Morrison*, 616, 616 n. 7.

43. *United States v. Lopez*, 581 (Kennedy, J., concurring).

44. *Board of Trustees of the University of Alabama v. Garrett*.

45. *Kimel v. Florida Board of Regents*.

46. The Religious Land Use and Institutionalized Persons Act of 2000 was designed to reach this broad category of cases, though it has encountered some Establishment Clause challenges.

47. Franklin D. Roosevelt, *The Public Papers of Franklin D. Roosevelt*, ed. Samuel I. Rosenman, vol. 5 (New York: Random House, 1938), 191.

48. That signal is all the clearer and more interesting for Justice Clarence Thomas's lone concurrence questioning whether those New Deal precedents can be reconciled with the originalist Constitution. *United States v. Lopez*, 584 (Thomas, J., concurring).

49. *U.S. v. Lopez*, 559.

50. See also Keith E. Whittington, "Taking What They Give Us: Explaining the Court's Federalism Offensive," 51 *Duke Law Journal* 477 (2001). This could change if, for example, the Court were to invalidate significant provisions of the Endangered Species Act or Clean Water Act.

51. The argument in the next two paragraphs is developed at greater length in Keith E. Whittington, "Dismantling the Modern State? The Changing Structural Foundations of Federalism," 25 *Hastings Constitutional Law Quarterly* 483 (1998).

52. Rehnquist, "Random Thought," 324, 325.

precedent.[3] In this view, the activism of the Court consists largely in the extent to which its decisions change the law. The scope of Court opinions is another factor in evaluating the activism of the Court, as in cases where judges write opinions much broader than strictly necessary to decide a case, which puts the emphasis more on their "public law" function of laying down constitutional guidelines for public policy than on their "private law" function of deciding cases. Judicial activism can also be defined by examining the forms of Court power. For example, a very broad equity power, which, in effect, authorizes courts to assert ongoing supervisory power over institutions such as schools, hospitals, and prisons, can be considered characteristic of judicial activism.

While none of these usages is illegitimate, I believe that in a constitutional democracy the most fundamental criterion for the characterization of the scope of judicial power should be the relation of judicial power to the Constitution and the law. The "ordinary" power of judges is the power to interpret law in order to decide cases (either alone, or with juries). In doing so, judges cooperate with other branches in carrying out the law. In Hamilton's classic formulation in *The Federalist*, the judiciary "may truly be said to have neither FORCE nor WILL, but merely judgment." This view was reflected in Chief Justice John Marshall's statement that the judicial department "has no will in any case. . . . Judicial power is never exercised for the purpose of giving effect to the will of the judge; always for the purpose of giving effect to the will of the legislature; or in other words, to the will of the law."[4] To the extent that this is true—that judges enforce, not their own will, but the will of the people contained in the law—the power of the judiciary may be said, despite its relatively undemocratic structural features (appointment rather than election, and effective life tenure except in the rare and extreme case of impeachment),[5] to be consistent with republican principles. The "democratic credentials" of judicial review—potentially the most undemocratic of judicial acts, because it involves unelected and relatively unaccountable judges striking down acts of democratically elected officials—lie in the Court's decisions being rooted in the Constitution. To the extent that such acts are "undemocratic," it is not because of the nature of judicial power, but because of the limits that constitutionalism itself sets to democracy: the fact that, as Jefferson observed (not happily), the dead can rule the living in certain respects.

The most striking feature of American constitutional history, however, is the dramatic movement away from judicial review rooted in the Constitution and in principles of constitutional democracy, an interpretive judicial review, to an essentially different form of judicial review, one that is fundamentally legislative, because it is rooted, not in judgment, but in judicial will, that is, judicial perceptions of what conduces to social welfare. This movement is not an incidental result of certain decisions, but is systemic, rooted in the nature and form of modern judicial review.

The key element in the transformation of judicial review was the rise of modern "balancing" (broadly understood).[6] This distinctively modern conception of judicial review treats constitutional provisions as general "presumptions" in favor of certain principles, and then weighs the importance of the presumption in a given case against countervailing state interests. So, for example, the First Amendment is treated as establishing a strong presumption in favor of free speech, which can, however, be overcome by a strong showing of opposing interests (e.g., certain cases of incitement, libel, obscenity, fighting words, and so forth). And during the period in which balancing was used to decide free exercise cases (1963–90), the importance of the religious claim made in a given case was weighed against competing state interests (e.g., the impingement on Amish belief and practice versus the importance of compulsory education, as applied to the Amish refusal to send their children to high school). And the due process clause is treated as containing a substantive component prohibiting "arbitrary" deprivation of "fundamental rights," such as privacy, and judges are called on to evaluate the importance of the privacy concerns vis-à-vis competing state interests (e.g., in the case of abortion, the state interest in maternal health and in the potential life of the fetus).

What is implicit in each of these cases of balancing (and others that we shall see) is that the modern notion of judicial review requires judges to evaluate the relative importance of the rights claim in the case, the relative importance of the asserted state interest(s), and then the relative importance of the rights claim versus the state interests. But, in doing so, the judges can make no reasonable claim that they are simply enforcing the will of the people contained in the Constitution, since the Constitution itself offers virtually no guidance whatsoever in the making of any of these determinations. Those determinations must be made on the basis of what Hamilton and Marshall characterized as "will," not judgment. As Justice Benjamin Cardozo made clear in the elegant prose of his classic, *The Nature of the Judicial Process*, the basis for these determinations is the judge's conception of what advances social welfare.[7]

A second aspect of modern judicial review is the jettisoning of legislative deference. This is, of course, characteristic of the balancing cases, in which there is, virtually by definition, no clear constitutional guidance in the decision making. It is also true, however, of other cases in which an analysis with merely plausible but not clear-cut constitutional foundations is made the basis for judicial review.

Legislative deference—according to which judges will strike down laws only in "clear" cases—is a necessary corollary of the traditional argument regarding the democratic credentials of judicial review. Judicial review does not consist in giving meaning to ambiguous constitutional provisions—provisions that can fairly be read in different ways. On what grounds, after all, could judges take one of two fair interpretations of the Constitution and, choosing one of them, override a similarly fair interpretation adopted by the legislature or executive? If the phrase is genuinely ambiguous, judges would not be in a position to say that they are exercising judgment—enforcing the will of the Constitution—rather than their own wills.

To forestall a likely misunderstanding, I want to emphasize that there is no pretense here of equating "clear" cases with "noncontroversial" cases. Judges themselves must decide what is clear, and the simple existence of some other vaguely "possible" interpretation does not prove that there is no clear meaning in a given case. The point is merely this: if judges, having carefully engaged in the appropriate methods of interpretation, arrive at the conclusion that the Constitution is not clear on a point, then they must defer to the legislature. The significance of this point as a limit on judicial power may seem to be undermined by the fact that it is the judges themselves who decide what is clear. That is mistaken, though. There is a large number of cases where no plausible argument can be made that a provision's meaning is clear. For example, the whole category of substantive due process and large swaths of modern equal protection law fit that description.

The most important criterion for judicial activism, then, is whether judicial review is exercised in the traditional form articulated by Hamilton and Marshall—dominant in theory and generally, I think (more controversially), in practice during the first part of American constitutional history—or in the modern form dominant in practice since at least the end of the nineteenth century, and more comprehensively (in theory as well as practice) since the appointment of justices holding modern ideas of judicial power (Holmes's legal realism) to the Court after 1937.

The question I want to ask in this chapter, then, is whether the Rehnquist Court should be considered to be a Court exercising "traditional judicial review" or one exercising "modern judicial review." I think that, with few exceptions, the answer is that the Rehnquist Court is modern in its jurisprudence, and that there has been no significant return to a principled judicial restraint characteristic of traditional judicial review.

Two brief caveats. First, among modern judges, who exercise essentially legislative judicial review and hence are activists, there are justices and Courts that are more or less activist. Frankfurter was a devout student of Holmes, who conceived of judicial acts as essentially legislative, but he wanted to exercise that power moderately, with caution, in a restrained way. In that sense he was a moderate or restrained judicial activist. More eccentrically, Justice Hugo Black disdained balancing and claimed to exercise a judicial review rooted in the text of the Constitution—that is, he embraced ideals more traditional than modern—and yet was a leader of the Warren Court revolution. The case that he was a judicial activist, then, must rest on rather different grounds: a showing that his readings of constitutional text were utterly implausible and so systematically as to constitute textual manipulation (however subjectively sincere).

Second, nothing I have said so far addresses the normative question. Accepting everything I have said about judicial activism and about the essential distinction between traditional and modern judicial review, one might be either a fervent advocate of judicial activism and modern judicial review, or a confirmed proponent of the traditional approach and determined opponent of judicial activism.

One final point. Someone might argue that my proposed understanding of judicial activism ought not to be adopted, because it is irrelevant and not useful, on the grounds that, even if there ever was such a thing as "traditional judicial review," all contemporary justices exercise modern judicial power, and therefore my understanding of judicial restraint (i.e., traditional judicial review) is, at best, of no more than historical interest. I think this is wrong, on two counts. First some contemporary justices do make a principled argument for a more traditional understanding of judicial power. In particular, Justices Antonin Scalia and Clarence Thomas generally embrace a principled, traditional understanding of judicial review. (Note that it is possible to maintain this, while at the same time recognizing that they have not always practiced traditional judicial review consistently.)[8] Second, these justices receive intellectual support from other judges and from various legal scholars—some of them represented in this book—and especially from those who are characterized in the contemporary debate as "originalists." On both these counts, then, the debate is a live one, and a traditional approach to judicial review is of more than merely historical interest.

THE REHNQUIST COURT

The first problem we confront when we ask whether the Rehnquist Court is a modern Court is the problem of who exactly constitutes the "Rehnquist Court."

Much of the discussion in this volume has concerned the case of *Planned Parenthood v. Casey*. This 1992 case was obviously decided by a Court presided over by Chief Justice William Rehnquist, and in that sense was obviously a "Rehnquist Court" decision. But, in another sense, that case seems more like a reincarnation of a Warren Court decision than a decision by a Court supposedly dominated by political and judicial conservatives. What this reflects is the complexity occasioned by the fact that the Rehnquist Court is composed of three different blocs: first, a politically liberal modern bloc (Stevens, Ginsberg, Breyer, and Souter), second, a centrist modern bloc that is typically, but not always, conservative (O'Connor, Kennedy), and third, a traditional bloc (Scalia, Thomas), with Rehnquist himself straddling the last two blocs. In cases where the centrist modern bloc and the traditional bloc unite, the character of the opinion will usually reflect the jurisprudential theory of the opinion writer. Where O'Connor or Kennedy (and sometimes Rehnquist) write, the opinion will typically reflect modern ideas of judicial power, and where Scalia or Thomas write, more traditional approaches will tend to take the fore. In addition, there are other decisions in which the "centrist" modern justices (O'Connor and/or Kennedy) will join with the liberal modern justices to produce a Court majority.

Accordingly, there are at least three main categories of "Rehnquist Court" opinions. First, cases like *Planned Parenthood v. Casey* and *Romer v. Evans* reflect the alliance of the modern "centrist" justices (who are liberal on certain key social issues) and modern liberals to produce a distinctly activist modern opinion. (The traditionalist dissenters in these cases base their opinions, not on culture-war conservatism, but on opposition to judicial activism.) Second, the five "conservatives" (Rehnquist, O'Connor, Kennedy, Scalia, and Thomas) vote together in cases like *Dolan v. Tigard*, with modern activist opinions written by one of the first three, or in a cases like *U.S. v. Lopez*, with opinions that fail to abide by traditional canons of legislative deference. Third, the five conservatives vote together in cases decided on more originalist grounds, written by Scalia or Thomas (or sometimes Rehnquist), such as *Lucas v. South Carolina Coastal Commission*. (There are other variations of these categories, of course. For example, *Employment Division, Department of Human Resources of Oregon v. Smith* was one of the most strikingly traditional or originalist of the Rehnquist Court's decisions—at least in its "bottom line," though not its handling of precedent. But because a modern centrist like O'Connor was committed to maintaining a balancing approach, the *Smith* Court opinion actually required a fifth vote from Justice Stevens, whose vote has to be explained on grounds very different from Scalia's, namely, the rigorous privatization of religion that results from his strict separationism.)

When one asks the question, "Is the Rehnquist Court an activist Court?" then, it is worthwhile asking, "Which Rehnquist Court?" My own conclusion is that only rarely in its best-known decisions does the Rehnquist Court act as a traditional rather than a modern or activist

Court. I want to provide some support for this claim in the balance of this chapter by examining a number of important Rehnquist Court decisions.

In fairness to the Court, I do want to make an important qualification. I concede that an examination of actual Rehnquist Court decisions understates the extent to which it has been a very substantial *obstacle* to judicial activism in ways that are more indirect and impossible to measure. Because it is (rightly) anticipated, on the basis of experience, that the Court will not be receptive to many activist claims (especially from the left, the source of most activist claims), many of those claims that might have been pursued had there been a liberal activist Supreme Court have not been pursued. In fact, ironically, many complaints about Rehnquist Court judicial activism come from political liberals who are upset that the Court has refused to endorse their activist legal claims (e.g., their efforts to read into the Constitution a prohibition of the death penalty, a rigid separation of church and state, expansive criminal defendants' rights, and so on).

THE REHNQUIST COURT AND BALANCING: THE BURGER COURT BACKGROUND

Much of the Rehnquist Court's constitutional jurisprudence essentially builds on trends that began in the Burger Court. Several Burger Court decisions exemplify the commitment of certain contemporary "conservative" justices to balancing as an approach to constitutional interpretation and judicial review.

The first example can be found in *U.S. Trust v. New Jersey* (1976). The contract clause had come pretty close to being read out of the Constitution in the 1934 case *Home Building and Loan v. Blaisdell*, which upheld a law only marginally different from the "stay laws" that were the precise object of the contract clause's prohibition. *U.S. Trust v. New Jersey* resurrected the clause, but in a typically modern form. The Court, through Justice Blackmun, rather than trying to identify a category of state laws that "impair the obligation of contract," (examples of which he rejected as "formalism")[9] in effect rewrote the constitutional provision, making it read that states shall make no law *unreasonably* impairing the obligation of contract. Moreover, it created a typically modern presumption against laws impairing the obligation of state contracts, because they involved the state's self-interest.[10]

A second example of Burger Court balancing by conservative judges appeared in the dissents in *Garcia v. San Antonio Metropolitan Authority* (1985), in which Blackmun's flip-flop led to the overruling of *National League of Cities v. Usery* (1976). The majority opinion in *Garcia* argued that none of the legal distinctions offered to justify limits on federal regulation of state employment law, such as the immunity of those activities that could be characterized as "integral governmental functions," held up under analysis and experience. (This is an analysis, I should note, for which I have substantial sympathy. While the Constitution justifies some reasonable concern about direct federal regulation of core state activities, it is hard for me to see that there is any judicially manageable standard that could meet the test of the requirement of legislative deference in unclear cases.) The responses of Justices Powell and O'Connor effectively adopted a balancing approach to the Tenth Amendment.

Justice Powell argued:

> Much of the Court's opinion is devoted to arguing that it is difficult to define a priori "traditional governmental functions." National League of Cities neither engaged in, nor required, such a task. The Court discusses and condemns as standards "traditional governmental functions," "purely historical" functions, "'uniquely' governmental functions," and "'necessary' governmental services." But nowhere does it mention that National League of Cities adopted a familiar type of balancing test for determining whether Commerce Clause enactments transgress constitutional limitations imposed by the federal nature of our system of government.[11]

In opting for a balancing approach, Justice Powell obviated the difficulties of identifying with any precise principle a category of state actions that are exempt from federal regulation: balancing permits justices to "specify" relatively vague general principles by making essentially ad hoc judgments.

Justice O'Connor followed a similar path:

> The problems of federalism in an integrated national economy are capable of more responsible resolution than holding that the States as States retain no status apart from that which Congress chooses to let them retain. The proper resolution, I suggest, lies in weighing state autonomy as a factor in the balance when interpreting the means by which Congress can exercise its authority on the States as States. It is insufficient, in assessing the validity of congressional regulation of a State pursuant to the commerce power, to ask only whether the same regulation would be valid if enforced against a private party. That reasoning, embodied in the majority opinion, is inconsistent with the spirit of our Constitution.[12]

So justices will have to weigh the importance of the congressional regulation, throw in some unspecified concern for state autonomy, and then decide whether the degree of impingement on state autonomy is warranted by the purposes and character of the congressional resolution. There is little or no guidance from the Constitution in this process: it merely specifies the vague general principles and then gives way to judicial decisions based on a Court majority's considered judgment as to what the broad social welfare requires.

Note, for the record, that I am not arguing that Powell and O'Connor have no important constitutional principles to rely on here. I think that federalism is an absolutely fundamental constitutional principle, and that the autonomy of state operations from federal regulation is a very relevant factor in evaluating the state of federalism. I think legislators should weigh that consideration heavily in their evaluation of proposed legislation. What I am skeptical about is the existence of clear constitutional principles that provide judicially manageable standards in this area. The plea of judicial conservatives here is for judicial legislation—a kind of judicial power to provide "necessary and proper laws"—to enforce important constitutional ideals that lack more specific protection in the text of the Constitution. But that is similar to various forms of liberal judicial activism about which judicial conservatives have rightly complained for a long time. (*Miranda* is judicial legislation designed to give effect to the constitutional ideal of no self-incrimination, *Mapp* is judicial legislation designed to give effect to the constitutional ideal of privacy, and so on and on and on.)

Powell and O'Connor, then, are good examples of justices who are considered "centrist" or "conservative," but whose jurisprudential approaches differ little from other modern justices. They (and similar justices like Anthony Kennedy) have often been the swing votes in both Burger Court and Rehnquist Court cases.

The Rehnquist Court and Balancing: The Takings Clause

One of the most obvious areas of balancing on the Rehnquist Court itself is its takings clause constitutional jurisprudence. That area is also interesting because it shows different ways in which various justices grapple with the issue.

The original meaning of the takings clause is reasonably clear from the paradigmatic case of a taking: when government exercises the power of eminent domain (takes private property for public use), it must provide just compensation to the property owners. The power the authors of the Fifth Amendment had in mind was the power to *take* property—physically. Over time, however, it became tempting to extend the principle of the takings clause to those regulations of the government that had a negative impact on property by diminishing its value. The problem, of course, is that an enormous amount of government regulation indirectly affects some property values to some degree. How is one to tell when compensation is required?

But the Court bit the apple of regulatory takings in *Pennsylvania Coal v. Mahon*. Justice Holmes acknowledged the problem straightforwardly:

> Government hardly could go on if to some extent values incident to property could not be diminished without paying for every such change in the general law. As long recognized, some values are enjoyed under an implied limitation and must yield to the police power. But obviously the implied limitation must have its limits, or the contract and due process clauses are gone. One fact for consideration in determining such limits is the extent of the diminution. When it reaches a certain magnitude, in most if not in all cases there must be an exercise of eminent domain and compensation to sustain the act. So the question depends upon the particular facts. The greatest weight is given to the judgment of the legislature, but it always is open to interested parties to contend that the legislature has gone beyond its constitutional power.[13]

Holmes went on to give an indication of exactly how clear a principle the Constitution provided in dealing with regulatory takings: "The general rule at least is, that while property may be regulated to a certain extent, if regulation goes too far it will be recognized as a taking. . . . As we already have said, this is a question of degree—and therefore cannot be disposed of by general propositions."[14] Such a rule simply authorizes ad hoc judicial decisions.

After a period of takings clause oblivion after the New Deal, conservative legal scholars and interest groups pushed to reinvigorate the takings clause at least from the 1970s, and the Rehnquist Court eventually answered their call. In a series of cases—especially *Nollan v. California Coastal Commission*, *Lucas v. South Carolina Coastal Commission*, and *Dolan v. City of Tigard*—the takings clause has been resuscitated. The key question for my purposes here is whether this was possible without employing a modern form of judicial review, that is, without engaging in judicial activism. I think the answer to that is no.

Justice Scalia makes an interesting effort to avoid judicial activism in *Lucas*, and it is possible that he succeeded, for narrow reasons associated with that case. The case came to the Supreme Court with South Carolina courts having already determined—and the Court accepting their judgment—that the prohibition of building on the land Lucas had bought rendered that property utterly worthless. Once that premise is granted, one might argue, it is possible to hold that an uncompensated regulatory taking of that sort is unconstitutional, on the grounds that it is effectively equivalent to a physical taking, and does not require judges to make precisely the distinctions that Holmes thought necessary—questions of "degree."

Questions of degree are at the heart of balancing and of the modern character of balancing cases. If a case involves a question of what degree of use of a power is legitimate, virtually by definition the Constitution can offer no guidance in deciding such a question. This point was at the heart of Marshall's observation in *McCulloch v. Maryland*, when he pointed out the advantages of relying on a particular theory of taxation (that state power of taxation corresponds to those objects over which the state is sovereign):

> If we measure the power of taxation residing in a State, by the extent of sovereignty which the people of a single State possess, and can confer on its government, we have an intelligible standard, applicable to every case to which the power may be applied. . . . We are relieved, as we ought to be, from clashing sovereignty; from interfering powers; from a repugnancy between a right in one government to pull down what there is an acknowledged right in another to build up; from the incompatibility of a right in one government to destroy what there is a right in another to preserve. We are not driven to the perplexing inquiry, so unfit for the judicial department, what degree of taxation is the legitimate use, and what degree may amount to the abuse of the power.[15]

Judges need "intelligible standards"—standards that flow from interpretation of the Constitution's text that allots, and withholds, different *kinds* of power from the federal and state governments. Questions of degree—"what degree of taxation is the legitimate use, and what degree may amount to the abuse of the power"—are "perplexing" inquiries "unfit for the judicial department." Why? They are perplexing for the judge, because he has no judicially manageable standards by which to make such a judgment—no standards deriving from a fair reading of the Constitution's text rather than from some political judgment as to what is the best point at which to say that the power ends.

In *Lucas*, Scalia struggles to find an intelligible standard to resolve the case. He notes the shift from physical to regulatory takings, and acknowledges that "our decision in Mahon offered little insight into when, and under what circumstances, a given regulation would be seen as going 'too far' for purposes of the Fifth Amendment." There are, however, he says, "at least two discrete categories of regulatory action" that are "compensable without case-specific inquiry into the public interest advanced in support of the restraint," namely, regulations involving a physical invasion of private property, and regulation denying "all economically beneficial or productive use of land."[16] *Lucas* seems to fit into the latter category.[17]

In a footnote, Scalia has the candor to admit, "Regrettably, the rhetorical force of our 'deprivation of all economically feasible use' rule is greater than its precision, since the rule does not make clear the 'property interest' against which the loss of value is to be measured." He expresses the hope that the "answer to this difficult question may lie in how the owner's reasonable expectations have been shaped by the State's law of property—i.e., whether and to what degree the State's law has accorded legal recognition and protection to the particular interest in land with respect to which the takings claimant alleges a diminution in (or elimination of) value." This is the principle that Scalia employs to resolve *Lucas*: "Where the State seeks to sustain regulation that deprives land of all economically beneficial use, we think it may resist compensation only if the logically antecedent inquiry into the nature of the owner's estate shows that the proscribed use interests were not part of his title to begin with."[18]

Dolan v. City of Tigard is a different kettle of fish. Chief Justice Rehnquist (as his earlier Court opinion in *Morrison v. Olson* suggested) does not hesitate to employ a modern balancing approach on some occasions. When the city of Tigard tried to condition a permit to expand a hardware store and pave its parking lot on the owner's dedication of a portion of her property along a floodplain for a greenway and another portion for a pedestrian/bicycle pathway, she invoked the takings clause. Rehnquist's Court opinion struck down the requirements as uncompensated takings. He found that there was an essential nexus between legitimate state interests and the permit condition, but he found that the conditions failed the second part of the test (dealing with "the degree of the exactions demanded")[19] that the city show a rough proportionality between its exactions and the projected impact of the proposed development. The city did not have to provide a precise mathematical calculation, the Court said, but it had to "make some sort of individualized determination that the required dedication is related both in nature and extent to the impact of the proposed development."[20] This looks pretty much like a straightforward balancing test.

Justice Stevens's dissent criticizes the Court for "abandoning the traditional presumption of constitutionality and imposing a novel burden of proof," and it goes on to argue that the "so-called 'regulatory takings' doctrine that the Holmes dictum kindled has an obvious kinship with the line of substantive due process cases that *Lochner* exemplified. Besides having similar ancestry, both doctrines are potentially open-ended sources of judicial power to invalidate state economic regulations that Members of this Court view as unwise or unfair."[21] This is a fair criticism, I think, and one that closely parallels many conservative criticisms of modern liberal judicial legislation. Given Justice Stevens's own activism in many areas, it is understandable that some conservatives are tempted to say that what is sauce for the goose (a wide range of liberal activist decisions) is sauce for the gander (conservative property rights activist decisions). A more principled position, however, will reject activism on both sides of the political spectrum.

It should also be noted that, for all his efforts to find "an intelligible standard" in *Lucas*—one that avoids a modern balancing approach—

Justice Scalia concurs *sub silentio* in the *Dolan* Court opinion (as does Justice Thomas).

The Rehnquist Court and Balancing: The Free Exercise Clause

The Rehnquist Court takes a quite different approach to balancing in *Employment Division, Oregon Department of Human Resources v. Smith*. This is one of the few modern Court decisions that actually seems to return to a more traditional standard. There are, however, some significant qualifications to that assertion.

The free exercise clause has long been interpreted to guarantee freedom of belief, and to guarantee freedom of action from religiously based discrimination, but traditionally religiously motivated action was subject to the ordinary constraints of secular laws. This "secular regulation rule," exemplified by *Reynolds v. U.S.*, in which the Court upheld a congressional prohibition of polygamy in the Utah territory, came under increasing attack in the modern era, on the grounds that it permitted limits on religious freedom on relatively insignificant secular grounds. In the 1963 case *Sherbert v. Verner*, the Court adopted one form of a modern balancing approach, with a heavy emphasis on the religious liberty side of the equation, requiring a compelling state interest to overcome claims of religious freedom. This approach lasted until *Smith* in 1990.

While Scalia generally recognizes the force of precedent, he rejects the legitimacy of certain precedents, especially those, like *Sherbert*, that compel judges to act like legislators, by asking them to weigh the sincerity, centrality, and importance of religious beliefs against countervailing state interests. He acknowledges the difficulties this may entail for religious minorities, but considers this preferable to judges engaging in essentially legislative activity:

> It may fairly be said that leaving accommodation to the political process will place at a relative disadvantage those religious practices that are not widely engaged in; but that unavoidable consequence of democratic government must be preferred to a system in which each conscience is a law unto itself or in which judges weigh the social importance of all laws against the centrality of all religious beliefs.[22]

The priority of neutral, generally applicable laws over religious objections is an intelligible judicial standard, while the compelling state interest test is essentially legislative, and improper for judges operating on traditional jurisprudential principles.

If the central thrust of the *Smith* opinion represents Scalia's more traditional approach, however, other aspects of the opinion should limit any inferences drawn from *Smith* about the Rehnquist Court's general approach. Scalia's opinion bears the marks of necessary compromise, in the form of some fairly fancy (though not particularly persuasive) footwork to harmonize this opinion with precedents. First, Scalia has to distinguish the case from a series of opinions that he characterizes as "hybrid" opinions, involving free exercise claims plus some other constitutional guarantee, e.g., the Court opinion in *Wisconsin v. Yoder*, which involved First Amendment parental rights as well as a free exercise claim.[23] Second, he has to distinguish *Sherbert* itself, by confining it to the unemployment compensation area, which is said to lend itself to individualized determinations. These distinctions may be imaginative, but they clearly represent profoundly transformed understandings of *Yoder* (and similar hybrid cases) and *Sherbert*.

Just as important in minimizing the import of *Smith*'s traditional opinion for the general character of the Rehnquist Court is the fact that Scalia has a majority in *Smith* only because he has a fifth vote from Justice Stevens, than whom there are few *less* traditional justices. Stevens' vote can be accounted for primarily by his rigidly separationist church-state views (sharply at odds with the original meaning of the establishment clause),[24] which minimize any public standing of religion.

Ironically, *Smith* went on to become, indirectly, the occasion for an even clearer demonstration of the essentially modern jurisprudential character of the Rehnquist Court.

THE REHNQUIST COURT AND JUDICIAL POWER: *CITY OF BOERNE V. FLORES*

Smith provoked an unusual coalition of interest group and congressional pro–minority rights liberals and proreligion conservatives to pass, by an overwhelming majority, the 1993 Religious Freedom Restoration Act (RFRA). The intent of RFRA was clearly to overturn *Smith* and to restore the rule of *Sherbert* for both federal and state governments. The fact that there were two issues in the case—the issue of Congress's power to define constitutional rights under Section 5 of the Fourteenth Amendment, and the *Smith*/free exercise issue—complicates an understanding of the case considerably. The Court, I will argue, wrote an opinion that would normally be wrong, but is right this time, almost, as it were, by accident.

In *Boerne*, the *Smith* majority holdovers (Rehnquist, Stevens, Scalia, Kennedy) join with two newcomers (Thomas and Ginsberg) to defend *Smith* against the congressional response.[25] They argue that the Supreme Court has the ultimate authority to interpret the Constitution, and that Congress's power under Section 5 is merely a remedial power, which does not authorize Congress to "decree the substance of the Fourteenth Amendment's restrictions on the States."[26] History and case law demonstrate, the Court says, that "[a]s enacted, the Fourteenth Amendment confers substantive rights against the States which, like the provisions of the Bill of Rights, are self-executing. . . . The power to interpret the Constitution in a case or controversy remains in the Judiciary."[27] After all, "If Congress could define its own powers by altering the Fourteenth Amendment's meaning, no longer would the Constitution be 'superior paramount law, unchangeable by ordinary means.' It would be 'on a level with ordinary legislative acts, and, like other acts, . . . alterable when the legislature shall please to alter it' " (quoting *Marbury v. Madison*).

The argument here parallels the argument of *Cooper v. Aaron* (1957), which argued that the oath of state officials to enforce the Constitution was an oath to enforce it *as it is understood by the Supreme Court*. In *Boerne*, the power of the Court under Section 5 to enforce the Fourteenth Amendment is simply a power to enforce it *as it is understood by the Supreme Court*.

But the matter is more complicated than that. As Lincoln noted in his speech on the *Dred Scott* decision, while Supreme Court interpretations of the Constitution are ordinarily authoritative, that is not always the case. To reverse the later words of Chief Justice Charles Evans Hughes, "The Constitution is *not always* what the Supreme Court says it is." The Court can get the Constitution wrong, and if other public officials are correct in believing that the Court has seriously erred, then they need not feel bound by its interpretation, though they will obey its decision in the particular case. They can legitimately act on their different understanding of the Constitution, in the meantime working to change the Court's mind (primarily through new appointments) should a new case be presented to the Court. So, for example, Lincoln claimed during his 1858 Senate campaign, that he would feel authorized to vote for a proposed law inconsistent with *Dred Scott*. The Court would still have the power to pass on acts of other branches (both state and federal), but in a sense the real "ultimate authority" is the American people (even short of a constitutional supermajority that can amend the Constitution), who can decide that the Court was wrong, elect officials who will act on an interpretation of the Constitution opposed to the Court's, and ultimately change the Court to vindicate that view. (They may be right or wrong about their interpretation of the Constitution, but the point is this: it is not simply a given that the Court's interpretation is by definition authoritative.)[28]

But Lincoln's argument about the limited authority of Supreme Court interpretations is not the only factor that must be considered. Another key factor completely ignored by the Court in *Boerne*—partly because it runs contrary to the fundamental assumptions of modern judicial review and partly because it genuinely is not at issue in *Boerne*—needs to be highlighted. What if the constitutional provision at issue is not *clear*? What if there is more than one "fair" interpretation of a provision?

The Court does not consider this in *Boerne*, and, in fact, it is not an issue in that case, because *Smith* is a very rare example of a modern Court decision that rests, not on the shaky legislative foundations of modern judicial review, but on the sound interpretive foundations of traditional judicial review. So the Court is right to say that, in this case, Congress is trying to overturn a clearly correct Court interpretation of the Constitution, and so its decision in *Boerne* is correct. That, presumably, is why the more traditional justices on the Court (particularly Scalia and Thomas) joined Kennedy's Court opinion. But, in doing so, they made the mistake of signing on to an opinion that asserted much too broad a view of judicial power and much too narrow a view of congressional power.

The much more common case in modern constitutional law is Court decisions that interpret an allegedly vague general provision of the Constitution and read it in one, perhaps plausible, but hardly compelling way. For example, what if Congress were to pass a law pursuant to Section 5 of the Fourteenth Amendment that in effect authorized states to adopt a "totality of circumstances" rule, rather than a rule requiring the Miranda warnings, in evaluating whether confessions violated Fourteenth Amendment procedural due process guarantees? It is an understatement to say that "due process" does not clearly demand the Miranda warnings, which are only one possible method of enforcing self-incrimination guarantees said to be implicit in the Fourteenth Amendment due process clause. On what grounds could the Court plausibly claim that what is merely its preferred approach to giving content to due process in the states trumps Congress's explicit authority under Section 5 to enforce the Fourteenth Amendment guarantee of due process? Under a proper understanding of the Court's limited constitutional powers, there are no such grounds.

This example could be multiplied extensively. Congressional authorization of alternatives to the exclusionary rule in search and seizure cases? Same result. Congressional power to prohibit partial-birth and other abortions—based, not on a strained reading of the commerce clause, but on an utterly plausible reading of the equal protection clause (one much more plausible than the flimsy substantive due process argument for abortion rights)? Same result. Congressional regulation of remedies employed in desegregation cases and other broad institutional litigation (even accepting, on grounds of precedent, the dubious equal protection standards that provide the foundation for the original finding of constitutional violations in those cases)? Same result.

Congressional power according to this understanding is not unlimited—Congress is not so unconstrained that it is free to define simply anything as being in or outside the language of the Fourteenth Amendment. Some constitutional provisions are clear—such as the secular regulation rule interpretation of the free exercise clause, which undergirds the decision in *Boerne* (assuming that application of the First Amendment to the states is settled). Other laws would clearly go beyond any plausible reading of Fourteenth Amendment rights, such as a modern privacy right (as opposed to the old Fourth Amendment–type privacy right). But within fairly broad limits, Congress would have a good deal of power under Section 5 to do precisely what the Court in *Boerne* denies that it can do: to "decree the substance of the Fourteenth Amendment's restrictions on the States" by adopting reasonable interpretations of the very general language of Section 1 (privileges and immunities, due process, and equal protection).

The Rehnquist Court's broad opinion in *Boerne*—and there were really no dissents, or even appropriate qualifying concurrences, on the broad judicial power issue—is an indication of how little it challenges modern latitudinarian notions of judicial power.

The Rehnquist Court and Legislative Deference

It is particularly in the area of constitutional adjudication of federalism issues that the Rehnquist Court has found itself accused of conservative judicial activism. This area includes commerce clause cases (*U.S. v. Lopez* and *U.S. v. Morrison*), "commandeering" cases (*New York v. U.S.* and *Printz v. U.S.*), and Eleventh Amendment cases (*Seminole Tribe v. Fla.* and *Alden v. Maine*). There can be no question that the Court's concerns here involve very important constitutional principles that have too often been given short shrift. It can even be argued that there has been an essential change in the nature of American federalism, from a federalism that constitutionally reserves certain questions to the final authority of states to a federalism based on Congress's discretionary decisions to leave certain questions to the states.

There is a serious question, however, as to whether there are judicially manageable standards for courts to deal with this issue. Some of the Rehnquist Court federalism doctrines may be defensible on grounds of traditional, interpretive judicial review. For my present purposes, however, I want to focus in the last part of this chapter on an area where I am inclined to think that such a defense is unsuccessful, namely, the commerce clause.

U.S. v. Lopez was the first Supreme Court decision in sixty years to strike down a law on the grounds that it exceeded Congress's authority under the commerce clause. After its switch in 1937, and subsequently bolstered by eight Roosevelt appointees, the Court wrote very broad opinions upholding federal power to regulate virtually any form of commercial activity. In *Wickard v. Filburn* (1942), the Court unanimously upheld a fine imposed on a small Ohio farmer who had grown wheat in excess of his government-assigned quota for use on his own farm. The regulation was valid because there was a substantial effect on interstate commerce here, if two factors were taken into consideration: first, Filburn had to be considered as one of a large class of similarly situated people, and second, even if the wheat never left the farm, it indirectly influenced how much wheat the farmer would have to sell in the interstate wheat market. Given these two criteria, it was doubtful that any economic activity could be considered not to have a substantial effect on interstate commerce.

This was arguably the result, not so much of a change in Court doctrine, as a change in the facts of economic life. When the Framers wrote the Constitution, the distinction between interstate and intrastate economic activity was a real distinction in practice: a great deal of economic activity occurred in and had no impact beyond a locality. With the growth of means of transportation and communication and other technology, the national market grew, and it could plausibly be argued that little, if any, exclusively "intrastate" economic activity was left.

By the 1960s, the commerce power was such a strong and successful basis for laws that Congress employed it as the foundation for the controversial Civil Rights Act of 1964, and the Court's decision upholding the law on those grounds was unanimous. Federal regulation even of noneconomic matters, based on their economic effects, now seemed unchallengeable under the commerce power.

It was not unusual, then, when Congress based the Gun-Free School Zones Act of 1990 on the commerce clause, and did not feel any need to provide an elaborate record to justify the law as a commerce clause regulation, since a talismanic invocation of the commerce clause was all that had been required for a long time. *U.S. v. Lopez*, then, came as something of a shock to many people, though others were aware that some conservative scholars had been raising the issue for a while (and obviously with enough success for an appeals court to strike down the law). The Court took advantage of the fact that earlier commerce clause opinions had maintained at least theoretical limits on the power;[29] it distinguished between economic and noneconomic activity, with regulation of the latter issues being more questionable; and it argued that it could not uphold the reasoning justifying government regulation in this case without transforming the commerce clause into a federal police power to regulate virtually anything.[30]

Subsequently, the Court also struck down a part of the Violence Against Women Act (which gave women subjected to violence a right to sue in federal court), in *U.S. v. Morrison* (2000). This time around, Congress had carefully put together an extensive record to justify the contention that such violence had a substantial impact on interstate commerce, but the Court responded that the record bore out its concern "that Congress might use the Commerce Clause to completely obliterate the Constitution's distinction between national and local authority" and it held that Congress could not "regulate noneconomic, violent criminal conduct based solely on that conduct's aggregate effect on interstate commerce."[31]

Is the Court's recent return to placing limits on Congress's commerce power an instance of conservative judicial activism? For reasons I have discussed elsewhere, in regard to an earlier Court's foray into this area, I am inclined to think so.[32] It is not that there is no serious constitutional issue here. The scope of federal power under the commerce clause is a very important issue, and if there is to be a genuine *constitutional* division of power between federal and state governments—if the federal government is to remain a government of enumerated powers rather than a government of general powers—then some limits on the commerce clause are essential. The problem is that there seem to be no clear-cut, judicially manageable standards for making the necessary distinction, and therefore the vindication of this constitutional principle, in practice, must be left to actors in the political process, to legislators and executives.

There is language in *Lopez* itself that suggests the problem: "Admittedly, a determination whether an intrastate activity is commercial or noncommercial may in some cases result in legal uncertainty"; "In Jones & Laughlin Steel, we held that the question of congressional power under the Commerce Clause 'is necessarily one of degree'"; "These are not precise formulations, and in the nature of things they cannot be."[33]

Even more clearly, Justice Kennedy's concurrence (joined by O'Connor) suggests the uncertainty of legal standards. After a negative review of earlier "formalistic" distinctions employed to limit federal commerce power, it quotes *Wickard* approvingly (with the rhetoric typical of modern judicial review) to the effect that "whatever terminology is used, the criterion is necessarily one of degree and must be so defined. This does not satisfy those who seek mathematical or rigid formulas. But such formulas are not provided by the great concepts of the Constitution."[34] The concurrence even concedes that, regarding federalism, "there seem[s] to be much uncertainty respecting the existence, and the content, of standards that allow the Judiciary to play a significant role in maintaining the design contemplated by the Framers."[35] But, while acknowledging the role of political officials, Kennedy concludes that judges must play a part as well: "the federal balance is too essential a part of our constitutional structure and plays too vital a role in securing freedom for us to admit inability to intervene when one or the other level of Government has tipped the scales too far."[36] And, in a statement that quotes *Marbury v. Madison*, but reflects a distinctively modern understanding of judicial power as the power to define unclear provisions, he says: "But as the branch whose distinctive duty it is to declare 'what the law is,' we are often called upon to resolve questions of constitutional law not susceptible to the mechanical application of bright and clear lines."[37] The bottom line is that this law goes too far, and therefore is unconstitutional.

Finally, and perhaps even more revealingly, Justice Thomas's more radical concurrence does *not* dismiss as "formalistic" the earlier Court cases limiting the power, and he seems, on the contrary, to be rather sympathetic toward a return to some such approach. He calls for reconsidering the substantial effects test "with an eye toward constructing a standard that reflects the text and history of the Commerce Clause without totally rejecting our more recent Commerce Clause jurisprudence."[38] His purpose in writing the concurrence, he says, includes the need to "point out the necessity of refashioning a coherent test that does not tend to 'obliterate the distinction between what is national and what is local and create a completely centralized government.'"[39]

What is revealing is that Justice Thomas does not tell us *what* the newly fashioned, coherent test would be. For the time being, he seems satisfied with the distinction between commercial and noncommercial activities,[40] but it seems clear that he wants a more substantial restriction on federal power. In *U.S. v. Morrison*, he repeats his call for the Court to "replace[] its existing Commerce Clause jurisprudence with a standard more consistent with the original understanding," but again does not offer an account of what that standard would be.[41]

Is he holding back because the standard he has in mind is the pre-1937 standard? If so, perhaps it is the staggering implications of a resuscitation of pre-1937 commerce clause jurisprudence that prevents him from being more forthcoming. Yet he says that "we ought to temper our Commerce Clause jurisprudence in a manner that both makes sense of our more recent case law and is more faithful to the original understanding of that Clause," which seems to imply a rejection of the idea of simply returning to the pre-1937 standards.[42] But, if there is some new standard that preserves at least much of the recent jurisprudence, while at the same time bringing it more in line with the (narrower) original understanding of the commerce power, what is it? The fact that Justice Thomas does not offer such a standard at least suggests this possibility: perhaps there is no judicially manageable standard. The distinction between interstate commerce and other, intrastate activities that affect it—especially in a society now so united or integrated by modern forms of transportation and communication—is simply not clear enough to serve as the basis for judicial review, according to traditional standards that require legislative deference unless the unconstitutionality of an act is clear.[43]

This does not mean that we should ignore the serious constitutional issues involved in federalism. But, as conservatives have long pointed out in other areas, not all constitutional issues need be resolved by the judiciary. The recognition of the constitutional responsibilities of a wide variety of actors (judges, legislators, executives, voters), which was dominant in early American history, needs to be resurrected. There are some signs that constitutional scholarship is taking that theme more seriously these days, under the pressure of a Supreme Court whose decisions are not as popular in the legal academy as the Warren Court's decisions were. Unfortunately, few seem to be drawing the conclusion that a significant curtailment of the scope of judicial review, much less a return to its more traditional form, is appropriate.

Conclusion

The criticism of the Rehnquist Court's constitutional jurisprudence that I am offering—based on its employment of standard modern balancing techniques and insufficient attention to the requirements of legislative deference where judicially manageable standards are not available—does not lead to much sympathy for its standard liberal critics today. Since most of those critics regularly and cheerfully advocate the use of a broad, legislative form of judicial review in civil liberties cases (such as *Casey* and *Romer*, the focus of trenchant criticism in earlier chapters of this volume), their rejection of cases such as *Lopez* has all the marks of special pleading: it is wrong because they do not like these particular results.

These critics are in the same category with Justice Brennan, who was outraged—yes, outraged!—in *National League of Cities v. Usery* that the Court would "repudiate principles governing judicial interpretation of our Constitution settled since the time of Mr. Chief Justice John Marshall."[44] This, from the same Justice Brennan who spearheaded the Warren Court revolution overturning large portions of "principles governing judicial interpretation of our Constitution settled since the time of Mr. Chief Justice John Marshall." It is tempting simply to point out that "what goes around, comes around," and that liberal judicial activists have little ground on which to object to a more conservative Court's activism.

It may be particularly tempting to some conservatives to use judicial power for their own purposes because, to the extent that conservatives are practitioners of judicial restraint and liberals are practitioners of judicial activism, it makes judicial activism a "win-win" situation for liberals: if liberals control the courts, they get to employ judicial activism for their purposes, and if conservative advocates of judicial self-restraint control the courts, liberals are no worse off.

But whatever the poetic justice of jurisprudential liberals being hoist on their own activist petard, conservatives ought to resist the invitation to use modern judicial power for their purposes, because they were right when they articulated principled criticisms of liberal Court activism, and they should stand fast to those principles when they are dealing with conservative Court activism. It is a matter of basic republican political morality that all public officials, who receive their power from the people via the fundamental law of the Constitution, should act in accord with the terms of that grant of power. In the case of judges, those terms are clear: judges are to exercise "neither FORCE nor WILL, but merely judgment."

NOTES

1. *First Things*, November 1996.

2. For example, see Larry Kramer, "Federalism and the Rehnquist Court," at http://www.aals.org/profdev/constitutional/kramer.html.

3. I cannot, regrettably, discuss the issue of precedent as much as I would like to in this chapter. It is an important, and very difficult, issue for originalists to address, because of the problem of how to deal with precedents that are settled, but clearly diverge from original intent. I have discussed the issue in *How to Read the Constitution* (Rowman and Littlefield, 1996), chap. 8.

4. *Osborne v. Bank of U.S.*, 9 Wheaton 738, 866.

5. Actually, impeachment and conviction are rare with respect to federal judges in general, but historically nonexistent with respect to a Supreme Court justice (only Justice Samuel Chase having been impeached, and he acquitted).

6. When I use the term "balancing" here, I am not referring to Justice Felix Frankfurter's somewhat more deferential standard of judicial review, which was essentially modern (legislative), but infused with a heavy dose of caution, based on a strong sense of the antimajoritarian character of judicial review. Balancing, as I use the term, applies equally to various tests that are more rigorous and less deferential to the political branches—e.g., "clear and present danger," "compelling state interest"—and share the general characteristic of requiring judges to weigh vague constitutional principles against various countervailing state interests.

7. Benjamin Cardozo, *The Nature of the Judicial Process* (New Haven: Yale University Press, 1921). While Cardozo's description of judicial power is, on the whole, a relatively moderate statement of modern judicial review, it makes

clear—following the thought of the greatest exponent of modern judicial power, Oliver Wendell Holmes Jr.—that judges *make* law. See Christopher Wolfe, *The Rise of Modern Judicial Review*, rev. ed. (Lanham, Md.: Rowman and Littlefield, 1994), chap. 10.

8. I am not referring here to the problem more traditional justices face in dealing with a large body of modern constitutional law precedents that are based on modern activist decisions. Traditional justices are not fairly taxed with activism when they properly accept and apply precedents (though they have reasonable grounds to resist some precedents, particularly those that impose legislative duties on them, in the form of balancing tests). The inconsistency I refer to at this point in the text does not involve precedent, but initiatives by conservative justices to expand judicial balancing for conservative purposes such as the protection of property rights.

9. 431 U.S. 1 (1977). See the references to "an outdated formalism," at 20, and "such formalistic distinctions," at 24.

10. At 25–26 (internal citations omitted):

> Although the Contract Clause appears literally to proscribe "any" impairment, this Court observed in Blaisdell that "the prohibition is not an absolute one and is not to be read with literal exactness like a mathematical formula." Thus, a finding that there has been a technical impairment is merely a preliminary step in resolving the more difficult question whether that impairment is permitted under the Constitution. In the instant case, as in Blaisdell, we must attempt to reconcile the strictures of the Contract Clause with the "essential attributes of sovereign power," necessarily reserved by the States to safeguard the welfare of their citizens.

> The Contract Clause is not an absolute bar to subsequent modification of a State's own financial obligations. . . . As with laws impairing the obligations of private contracts, an impairment may be constitutional if it is reasonable and necessary to serve an important public purpose. In applying this standard, however, complete deference to a legislative assessment of reasonableness and necessity is not appropriate because the State's self-interest is at stake.

Note that talk of less than "complete" deference is a polite way of saying there's fundamentally no deference, period. For parallels, see Brandeis regarding deference and the First Amendment, in *Whitney v. California* (a state law on speech creates "merely a rebuttable presumption" 274 U.S. 379, which turns out to be no presumption at all), and the *Carolene Products* footnote (which speaks of a "narrower scope for operation of the presumption of constitutionality," 304 U.S. 152, i.e., no scope at all for it).

11. 469 U.S. at 561–62 (internal citations and notes omitted). Justice Powell also says that "[i]n reading National League of Cities to embrace a balancing approach, JUSTICE BLACKMUN quite correctly cited the part of the opinion that reaffirmed Fry v. United States, 421. The Court's analysis reaffirming Fry explicitly weighed the seriousness of the problem addressed by the federal legislation at issue in that case, against the effects of compliance on state sovereignty. 426 U.S., at 852–853. Our subsequent decisions also adopted this approach of weighing the respective interests of the States and Federal Government. Ibid, at 562–63."

12. *Garcia*, 588. She goes on to say: "It has been difficult for this Court to craft bright lines defining the scope of the state autonomy protected by National League of Cities. Such difficulty is to be expected whenever constitutional concerns as important as federalism and the effectiveness of the commerce power come into conflict. Regardless of the difficulty, it is and will remain the duty of this Court to reconcile these concerns in the final instance." *Garcia* at 588–89. "Difficulty crafting bright lines" is often another way of saying that the Court is not able to identify clear principles to distinguish what is constitutional and unconstitutional, and hence will engage in ad hoc balancing.

13. 260 U.S. 393 (1922), at 413.

14. Ibid., 415–16. Note not only that since 1937 the due process clause—in the form of judicial review of the reasonableness of economic regulation—has been "gone," but also that before the Civil War no such federal due process power had been exercised, with the single, lamentable exception of *Dred Scott v. Sanford*.

15. 4 Wheaton 316, 429–30 (1819).

16. 505 U.S. 1003, 1015 (1992).

17. Scalia points out two jurisprudential advantages of employing this principle. First, "total deprivation of beneficial use is, from the landowner's point of view, the equivalent of a physical appropriation" and second, "the functional basis for permitting the government, by regulation, to affect property values without compensation—that [citing *Mahon*] 'Government hardly could go on if to some extent values incident to property could not be diminished without paying for every such change in the general law'—does not apply to the relatively rare situations where the government has deprived a landowner of all economically beneficial uses." Ibid., 1017.

18. Ibid., 1027.

19. 512 U.S. 374, 388 (1994).

20. Ibid., 391. The requirement of only "very generalized statements as to the necessary connection between the required dedication and the proposed development" required by some state courts is "too lax," while "a very exacting correspondence" (the "specific and uniquely attributable" test) goes too far. The Court adopts an "intermediate position" requiring the showing of a "reasonable relationship," but it prefers the "rough proportionality" language, "partly because the term 'reasonable relationship' seems confusingly similar to the term 'rational basis' which describes the minimal level of scrutiny under the Equal Protection Clause of the Fourteenth Amendment." Ibid., 389–91.

The repetition several times that no "precise mathematical calculation is necessary" suggests to me almost a sort of guilty conscience, the Court understanding that the determination required by the test is one made effectively without any real guidance from the law.

21. Ibid., 406 and 406–7.

22. 494 U.S. 872, 890 (1990).

23. Note the additional problem that this particular hybrid right creates for Scalia, since the constitutional foundations of parental rights are found in the Court's substantive due process jurisprudence, of which Scalia is rightly a strong critic.

24. On the original meaning of the establishment clause, see Gerard V. Bradley, *Church-State Relationships in America* (New York: Greenwood Press, 1987).

25. O'Connor, Souter, and Breyer dissented, based on their rejection of *Smith* as a precedent. For them, once *Smith* is rejected, RFRA simply supports the Court's decision, so there is no real Section 5 issue.

26. 521 U.S. 507, 519 (1997).

27. Ibid., 524.

28. And, for the record, one can search high and low in *Marbury v. Madison* to find an argument contrary to this one, but it will not be found, because it is not there.

29. "But even these modern-era precedents which have expanded congressional power under the Commerce Clause confirm that this power is subject to outer limits. In Jones & Laughlin Steel, the Court warned that the scope of the interstate commerce power 'must be considered in the light of our dual system of government and may not be extended so as to embrace effects upon interstate commerce so indirect and remote that to embrace them, in view of our complex society, would effectually obliterate the distinction between what is national and what is local and create a completely centralized government.'" 514 U.S. 549, at 556–57.

30. "To uphold the Government's contentions here, we would have to pile inference upon inference in a manner that would bid fair to convert congressional authority under the Commerce Clause to a general police power of the sort retained by the States. Admittedly, some of our prior cases have taken long steps down that road, giving great deference to congressional action. The broad language in these opinions has suggested the possibility of additional expansion, but we decline here to proceed any further. To do so would require us to conclude that the Constitution's enumeration of powers does not presuppose something not enumerated, and that there never will be a distinction between what is truly national and what is truly local. This we are unwilling to do." Ibid., 567–68 (internal citations omitted).

31. 529 U.S. 598, 615, 617 (2000).

32. See Wolfe, *Rise of Modern Judicial Review*, 172–78.

33. *U.S. v. Lopez*, 566 (internal citation omitted); and at 567.

34. Ibid., 574.

35. Ibid., 575.

36. Ibid., 577 (internal citation omitted).

37. Ibid., 579 (internal citation omitted).

38. Ibid., 654.

39. Ibid.

40. Ibid., 601 n. 9.

41. *U.S. v. Morrison*, 627.

42. *U.S. v. Lopez*, 584. He also says "In an appropriate case, I believe that we must further reconsider our 'substantial effects' test with an eye toward constructing a standard that reflects the text and history of the Commerce Clause *without totally rejecting our more recent Commerce Clause jurisprudence*" (585; emphasis added).

43. I acknowledge that authors genuinely oriented toward traditionalist principles have attempted to make a case for the decision in *Lopez*. I simply am not convinced that they offer standards that judges can use with sufficient clarity to justify judicial review, especially in light of familiar "slippery slope arguments." See especially Robert P. George and Gerard V. Bradley, "Outer Limits: The Commerce Clause and Judicial Review," in *The Supreme Court and American Constitutionalism*, ed. B. Wilson and K. Masugi (Lanham, Md.: Rowman and Littlefield, 1998).

44. 426 U.S. 833, 857 (1976).

Index

Note: A page in parenthesis following an endnote reference indicates a subject occuring on but not directly identified on that page.

NEW FORUM BOOKS

New Forum Books makes available to general readers outstanding original inter-disciplinary scholarship with a special focus on the juncture of culture, law, and politics. New Forum Books is guided by the conviction that law and politics not only reflect culture but help to shape it. Authors include leading political scientists, sociologists, legal scholars, philosophers, theologians, historians, and economists writing for nonspecialist readers and scholars across a range of fields. Looking at questions such as political equality, the concept of rights, the problem of virtue in liberal politics, crime and punishment, population, poverty, economic development, and the international legal and political order, New Forum Books seeks to explain—not explain away—the difficult issues we face today.